AFRICAN POLITICAL, ECONOMIC, AND SECURITY ISSUES

SUB-SAHARAN AFRICA

U.S. AND CHINESE ECONOMIC ENGAGEMENT

African Political, Economic, and Security Issues

Additional books in this series can be found on Nova's website under the Series tab.

Additional E-books in this series can be found on Nova's website under the E-book tab.

Global Economic Studies

Additional books in this series can be found on Nova's website under the Series tab.

Additional E-books in this series can be found on Nova's website under the E-book tab.

AFRICAN POLITICAL, ECONOMIC, AND SECURITY ISSUES

SUB-SAHARAN AFRICA

U.S. AND CHINESE ECONOMIC ENGAGEMENT

JACQUELINE S. SANTIAGO
EDITOR

nova publishers

New York

For permission to use material from this book please contact us:
Telephone 631-231-7269; Fax 631-231-8175
Web Site: http://www.novapublishers.com

Library of Congress Cataloging-in-Publication Data

ISBN: 978-1-62618-433-6

Published by Nova Science Publishers, Inc. † New York

CONTENTS

Preface		**vii**
Chapter 1	Sub-Saharan Africa: Trends in U.S. and Chinese Economic Engagement *United States Government Accountability Office*	**1**
Chapter 2	Sub-Saharan Africa: Case Studies of U.S. and Chinese Economic Engagement in Angola, Ghana, and Kenya *United States Government Accountability Office*	**59**
Chapter 3	U.S. Trade and Investment Relations with sub-Saharan Africa and the African Growth and Opportunity Act *Vivian C. Jones and Brock R. Williams*	**103**
Chapter 4	U.S. Strategy Toward Sub-Saharan Africa *The White House*	**141**
Index		**151**

PREFACE

Since 2001, China has rapidly increased its economic engagement with sub-Saharan African countries. The United States has increased aid to sub-Saharan Africa and in 2010 provided more than a quarter of all U.S. international economic assistance to the region. According to some observers, China's foreign assistance and investments in Africa have been driven in part by the desire for natural resources and stronger diplomatic relations. Some U.S. officials and other stakeholders also have questioned whether China's activities affect U.S. interests in the region. This book examines the goals and policies in sub-Saharan Africa; trade, grants, loans, and investment activities in the region; and engagement in three case-study countries-Angola, Ghana, and Kenya.

Chapter 1 – Since 2001, China has rapidly increased its economic engagement with sub-Saharan African countries. The United States has increased aid to sub-Saharan Africa and in 2010 provided more than a quarter of all U.S. international economic assistance to the region. According to some observers, China's foreign assistance and investments in Africa have been driven in part by the desire for natural resources and stronger diplomatic relations. Some U.S. officials and other stakeholders also have questioned whether China's activities affect U.S. interests in the region.

GAO was asked to review the nature of the United States' and China's engagement in sub-Saharan Africa. This report examines (1) goals and policies in sub-Saharan Africa; (2) trade, grants and loans, and investment activities in the region; and (3) engagement in three case-study countries—Angola, Ghana, and Kenya. GAO obtained information from, among others, 11 U.S. agencies, U.S. firms, and host-government officials. GAO was not able to meet with Chinese officials. GAO did not include U.S. and Chinese security engagement in the scope of this study.

Chapter 2 – Sub-Saharan Africa: Case Studies of U.S and Chinese Economic Engagement in Angola, Ghana, and Kenya, by United States Government Accountability Office.

Chapter 3 – Following the end of the apartheid era in South Africa in the early 1990s, the United States sought to increase economic relations with sub-Saharan Africa (SSA). President Clinton instituted several measures that dealt with investment, debt relief, and trade. Congress passed legislation that required the President to develop a trade and development policy for Africa. Between 1960 and 1973, Africa's economic growth was relatively strong, followed by a period of stagnation and decline for the subsequent two decades in many SSA countries. Current perspectives, however, indicate that many of the fastest-growing countries in the world are on the African continent, and the International Monetary Fund (IMF) projects that the SSA region will grow in terms of real GDP by 5.3% in 2012 and 2013.

In 2000, Congress approved new U.S. trade and investment legislation for SSA in the African Growth and Opportunity Act (AGOA; Title I, P.L. 106-200). According to U.S. trade statistics, U.S. trade with SSA has comprised 1% to 2% of U.S. total trade with the world. AGOA extends preferential treatment to U.S. imports from eligible countries that are pursuing market reform measures. Data show that U.S. imports under AGOA are mostly energy products, but imports of other products have grown significantly. AGOA mandated that U.S. officials meet regularly with their counterparts in SSA, and 11 of these meetings have been held to date. The 11th AGOA Forum was held from June 14 to June 15, 2012, in Washington, DC. AGOA also directed the President to provide U.S. government technical assistance and trade capacity support to AGOA beneficiary countries. Government agencies that have roles in this effort include the U.S. Agency for International Development, the Assistant U.S. Trade Representative for Africa (established by statute under AGOA), the Overseas Private Investment Corporation, the Export-Import Bank, the U.S. and Foreign Commercial Service, and the Trade and Development Agency. In AGOA, Congress declared that free-trade agreements should be negotiated, where feasible, with interested SSA countries. Related to this provision, negotiations on a free-trade agreement with the Southern African Customs Union (SACU), which includes South Africa and four other countries, began in June 2003, but were suspended in April 2006.

The 112th Congress enacted legislation to extend through September 2015 an expiring provision in AGOA, which allows apparel made in lesser-developed countries to be made of yarns and fabrics from any country and still receive duty-free treatment, subject to a cap (P.L. 112-163). This amendment to AGOA also added South Sudan to the list of SSA countries eligible for AGOA benefits. Eligible countries may become AGOA beneficiaries subject to approval by the Administration.

Legislation is pending to further enhance U.S.-SSA trade relations. H.R. 4221 and S. 2215 seek to increase U.S. exports to Africa, in part, through strategies aimed at further developing relationships between the United States and African countries on a government-to-government level, fostering private sector U.S.-African ties, and targeting more U.S. export financing toward trade with Africa. An amended version of S. 2215 was ordered reported by the Senate Foreign Relations Committee in September 2012. H.R. 656, a separate initiative, would create at the State Department a Special Representative for United States-Africa Trade, Development, and Diaspora Affairs that would also promote U.S. trade and investment ties with SSA.

Chapter 4 – Upon taking office, President Obama committed to supporting strong, open, and accountable governments and sustainable development in Africa. In his speech before the Ghanaian Parliament in July 2009, the President asserted that Africa is a fundamental part of our interconnected world, and called for a partnership with Africa that is "grounded in mutual responsibility and mutual respect."

The National Security Strategy, released in May 2010, reinforces this vision, and calls for partnership with African nations as they grow their economies and strengthen their democratic institutions and governance. In June 2012, the President approved a Presidential Policy Directive that outlines his vision with respect to U.S. policy toward sub-Saharan Africa. This document is drawn from and reflects that Directive.

In: Sub-Saharan Africa
Editor: Jacqueline S. Santiago

ISBN: 978-1-62618-433-6

Chapter 1

SUB-SAHARAN AFRICA: TRENDS IN U.S. AND CHINESE ECONOMIC ENGAGEMENT*

United States Government Accountability Office

WHY GAO DID THIS STUDY

Since 2001, China has rapidly increased its economic engagement with sub-Saharan African countries. The United States has increased aid to sub-Saharan Africa and in 2010 provided more than a quarter of all U.S. international economic assistance to the region. According to some observers, China's foreign assistance and investments in Africa have been driven in part by the desire for natural resources and stronger diplomatic relations. Some U.S. officials and other stakeholders also have questioned whether China's activities affect U.S. interests in the region.

GAO was asked to review the nature of the United States' and China's engagement in sub-Saharan Africa. This report examines (1) goals and policies in sub-Saharan Africa; (2) trade, grants and loans, and investment activities in the region; and (3) engagement in three case-study countries—Angola, Ghana, and Kenya. GAO obtained information from, among others, 11 U.S. agencies, U.S. firms, and host-government officials. GAO was not able to meet with Chinese officials. GAO did not include U.S. and Chinese security engagement in the scope of this study.

WHAT GAO FOUND

The United States and China have emphasized different policies and approaches for their engagement with sub-Saharan Africa. U.S. goals have included strengthening democratic institutions, supporting human rights, using development assistance to improve health and education, and helping sub-Saharan African countries build global trade. The Chinese

* This is an edited, reformatted and augmented version of the Highlights of GAO-13-199, a report to congressional requesters, dated February, 2013.

government, in contrast, has stated the goal of establishing closer ties with African countries by seeking mutual benefit for China and African nations and by following a policy of noninterference in countries' domestic affairs.

Both the United States and China have seen sharp growth in trade with sub-Saharan Africa over the past decade, with China's total trade in goods increasing faster and surpassing U.S. trade in 2009. Petroleum imports constitute the majority of U.S. and Chinese imports from sub-Saharan Africa, with China also importing a large amount of other natural resources. China's exports of goods to the region have grown and far exceed U.S. exports of goods. Information on other key aspects of China's engagement in sub-Saharan Africa is limited in some cases, since China does not publish comprehensive data on its foreign assistance or government-sponsored loans to the region. Data-collection efforts focused on specific countries, as GAO's case-study analysis shows, can provide further insights but do not fully eliminate these information gaps.

Both the United States and China chiefly import natural resources from sub-Saharan Africa, but data from Angola, Ghana, and Kenya suggest that U.S. and Chinese patterns of engagement have differed in other respects. The United States has primarily provided grants to Kenya for health and humanitarian programs. Data from Ghana and Kenya suggest that China has provided much smaller amounts of grant assistance and pursued increasing engagement through loans for large-scale infrastructure projects. Information from Angola, Ghana, and Kenya indicates that direct competition between U.S. and Chinese firms is limited, with U.S. firms concentrated in higher-technology areas. Further, differences across the three countries suggest that host-government requirements, such as regulations on hiring local labor, influence Chinese and U.S. firms' engagement in each case-study country.

ABBREVIATIONS

AGOA	African Growth and Opportunity Act
BEA	Bureau of Economic Analysis
Commerce	Department of Commerce
China	Ex-Im Export-Import Bank of China
FOCAC	Forum on China-Africa Cooperation
GDP	gross domestic product
GSP	Generalized System of Preferences
IMF	International Monetary Fund
MCC	Millennium Challenge Corporation
NGO	nongovernmental organization
OECD	Organization for Economic Cooperation and Development
OPIC	Overseas Private Investment Corporation
State	Department of State
Treasury	Department of the Treasury
UN	United Nations
USAID	U.S. Agency for International Development
U.S. Ex-Im	Export-Import Bank of the United States
USTR	Office of the U.S. Trade Representative

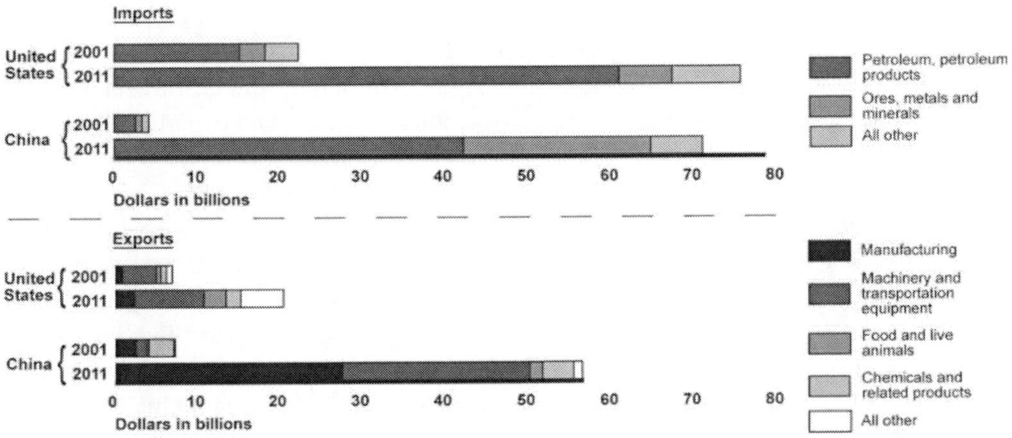

Source: GAO analysis of UN data.

U.S. and Chinese Imports from, and Exports to, Sub-Saharan Africa, 2001 and 2011.

February 7, 2013

The Honorable James M. Inhofe
United States Senate
The Honorable Jack Kingston
House of Representatives

China's economic ties with sub-Saharan Africa, including its rapidly rising trade and investment in the region, have drawn global attention. While U.S. trade with the region has also increased, the United States has generally focused on providing development and humanitarian assistance to African countries, directing more than a quarter of its foreign economic assistance to the region in 2010. Since 2001, China has substantially increased its economic engagement with sub-Saharan African countries, with strong growth in both imports and exports. According to some observers, China's foreign assistance and investments throughout Africa since that time have been driven in part by the Chinese government's desire to obtain a share in Africa's natural resources as well as by its interest in establishing diplomatic relations with countries in the region. Various U.S. officials and members of the U.S. business community have questioned whether China's role in the region is affecting U.S. interests and opportunities for U.S. firms in sub-Saharan Africa.

You asked us to review the nature of the United States' and China's engagement in sub-Saharan Africa.[1] This report examines (1) U.S. and Chinese goals and policies for sub-Saharan Africa; (2) the United States' and China's trade, grants and loans, and investment activities in sub-Saharan Africa; and (3) aspects of the United States' and China's engagement in three sub-Saharan African countries—Angola, Ghana, and Kenya.

To review U.S. and Chinese goals and policies with respect to sub-Saharan Africa, we used U.S. government documents, publicly available Chinese government documents, and statements from U.S. government officials. To examine the United States' and China's engagement through trade, grants and loans, and investment in sub-Saharan Africa, we analyzed available data for the United States and China from a variety of U.S., multilateral, and Chinese government sources,[2] generally for 2001 through 2010 or 2011.[3] We did not include security issues within the scope of this study. To identify the best available data, as well as data limitations, we interviewed U.S. government officials and experts in Washington, D.C. We also analyzed information on U.S. programs and funding from the U.S. Department of Commerce (Commerce), the Millennium Challenge Corporation (MCC), the Overseas Private Investment Corporation (OPIC), the Export-Import Bank of the United States (U.S. Ex-Im), and the U.S. Agency for International Development (USAID). In addition, we analyzed publicly available information from Chinese government entities, such as the Ministry of Commerce; the World Bank; the International Monetary Fund (IMF); and scholarly literature, among other sources, and we obtained some data from case-study country governments. To compare in depth the nature of the United States' and China's engagement in sub-Saharan Africa, we conducted case studies of Angola, Ghana, and Kenya. We selected these countries on the basis of our assessment of the levels, types, and intersection of the United States' and China's engagement in trade, grants and loans, and investment activity in each country; the three countries' geographic diversity; and input from U.S. government officials and experts on China's role in Africa. These case studies are meant to be illustrative and are not generalizable. We conducted work in Washington, D.C., and in Angola, Ghana, and Kenya, including meetings with officials from U.S. agencies, host-government ministries, U.S. businesses, other donors, and nongovernmental organizations (NGO). Despite our requests, we were unable to meet with Chinese government officials in Africa or in Washington, D.C. We have noted data limitations as appropriate, such as lack of available data on China's grants and loans to the region and likely underreporting of China's investment data. Overall, we determined the data presented in this study to be generally reliable for the purposes for which they are used. Appendix I provides a more detailed discussion of our objectives, scope, and methodology. Additional information on the United States' and China's trade, grants and loans, and investment activities in Angola, Ghana, and Kenya is presented in a separate supplemental report, GAO-13-280SP.

We conducted this performance audit from November 2011 to February 2013 in accordance with generally accepted government auditing standards. Those standards require that we plan and perform the audit to obtain sufficient, appropriate evidence to provide a reasonable basis for our findings and conclusions based on our audit objectives. We believe that the evidence obtained provides a reasonable basis for our findings and conclusions based on our audit objectives.

BACKGROUND

Sub-Saharan Africa comprises 49 countries,[4] including 4 of the 10 economies worldwide that grew most rapidly from 2001 through 2011.[5] Since 1990, overall decreases in maternal and child mortality rates, as well as improvements in indicators measuring education and poverty rates, have shown that economic and social conditions are improving in the region. However, countries in sub-Saharan Africa, including our three case-study countries—Angola, Ghana, and Kenya—continue to face significant development challenges, such as those related to governance and government transparency, and overall low income levels.

Indicator	Sub-Saharan Africa[a]	Angola	Ghana	Kenya
Population (in millions)	875	20	25	42
GDP per capita[b]	$2,363	$5,930	$1,884	$1,718
Income level[c]	Varying	Upper middle income	Lower middle income	Low income
Population living on less than $1.25 per day (percentage)	N/A	54	30	20
Human Development Index[d]	N/A	Ranked 148 of 187	Ranked 135 of 187	Ranked 143 of 187
Life expectancy at birth (years)	54	51	64	57
Adult literacy rate (percentage)	69	70	67	87
Corruption Perceptions Index[e]	N/A	Ranked 168 of 183	Ranked 69 of 183	Ranked 154 of 183

Source: GAO analysis data from the World Bank, United Nations, and Transparency International.
Note: Data shown are the most recent available.

[a] Some data sources did not consistently classify countries in sub-Saharan Africa. For example, data for sub-Saharan Africa from the Human Development Index did not include Sudan. In addition, some data were not available for the sub-Saharan Africa region.

[b] Gross domestic product (GDP) per capita is based on purchasing power parity, which equalizes the purchasing power of different currencies in their home countries by taking into account the relative cost of living and the inflation rates of different countries, rather than by comparing the countries' nominal GDP data.

[c] The World Bank classified income level by gross national income per capita as follows: low income, $1,025 or less; lower-middle income, $1,026 to $4,035; upper-middle income, $4,036 to $12,475; and high income, $12,476 or more.

[d] The Human Development Index provides a composite measure of three basic dimensions of human development: health, education, and income, where a ranking of 1 indicates a country with high social and economic development.

[e] Based on the perceived level of corruption of a country's public sector, where a ranking of 1 indicates the lowest level of perceived corruption relative to other countries included in the index.

Figure 1. Selected Economic and Development Indicators for Sub-Saharan Africa Compared with Angola, Ghana, and Kenya.

Figure 1 shows the location and selected characteristics of the sub-Saharan Africa region and our case-study countries.

- *Angola.* In 2002, Angola officially ended a 27-year civil war that resulted in the deaths of up to 1.5 million people and destroyed the country's infrastructure. Since 2001, Angola has become one of the largest crude oil-producing countries in sub-Saharan Africa, and high international oil prices have driven the country's high growth rate in recent years. The country's efforts to rebuild following the war spurred a construction boom and—although the country imports half of its food—an increased focus on agriculture. Despite Angola's oil reserves and relatively high income level per capita, the UN classifies Angola as a least developed country, on the basis of its low ratings on human development indicators and the weakness of its economy. More than 54 percent of Angola's population—the highest percentage among our three case-study countries—lives on the equivalent of less than $1.25 per day. In 2011, Transparency International ranked Angola's public sector among the most corrupt in sub-Saharan Africa, and other sources have noted significant challenges including corruption and lack of transparency, particularly in the extractive industries.[6]

- *Ghana.* In 1957, Ghana became the first sub-Saharan country in colonial Africa to gain its independence. Ghana's economy has generally been strengthened by a quarter century of relatively sound management, a competitive business environment, and sustained reductions in poverty levels. The country is well endowed with natural resources, and oil production that began in 2010 is expected to boost Ghana's economic growth. Agriculture accounts for roughly one-quarter of Ghana's gross domestic product (GDP) and employs half of the workforce. In 2011, the year that Ghana began to export oil, the World Bank elevated Ghana to lower-middle-income status based on its per capita income.[7]
- *Kenya.* Kenya is considered a hub for trade and finance in the East Africa region of sub-Saharan Africa and is that region's largest economy. Kenya's economic growth has been affected by increasing inflation, high energy and food prices, and the 2011 drought in the Horn of Africa. In addition, contested national elections in 2008 and the resulting violence negatively affected the economy and foreign investments in Kenya. Although economic recovery continues, the country faces challenges including a growing trade imbalance, corruption, and rural and urban poverty. Kenya also faces challenges in its manufacturing and drought-affected agricultural sectors, which affect the country's economic stability. The overall welfare of Kenyans has improved in the past decade, with a general decline in national poverty and rising primary education enrollment rates. However, because of Kenya's low per-capita income levels, the World Bank classifies it as a low-income country. The World Bank has noted that poverty and climate change issues remain among the country's top development challenges.

U.S. and Chinese Economies

The United States is the world's largest trader in goods—that is, total imports and exports—and its market-based economy is the world's largest economy, producing one-fifth of total global economic output.8 In addition, the United States is the largest exporter of services, primarily education services; financial services; and business, professional, and technical services, among others. As a member of the Organization for Economic Cooperation and Development (OECD), the United States collaborates with other countries and helps set international standards on economic, social, and scientific issues, to help member and nonmember countries promote economic growth, free markets, and efficient use of resources.9 The United States also coordinates its development assistance activities with other members of the OECD Development Assistance Committee, a forum of many of the largest funders of aid that has a mandate to promote development cooperation and other policies for sustainable development. In accordance with the 2005 Paris Declaration on Aid Effectiveness, the U.S. government generally does not condition its aid on, or "tie" it to, the recipient country's use of the aid to procure goods or services from the United States.

China is the world's largest manufacturer and exporter of goods,[10] with overall economic output second only to the United States'.[11] In 2010, China was the fourth-highest-ranked global exporter of services, although it still imports more services than it exports. Unlike the United States, China is not a member of OECD. However, China's entry into the World Trade Organization in 2001 has helped the country expand its economic integration with the global economy, and such integration is expected to help China increase its efficiency, innovation, and global competitiveness.[12] Over the past 3 decades, China has been transitioning from a rural, agricultural society to an urban, industrial society and from a planned economy, where the government makes key decisions about goods and production, toward one that is, like the U.S. economy, more market based. During this transformation, China's growth has been driven by manufacturing, in part because of its relatively low labor costs. However, China's overall growth has imposed increased pressure on the availability of natural resources. Moreover, according to a joint study by the World Bank and the Chinese government, state-owned enterprises are not yet clearly distinguished from the private sector.[13] This study notes that, more than in other economies, China's state-owned enterprises and government are closely connected and generally are mutually supportive and that China's large private enterprises also benefit from government financing and commercial diplomacy.[14]

Anticorruption Laws for U.S. and Chinese Firms

U.S. companies are subject to various regulations with respect to commercial activities abroad, including the Foreign Corrupt Practices Act of 1977, which prohibits payments to foreign government officials to assist in obtaining or retaining business.[15] The Foreign Corrupt Practices Act applies to all U.S. persons, including corporations, as well as foreign firms that issue securities regulated pursuant to the Securities Exchange Act of 1934. The United States also adopted the OECD Anti-Bribery Convention in 1998.[16] In 2011, the Chinese government amended its anticorruption laws to outlaw bribery of foreign public officials by Chinese nationals, companies, and residents for commercial benefit. Both the United States and China signed the United Nations Convention against Corruption in 2003.[17] According to Transparency International, in 2011, firms from China were perceived as among the most likely to pay bribes abroad, ranked at 27 among firms from 28 countries; U.S. firms, ranked at 10, were perceived as less likely to pay bribes abroad.[18]

U.S. and Chinese Government Agencies Engaged in Sub-Saharan Africa

U.S. Government Entities

Multiple U.S. agencies oversee and implement U.S. aid, trade, and investment activities in sub-Saharan Africa. Table 1 lists selected U.S. government entities' roles and responsibilities and areas of involvement.

Chinese Government Entities

China's Ministry of Commerce formulates and implements policies for foreign trade, economic cooperation, and overseas investments, in collaboration with other agencies.[19] The

Ministry of Commerce also leads China's foreign aid by selecting projects and organizing the implementation of aid activities. Table 2 lists selected Chinese government entities' roles and responsibilities and areas of involvement.

Table 1. Selected U.S. Government Entities' Roles and Areas of Involvement in Sub-Saharan Africa

U.S. government entity	Roles and responsibilities	Area(s) of involvement
Department of State (State)	Oversees policy development and bilateral relations; provides diplomatic presence supporting U.S. aid, trade, investment activities; supports Commerce's commercial diplomacy activities, especially where Commerce is not present.	Trade, aid, investment
Department of Commerce (Commerce)	Provides Commercial Service presence and supports trade missions to facilitate U.S. export and investment opportunities; helps U.S. firms resolve market-access problems and address trade-agreement compliance issues; assists U.S. firms competing for foreign-government contracts through its Advocacy Center.	Trade, investment
Department of the Treasury (Treasury)	Advocates for improvements to regulatory frameworks, transparency, and governance through multilateral development banks, such as the World Bank, to enhance private-sector investment; provides bilateral technical assistance in areas such as budget and economic policy.	Aid, investment
Office of the U.S. Trade Representative (USTR)	Develops and coordinates implementation of U.S. trade and investment policy, including trade preferences; leads discussions with Trade and Investment Framework Agreement partners; negotiates bilateral investment treaties and other trade agreements.	Trade, investment
U.S. Agency for International Development (USADI)	Formulates U.S. development policies; implements U.S. development assistance activities through grants.	Aid
Millennium Challenge Corporation (MCC)	Implements bilateral compacts for grant-funded development projects, including infrastructure construction; has signed compacts with 13 sub-Saharan African countries.	Aid
Export-Import Bank of the United States (U.S. Ex-Im)	Provides financing—such as working capital guarantees (preexport financing), export credit insurance, loan guarantees, and direct loans (mostly nonconcessional)—to promote U.S. exports.	Trade
Overseas Private Investment Corporation (OPIC)	Assists U.S. private sector investors overseas through direct loans, loan guarantees, political risk insurance, and support for private equity investment funds.	Investment
U.S. Trade and Development Agency	Funds project-planning activities, such as feasibility studies, and U.S. visits for African entrepreneurs to facilitate exports of U.S. goods. and services	Trade, investment

Source: GAO analysis of information from State, Commerce, Treasury, USTR, USAID, MCC, U.S. Ex-Im, OPIC, and the U.S. Trade and Development Agency.

Table 2. Selected Chinese Government Entities' Roles and Areas of Involvement in Sub-Saharan Africa

Chinese government entity	Roles and responsibilities	Areas of involvement
Ministry of Commerce	Formulates and implements policies on foreign trade and investment activities; leads foreign aid efforts.	Trade, aid, investment
Ministry of Finance	Supervises and audits implementation of foreign aid budget.	Aid
Ministry of Foreign Affairs	Coordinates with other Chinese ministries on issues including foreign trade and economic cooperation and assistance.	Trade, aid, investment
Export-Import Bank of China (China Ex-Im)	Supports Chinese government policy to promote Chinese exports and investment through export credits, international guarantees, concessional and nonconcessional loans for overseas construction and investment, and official lines of credit.	Trade, aid, investment
China Development Bank	Serves Chinese government's policy to promote trade and investment by providing large-scale, long-term funding for construction of infrastructure and industrial projects; oversees China-Africa Development Fund, which encourages Chinese investments in Africa.	Trade, investment

Source: GAO analysis of information from the Brookings Institution, the Center for Global Development, the government of China, the World Bank, and China scholar Deborah Brautigam.

Note: Although China does not have an official aid agency, China's Ministries of Commerce, Finance, and Foreign Affairs and the Export-Import Bank of China are among the entities involved in China's development assistance activities.

China Ex-Im and the China Development Bank, two of the Chinese government's financing institutions, promote the government's goals overseas. China Ex-Im maintains sole responsibility for concessional loans to support China's exports to sub-Saharan Africa and promotes Chinese exports and investment through export credits, international guarantees, and concessional and nonconcessional loans for overseas construction and investment. The China Development Bank provides large-scale, long-term funding for infrastructure construction and industrial projects; provides market-rate (nonconcessional) loans; and oversees the China-Africa Development Fund, to encourage Chinese investments throughout Africa.

U.S. Goals Have Emphasized Democracy and Development in Sub-Saharan Africa, while China's Policy Underscores Mutual Benefit and Noninterference

The United States' key priorities in sub-Saharan Africa include, among others, building democracy, promoting development, supporting commerce, and strengthening security. Also, in 2000, Congress passed the African Growth and Opportunity Act (AGOA), which extended trade preferences to eligible countries in the region.[22] The Chinese government has published policy papers that articulate its goal of establishing closer ties with African countries and state its principles of engagement, which include seeking mutual benefit for China and African nations and not interfering in African countries' domestic affairs.

U.S. Goals and Programs for Sub-Saharan Africa Include Focus on Development and Emphasis on Democracy and Economic Growth

The U.S. government has articulated its goals for sub-Saharan Africa through annual Department of State (State) bureau plans for the region and through a U.S. strategy announced in June 2012. The fiscal year 2013 State bureau plan for sub-Saharan Africa identifies a number of goals, including strengthening democratic institutions, building respect for human rights, ensuring countries are free of conflict, using U.S. development assistance to improve health and education indicators, and helping sub-Saharan African countries build their share of global trade.[23] According to State officials, State's annual bureau plan had served as the primary U.S. strategy for the region. However, in June 2012, the U.S. government publicly issued its interagency "U.S. Strategy Toward Sub-Saharan Africa."[24] In his letter introducing the current strategy, President Obama highlighted goals related to strengthening democratic institutions and growing Africa's economy as priority efforts critical to the region. The 2012 U.S. strategy articulates four objectives for U.S. interaction with the region that are consistent with the goals in State's bureau plan: strengthen democratic institutions; spur economic growth, trade, and investment; advance peace and security; and promote opportunity and development.

According to U.S. officials, the 2012 strategy is intended to encourage an interagency approach for engagement with sub-Saharan Africa, with greater emphasis on economic and commercial activities.[25] State, Commerce, USAID, and USTR officials said that several agencies are developing plans to coordinate in implementing the strategy's four objectives. Furthermore, according to a State document, U.S. agencies are working to better link trade policy and development objectives. In addition, State has issued a directive to prioritize economic issues in U.S. foreign policy worldwide, including efforts to improve regional economic integration and introduce U.S. businesses to new markets in sub-Saharan Africa. In October 2011, Secretary of State Hillary Clinton stated that, as part of this effort, the U.S. government is evolving its development efforts throughout Africa to increase investments and reinforce, but not replace, what these markets can achieve independently. The President's 2011 Trade Policy Agenda, coordinated by USTR, also states an interest in expanding markets for U.S. goods and services in sub-Saharan Africa and building the region's economic development through trade.[26]

Increased trade with sub-Saharan Africa was identified as a primary U.S. goal in the African Growth and Opportunity Act (AGOA), which was signed into law in 2000 to promote stable and sustainable economic growth and development in the region. AGOA allows eligible sub-Saharan African countries[27] to export to the United States, without import duties, qualifying goods from a list of more than 6,000 items.[28] Currently, 39 countries are eligible for AGOA benefits. As part of AGOA's "third-country fabric provision," a subset of those countries can export to the United States, subject to a cap, apparel made with yarns and fabrics originating anywhere in the world.[29] AGOA also called for an annual forum, known as the U.S.–Sub-Saharan Africa Trade and Economic Forum—a high-level economic dialogue among U.S. and African senior government officials, members of their respective private sectors, and representatives of civil society. U.S. officials have described the annual forum, which has been held in Washington, D.C., and various locations in Africa, as a way to link trade capacity building and trade opportunities. The U.S. government released the "U.S. Strategy Toward Sub-Saharan Africa" at the 2012 forum, which was held in Washington, D.C., and focused on sub-Saharan Africa's infrastructure development to promote trade among the countries of the region and with the United States.

The U.S. government also established trade and investment agreements with sub-Saharan African countries and regional economic communities to promote cooperation on trade and investment issues, including strengthening bilateral ties, improving the business environment, and building trade capacity.[30] These agreements include bilateral investment treaties, which establish some protections and regulations for U.S. investments in partner countries.[31]

In addition, the U.S. government maintains a number of development assistance programs in sub-Saharan Africa to help meet stated goals on promoting opportunity and development.[32] These programs include the Global Health Initiative, which integrates U.S.-funded global health efforts such as HIV/AIDS and malaria; Feed the Future, the U.S. government-wide strategy to address global hunger and food security; the Global Climate Change Initiative, which is intended to better integrate climate-change considerations into U.S. foreign assistance; Millennium Challenge Corporation (MCC) compacts and other programs, which provide grants for development projects to eligible countries; and Partnership for Growth, a U.S. partnership with select countries to promote economic growth through country ownership and joint decision making.[33]

China's Stated Policy for Africa Emphasizes Mutual Benefit and Noninterference

The Chinese government's policies and goals toward sub-Saharan Africa, while not specifically defined for the region, are reflected in two publicly released documents—its African Policy, issued in 2006,[34] and its policy on foreign aid, issued in 2011.[35] The 2006 African Policy states that China's objective in Africa is to promote long-term China-Africa relations in a mutually beneficial manner. The 2006 policy document outlines an approach that includes the principles of respecting African countries' independence and equality; seeking mutual benefit in economic development and cooperation on social development; fostering cooperation with Africa in the United Nations and other multilateral systems; and enhancing mutual learning in areas such as governance and development. Additionally, the 2006 document states that to establish relations with China, a country must adhere to the "one China" principle—that is, cease official relations with Taiwan.[36]

Regarding trade relations with Africa, China's 2006 African Policy includes plans to facilitate access for African commodities to the Chinese market and provide duty-free treatment for imports of some goods from least developed countries, including those in Africa. Additionally, the 2006 policy document expresses support for Chinese investments in Africa and announces continued assistance for Chinese firms through loans and credit lines with preferential terms.[37]

China's published policy on foreign aid, released in 2011, specifies goals that include helping recipient countries, including those in Africa, build development capacity, improve livelihoods, and promote economic growth and social progress. The 2011 policy document emphasizes “South-South cooperation” on foreign aid, indicating that China views itself as a developing country mutually engaged with other developing countries. Similar in content to China’s African Policy, the 2011 policy document notes the following principles of China’s foreign aid policy:

- helping countries build their own capacity for development and self-reliance by fostering local personnel and technical capacity, building infrastructure, and using domestic resources;
- not imposing political conditions or interfering in countries’ internal affairs, and respecting recipient countries’ role in guiding their own development;
- fostering equality and mutual benefit and accommodating recipient countries’ interests;
- maintaining a realistic sense of China’s capacity and resources to provide assistance, while recognizing the needs of recipient countries; and
- attending to reform and innovation to improve the outcomes of foreign aid.

China’s 2011 policy document also indicates that China provides resources for foreign aid through grants, and interest-free and concessional loans.

China offers foreign aid in the form of projects, goods and materials, emergency aid, and debt relief, among others. Moreover, the 2011 document states that 40 percent of China’s global foreign aid expenditures in recipient countries worldwide are for construction projects in which China provides some or all of the financing, services, materials, and labor. Unlike the United States and other nations, China is not a member of the OECD’s Development Assistance Committee and has not agreed to eliminate the tying of aid to the use of its own goods and services.[38]

However, U.S. officials said that China’s participation in the Fourth High-Level Forum on Aid Effectiveness in Busan, South Korea, in November 2011, along with 100 other countries that also are not OECD members, reinforced support for the 2005 Paris Declaration on Aid Effectiveness and represented a significant recognition of China’s role in development assistance.

China’s 2011 policy document states that Chinese experts working on construction projects will adopt the same standards of living as experts in the recipient country. In addition, China’s 2006 African Policy states that the government supports continued financing for Chinese enterprises’ investment and business engagement in Africa. Scholars and U.S. officials have also said that China actively uses its financing and assistance activities to facilitate opportunities for Chinese firms.

The Chinese government has also articulated aspects of its policy toward Africa, including sub-Saharan Africa, at the Forum on China-Africa Cooperation (FOCAC). The Chinese government initiated FOCAC in 2000 as a high-level platform to announce major Chinese initiatives, such as large infrastructure financing packages and trade preferences for Africa, and has convened high-level Chinese and African officials every 3 years since 2000. At the 2012 FOCAC, held in Beijing, the Chinese government reiterated principles from prior meetings and previously issued policy documents, including maintaining high-level engagement, strengthening China-Africa dialogue, and enhancing mutual trust. At that meeting, China also doubled its commitments for financing infrastructure and other development in Africa to $20 billion, from the $10 billion commitment that it announced in

2009; expanded duty-free treatment for certain African exports to China; and reiterated use of the China-Africa Development Fund, which was established in 2006 to fund up to $5 billion in Chinese firms' investments in Africa in sectors such as agriculture, infrastructure, and natural resources.

According to an article from the Centre for Chinese Studies in South Africa, the South African president's critical statements about aspects of China's presence in Africa made at the 2012 FOCAC showed Africans taking a greater stake in shaping the dialogue with China, in contrast to previous FOCAC sessions.[39] In addition, in a speech delivered before the start of the 2012 FOCAC, Chinese Premier Wen Jiabao spoke about unresolved issues in China's relationship with Africa, including the need to diversify trade and investments and increase technology transfer. Figure 2 presents a timeline of key FOCAC announcements in 2000 through 2012.

Data Show Growth in U.S. and Chinese Trade with Sub-Saharan Africa since 2001, but Data on China's Grants, Loans, and Investments Are Limited

Both U.S. and Chinese trade in goods with sub-Saharan Africa increased from 2001 through 2011, with Chinese trade increasing faster and surpassing U.S. trade in 2009. Imports of crude oil have dominated both countries' trade with sub-Saharan Africa. U.S. government aid in the form of grants increased from 2001 through 2010, and U.S. government loans to support U.S. exports and investments increased from 2001 through 2011; data on Chinese government grants and loans to sub-Saharan Africa are limited. Data for 2007 through 2011 suggest that U.S. foreign direct investment flows to the region were larger than China's.40 Mining, including petroleum extraction, was the top investment sector in sub-Saharan Africa for both countries.[41]

U.S. and Chinese Trade in Goods with Sub-Saharan Africa Increased from 2001 to 2011

China overtook the United States as sub-Saharan Africa's largest trading partner in 2009. The United States' and China's total trade in goods with sub-Saharan Africa increased each year from 2001 through 2011, except in 2009 when total trade declined during the global economic crisis (see figure 3).[42]

During that year, China's trade declined by less than the United States', and China overtook the United States as sub-Saharan Africa's largest trading partner. For the United States, growth in imports accounted for 80 percent of growth in total trade from 2001 through 2011; for China, growth in imports accounted for 56 percent of growth in total trade for the same period. China's exports overtook U.S. exports in 2003, with the value of China's exports almost triple the level of U.S. exports in 2011.

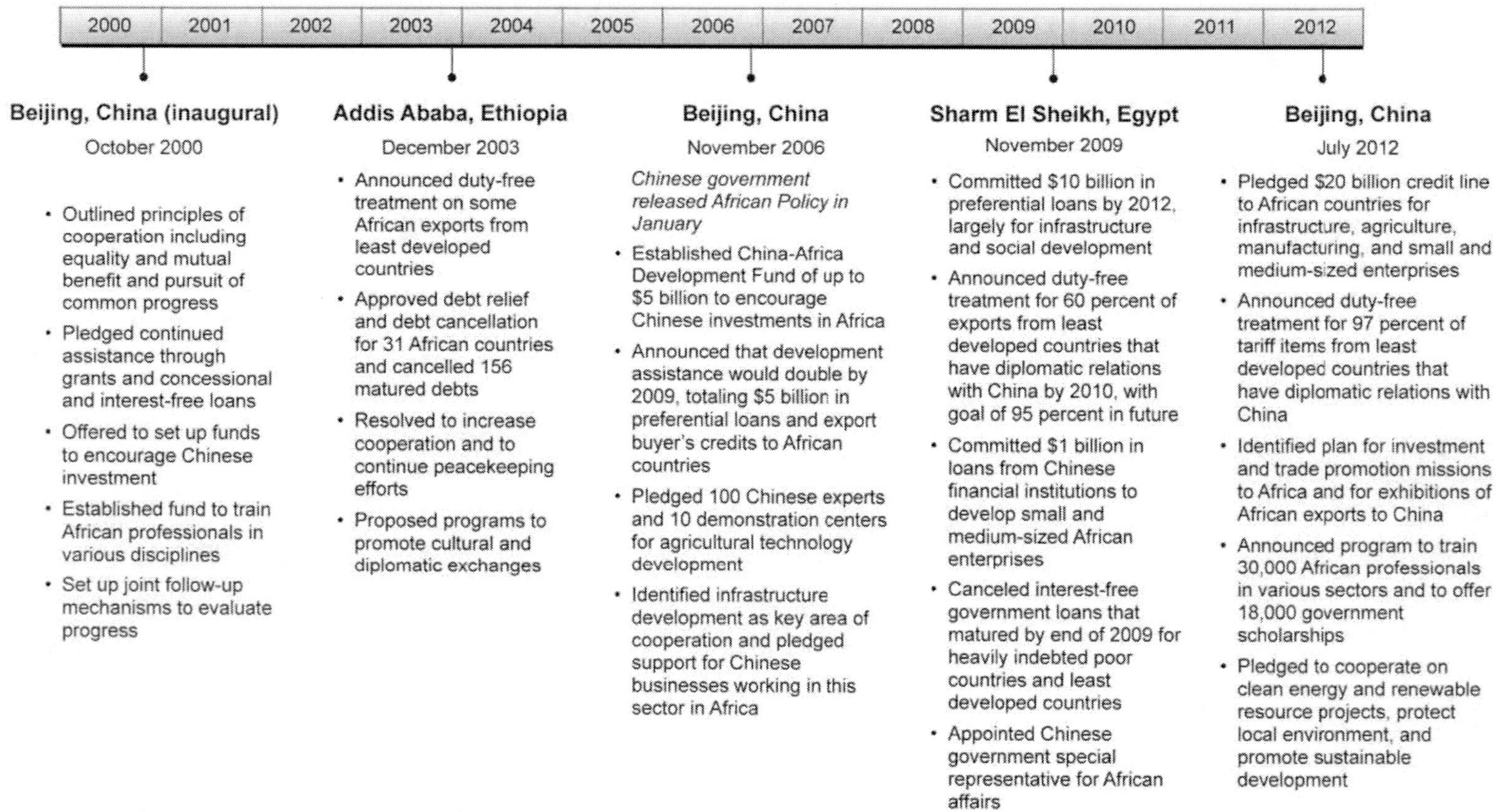

Source: GAO analysis of Chinese government information.

Figure 2. Key Chinese Government Announcements at the Forum on China-Africa Cooperation (FOCAC), 2000-2012.

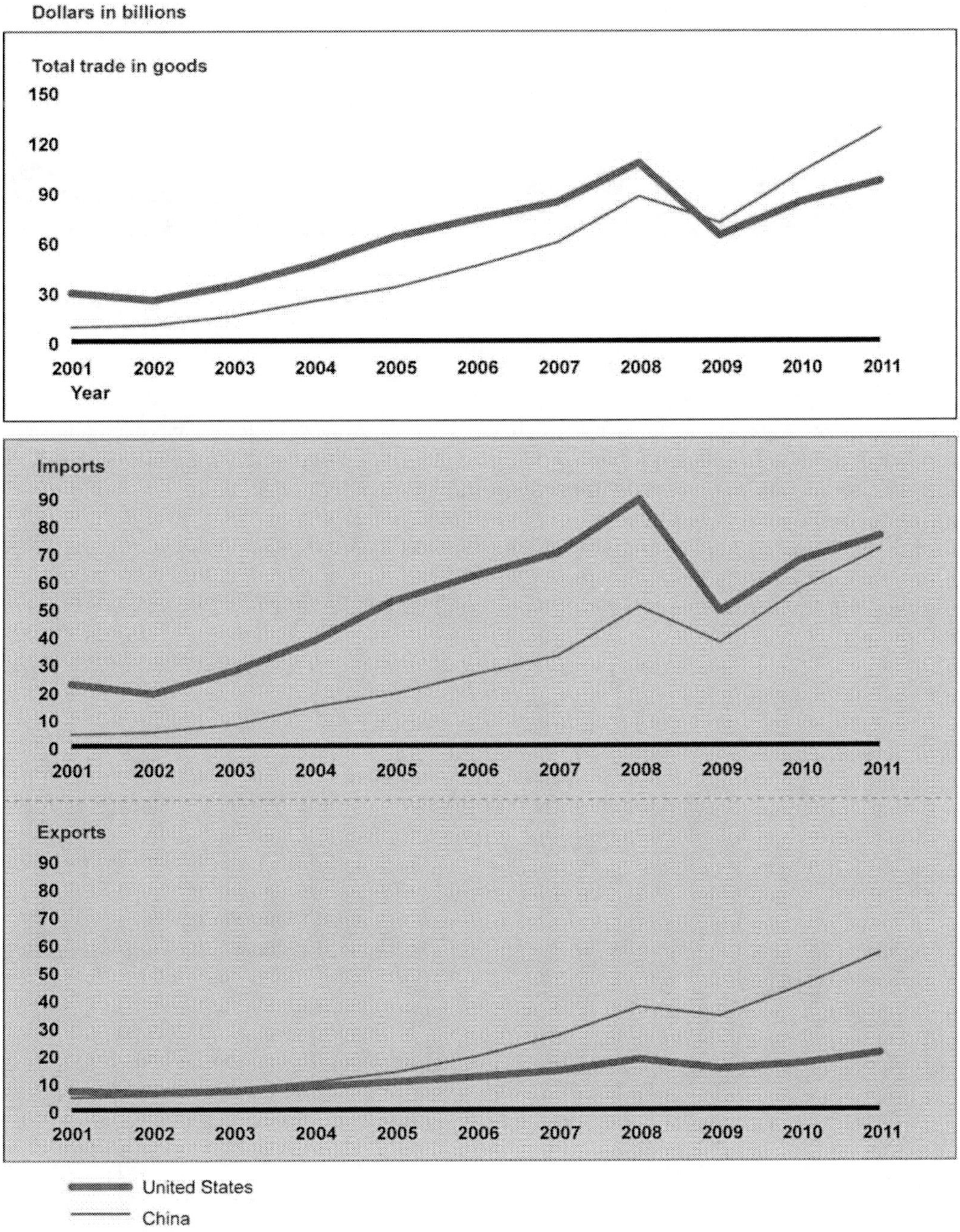

Source: GAO analysis of UN data.

Notes: Total trade in goods is defined as imports plus exports. Trade data are shown in nominal values. Changes in values over time are due in part to changes in the prices of traded goods, such as substantial increases in the price of oil. Data for Chinese imports have been adjusted to exclude imports of a category of goods labeled "special transactions," for consistency with figures reported by the IMF's Direction of Trade Statistics and the World Trade Atlas.

Figure 3. U.S. and Chinese Total Trade, Imports, and Exports of Goods to Sub-Saharan Africa, 2001-2011.

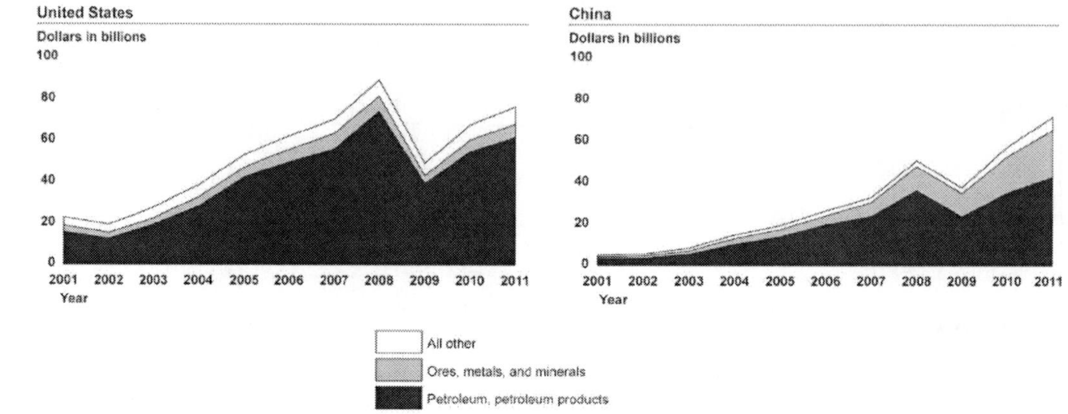

Source: GAO analysis of UN data.

Notes: Import values are shown in nominal dollars. Data for Chinese imports have been adjusted to exclude imports of a category of goods labeled "special transactions," for consistency with data reported by the IMF's Direction of Trade Statistics and the World Trade Atlas.

Figure 4. U.S. and Chinese Imports of Goods from Sub-Saharan Africa, 2001-2011.

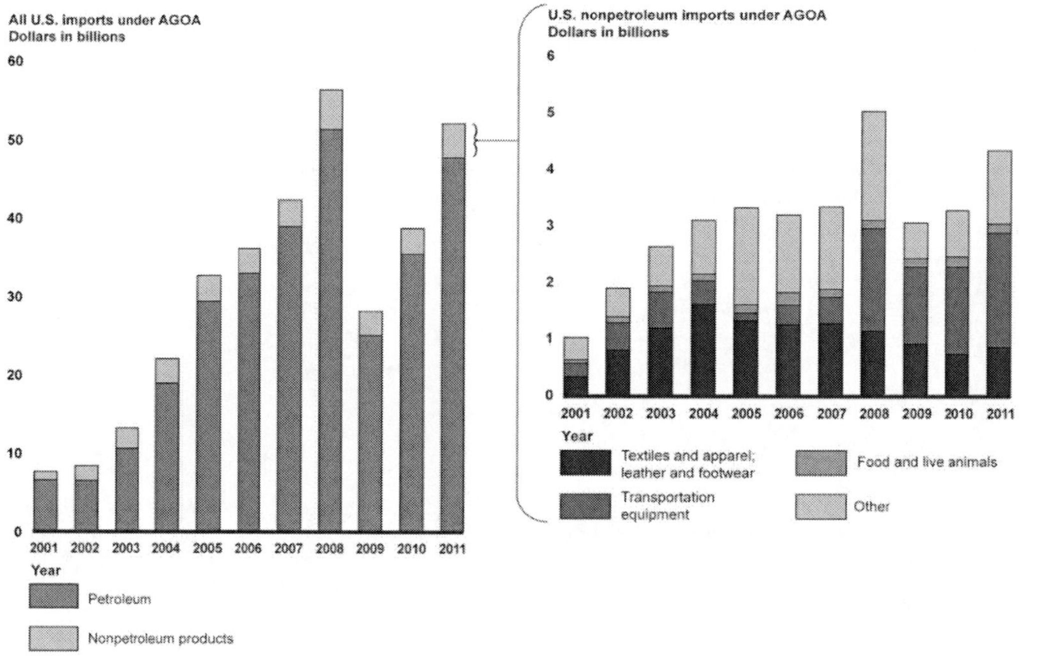

Source: GAO analysis of Department of Commerce Data.

Note: Import values are shown in nominal dollars.

Figure 5. U.S. Imports of Goods from Sub-Saharan Africa under AGOA, 2001-2011.

Crude Oil and Other Natural Resources Have Dominated U.S. and Chinese Imports of Goods from Sub-Saharan Africa

Natural resources have constituted the bulk of U.S. and Chinese imports from sub-Saharan Africa. In 2011, petroleum and petroleum products, primarily crude oil, accounted for 81 percent of the value of U.S. imports, while ores, metals, and minerals accounted for 9 percent. By comparison, petroleum and petroleum products, almost exclusively crude oil, accounted for 59 percent of the value of Chinese imports, while ores, metals, and minerals accounted for 32 percent.[43] As figure 4 shows, U.S. and Chinese imports of petroleum and petroleum products, as well as Chinese imports of ores, metals, and minerals, from sub-Saharan Africa have increased since 2001.[44]

The majority of U.S. imports from sub-Saharan Africa enter the United States without tariffs under AGOA. In 2011, imports under AGOA were approximately 70 percent of the total value of U.S. imports from sub-Saharan Africa.[45] Petroleum imports, primarily from Nigeria and to a lesser extent from Angola, constituted almost 92 percent of AGOA imports, while two categories of goods—transportation equipment and textiles, apparel, leather and footwear—were the primary nonpetroleum AGOA imports (see figure 5).[46]

Almost all Chinese imports from least developed countries in Africa enter China without tariffs.[47] In 2003, China announced that some commodities from least developed countries in Africa would be given duty-free status. By 2007, according to a report by the World Trade Organization that cited Chinese officials, 98 percent of the total value of Chinese imports from least developed countries, including sub-Saharan African countries, was exported to China duty free.[48]

Chinese Exports of Machinery, Transport Equipment, and Manufactured Goods Exceeded U.S. Exports of Goods to Sub-Saharan Africa

Chinese exports to sub-Saharan Africa increased more rapidly than U.S. exports from 2001 through 2011. The value of U.S. exports tripled during this period, from $6.8 billion to $20.3 billion, while the value of Chinese exports grew by a factor of nearly 13, from $4.4 billion to $56.3 billion. The largest category of U.S. exports to sub-Saharan Africa by value was machinery and transport equipment; the largest categories of Chinese exports were manufactured goods and machinery and transport equipment (see figure 6). The United States and China generally exported different types of machinery and transport equipment: motor vehicles and civil-engineering equipment were key U.S. exports, while ships and telecommunications equipment were key Chinese exports. In 2011, U.S. and Chinese exports of machinery and transport equipment to sub-Saharan Africa represented 41 percent and 40 percent, respectively, of the value of the two countries' total exports to sub-Saharan Africa, with China's exports of machinery and transport equipment almost triple the value of the United States'. China's largest category of exports was manufactured goods—for example, cotton fabrics and footwear—representing 49 percent of the value of its exports.

United States and China Have Several Common Trading Partners in Sub-Saharan Africa, but China's Reach Is Greater

In 2011, the United States imported more than $1 billion in goods from each of eight sub-Saharan African countries, and China imported more than $1 billion in goods from each of nine countries. The United States and China each imported more than $1 billion in goods from Nigeria, Angola, South Africa, the Republic of the Congo, and Equatorial Guinea. The United States also imported more than $1 billion in goods from Gabon, Chad, and Côte d'Ivoire, while China imported more than $1 billion in goods from the Democratic Republic of the Congo, Zambia, Sudan, and Mauritania.[49]

With respect to exports, the United States exported more than $1 billion in goods to each of 4 countries in sub-Saharan Africa in 2011, whereas China exported at a similar level to 10 countries (see figure 8). Both countries exported more than $1 billion in goods to South Africa, Nigeria, Angola, and Ghana.[50] In addition, China exported more than $1 billion in goods to Benin, Kenya, Tanzania, Togo, Liberia, and Sudan.

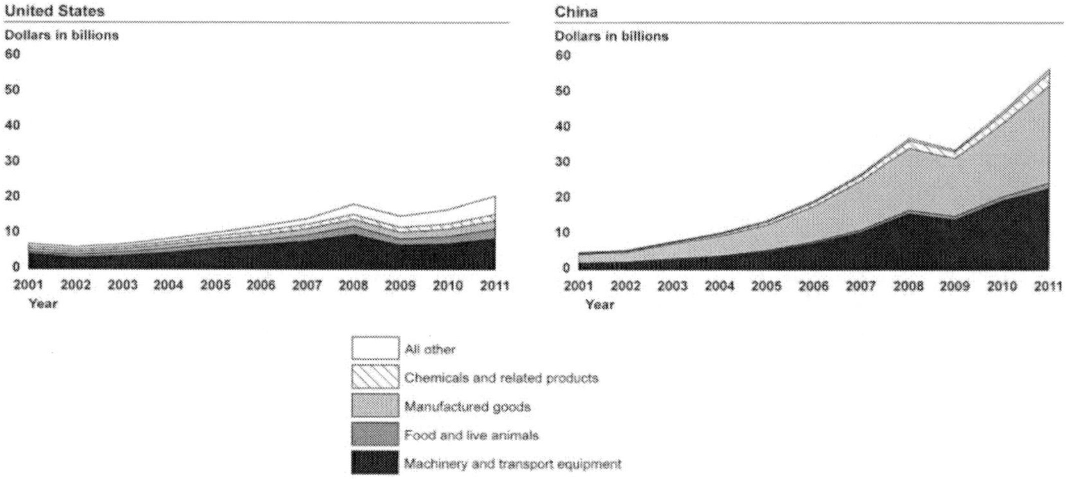

Source: GAO analysis of UN data.
Note: Export values are shown in nominal dollars.

Figure 6. U.S. and Chinese Exports of Goods to Sub-Saharan Africa, 2001-2011.

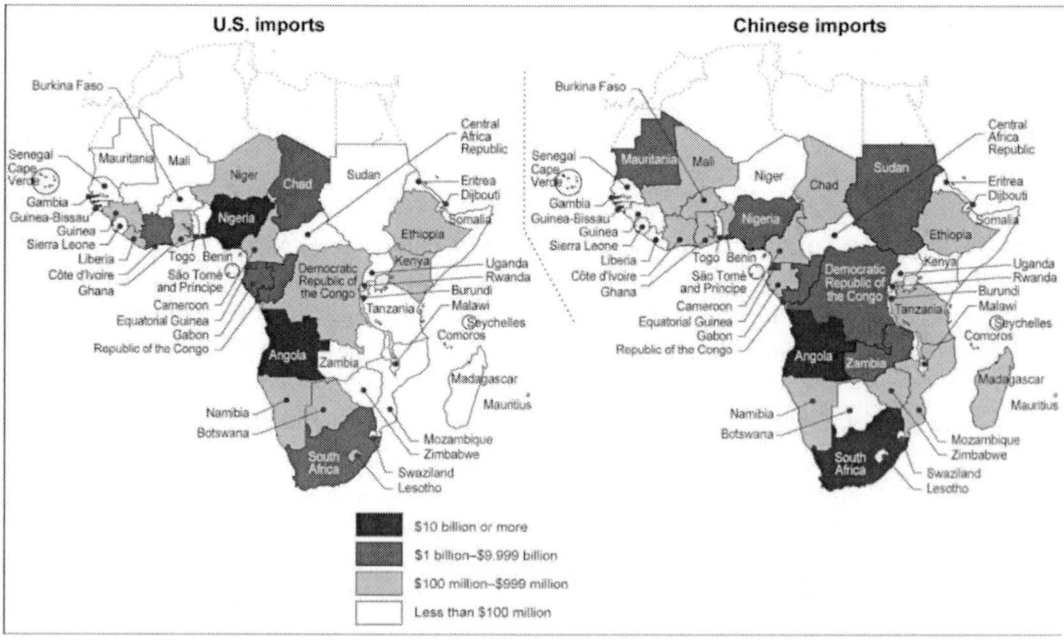

Source: GAO analysis of UN data. Map Resources (map).

Figure 7. U.S. and Chinese Imports of Goods from Sub-Saharan Africa, by Value of Imports and Country of Origin, 2011.

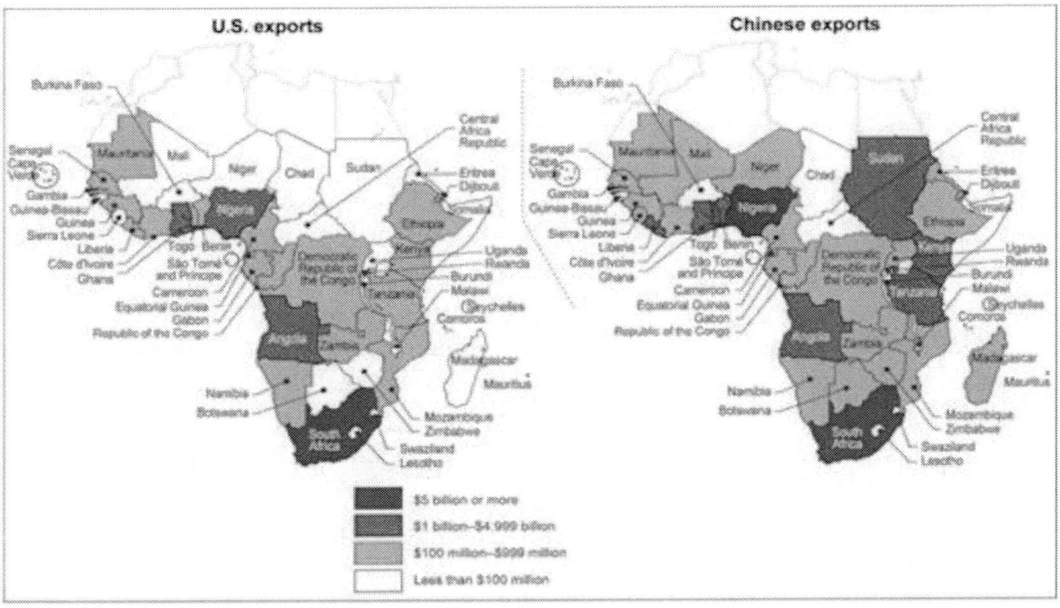

Source: GAO analysis of UN data. Map Resources (map).

Figure 8. U.S. and Chinese Exports of Goods to Sub-Saharan Africa, by Value of Exports and Destination, 2011.

U.S. Trade in Services with Sub-Saharan Africa Is Estimated to Exceed $11 Billion per Year, but Data on China's Trade in Services with the Region Are Unavailable

Estimates on U.S. trade in services indicate that the United States had a surplus in trade in services with sub-Saharan Africa from 2006 through 2011.[51] U.S. imports of services, excluding travel and passenger fares, averaged about $2.6 billion per year, and U.S. exports of services averaged about $9.1 billion per year.[52]

The largest service sectors for U.S. imports were business, professional, and technical services; travel and passenger fares; and financial services.

The largest service sectors for U.S. exports were business, professional, and technical services and travel and passenger fares.[53] Illustrating that business, professional, and technical services was a top sector for U.S. exports of services, data on contracts financed by the World Bank in sub-Saharan Africa from 2001 through 2011 show that most of U.S. firms' contracts were for consulting services and that these services accounted for 72 percent of the combined value of the U.S. firms' contracts.[54]

We were unable to obtain comparable data for China's trade in services with sub-Saharan Africa, in part because China does not publish regional or country-specific data.[55] However, according to experts and U.S. officials, China has been active in providing construction services.

In addition, the data on World Bank–financed contracts show that most of Chinese firms' contracts were for construction services and that these services accounted for 91 percent of the combined value of the Chinese firms' contracts.[56] Figure 9 illustrates the data on World

Bank–financed contracts with firms from the United States, China, and other countries in sub-Saharan Africa.

U.S. Government Grants and Loans to Sub-Saharan Africa Have Increased since 2001, but China Does Not Publish Data on Its Financing

U.S. government development assistance, predominantly grants, to sub-Saharan Africa increased from $1.4 billion in 2001 to $9.2 billion in 2010 (see figure 10).[57] This increase was driven primarily by growth in health assistance, resulting in part from the authorization of the President's Emergency Plan for AIDS Relief in 2003.[58] In 2010, health assistance and humanitarian aid were the largest categories of development assistance in sub-Saharan Africa.

The Chinese government does not regularly report data on its development assistance to sub-Saharan Africa.[59]

However, a white paper describing the Chinese government's foreign aid policy, published by the Information Office of China's State Council for the first time in 2011, states the value and type of development assistance provided worldwide.[60] According to the white paper, between 1950 and 2009, the Chinese government provided $38.8 billion globally in grants, interest-free loans, and concessional loans as foreign aid, with the type of assistance varying by the scale of the project.[61]

The white paper states that Chinese government grants are primarily for social welfare projects such as schools, hospitals, and water-supply projects; technical cooperation; and emergency humanitarian assistance, while the Chinese government's interest-free loans are primarily for construction of public facilities. The paper also states that the Chinese government's concessional loans are primarily for large and medium-sized infrastructure that generates economic and social benefits. An expert in China–Africa relations estimated that the Chinese government provided a total of about $6 billion in aid, including grants and concessional loans, to all of Africa between 2001 and 2009.[62]

U.S. government loans and related financing to support U.S-made products and firms' investments in sub-Saharan Africa increased from 2001 through 2011. U.S. Ex-Im's and OPIC's combined commitments, totaling more than $11.6 billion for this period, rose from an annual average of $858 million for 2001 through 2005 to $1.2 billion for 2006 through 2011.[63] The commitments varied considerably over this period. As figure 11 shows, U.S. Ex-Im's commitments ranged from $342 million in 2009 to about $1.7 billion in 2011, and OPIC's commitments ranged from about $149 million in 2002 to $948 million in 2011. During this period, U.S. Ex-Im financing was largely concentrated in Nigeria, South Africa, Ethiopia, Angola, Kenya, and Ghana, which represented 89 percent of Ex-Im financing committed for sub-Saharan Africa. For example, U.S. Ex-Im provided a direct loan of $806 million to a South African buyer for a U.S. firm's engineering services and provided loan guarantees of $605 million in Ethiopia and $256 million in Angola for lenders' financing to Ethiopian and Angolan buyers of aircraft.[64] OPIC committed its largest amounts of financing in the region for projects such as oil and gas extraction, electric power generation, local banks, and medical equipment sales.

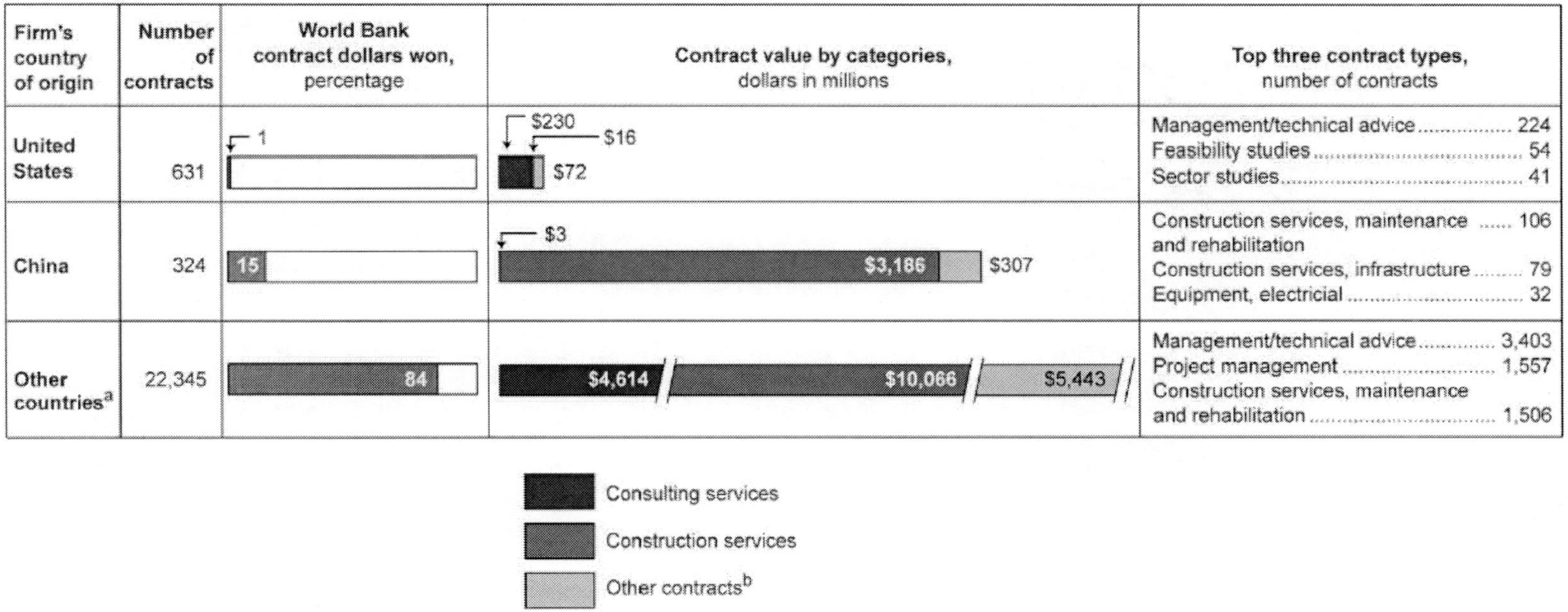

Source: GAO analysis of World Bank data.

Notes: According to the World Bank, data shown include only contracts reviewed by World Bank staff prior to award. In general, these types of contracts constitute about 40 percent of total World Bank investment lending. In addition, the nationality of a firm reflects the country in which it is registered, although the firm's parent may be headquartered in another country.

[a] Firms from at least 135 other countries won World Bank contracts, with firms from Ghana, Nigeria, Senegal, and Tanzania winning the largest numbers of contracts.

[b] Other contracts primarily represent contracts for goods such as transportation equipment, medical equipment and products, and information technology equipment.

Figure 9. World Bank–Financed Contracts Won by Firms from the United States, China, and Other Countries in Sub-Saharan Africa, 2001-2011.

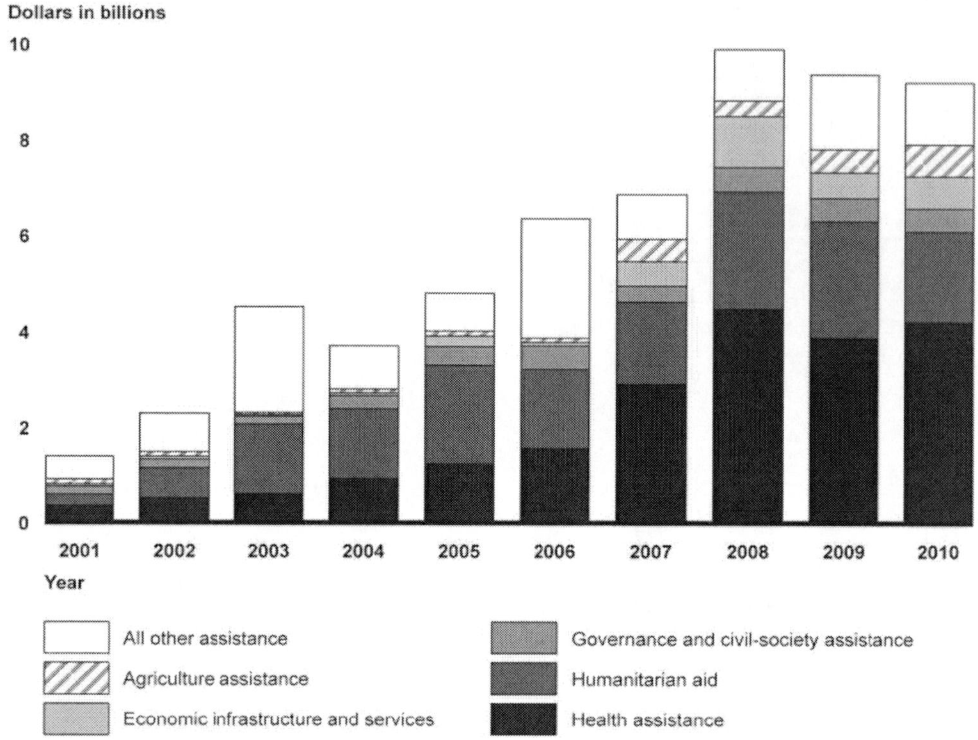

Source: GAO analysis of data fron USAID.

Note: Amounts of aid represent commitments and are shown in nominal dollars. Data for 2011 were not available.

Figure 10. U.S. Government Development Assistance to Sub-Saharan Africa, 2001-2010.

The Chinese government does not publish data on its loans to sub-Saharan Africa.[65] However, according to a World Bank study as well as host-government officials in our case study countries, the Chinese government provides financing such as loans for infrastructure projects that promote the use of Chinese companies and materials.[66] In addition, Chinese officials have provided some general information on the government's loans to all of Africa. In a July 2012 interview with official Chinese media, the president of China Ex-Im stated that in the last 7 to 8 years, China Ex-Im completed about 600 projects and provided approximately $38 billion in loans for all of Africa. In contrast, U.S. Ex-Im authorized approximately $9.8 billion in loans and other financing for all of Africa in the last 8 years. In a May 2012 interview with official Chinese media, the vice president of China Development Bank's China-Africa Development Fund stated that by the end of 2008, the fund had invested about $400 million in 20 projects in Africa.

Reported U.S. Investment in Sub-Saharan Africa Exceeded China's Reported Investment for 2007 through 2011

Data on the United States' and China's investments in sub-Saharan Africa suggest that U.S. foreign direct investment flows exceeded China's reported foreign direct investment flows from 2007 through 2011.[67] During this period, U.S. foreign direct investment flows to sub-Saharan Africa were $16.6 billion and Chinese reported foreign direct investment flows were $12.7 billion.

Figure 12 shows reported annual foreign direct investment flows from the United States and China to sub-Saharan Africa in 2007 through 2011. According to experts, China's foreign direct investment flows are likely underreported and have other limitations.[68] The U.S. foreign direct investment flows shown in figure 12 are less than actual flows, in part because data for some countries in some years are confidential and have not been released; however, the data that have been released are considered generally reliable for the years and countries to which they pertain.

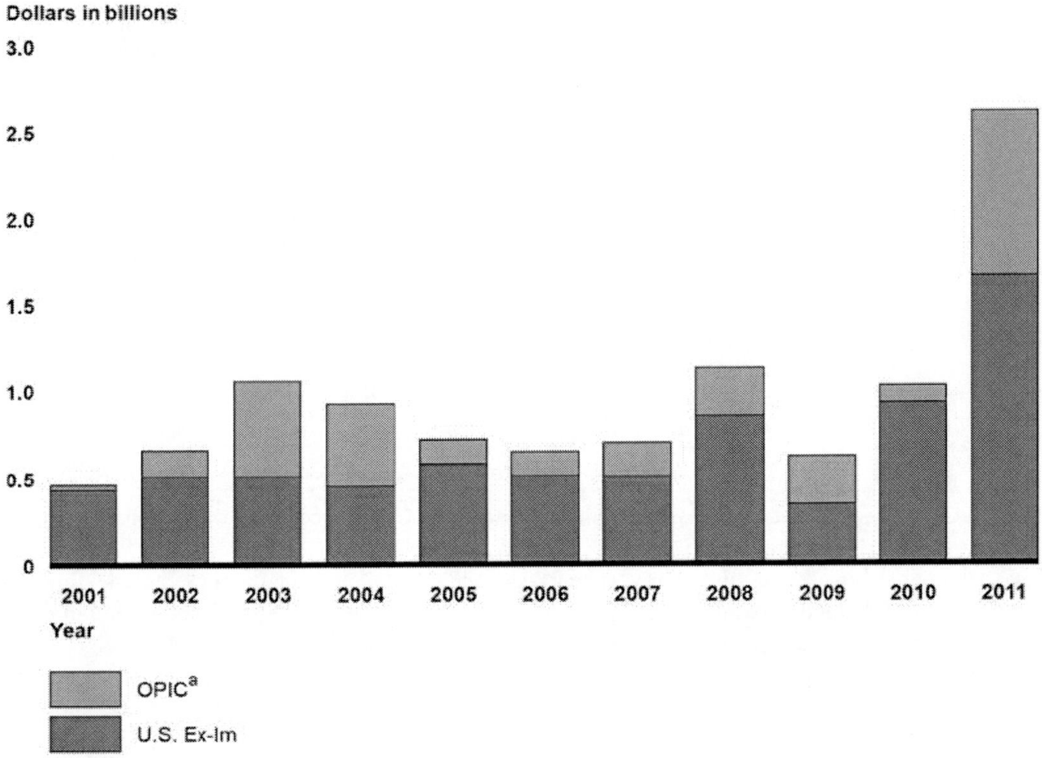

Source: GAO analysis of data from U.S. Ex-Im and OPIC.

Notes: Loans and other financing values are shown in nominal dollars by calendar year. In addition, these values are shown by calendar year, although U.S. Ex-Im and OPIC typically report data by fiscal year.

[a] OPIC may report data for some financing commitments, such as investment funds, only at the regional level. Data shown do not reflect OPIC investment funds for regional use in sub-Saharan Africa. OPIC's net commitments of regional investment funds to sub-Saharan Africa in fiscal years 2001 to 2011 amounted to $659.7 million. According to OPIC officials, because recipients of OPIC investment assistance may choose to invest in a set of countries, OPIC may initially lack information about the use of the assistance, such as the countries where such investments are made. In addition, according to OPIC officials, in countries with limited investment activity, business confidentiality agreements may prevent the disclosure of data that would reveal details of individual transactions.

Figure 11. U.S. Government Loans and Related Financing Committed for U.S.-Made Products and U.S. Firms' Investments in Sub-Saharan Africa, 2001-2011.

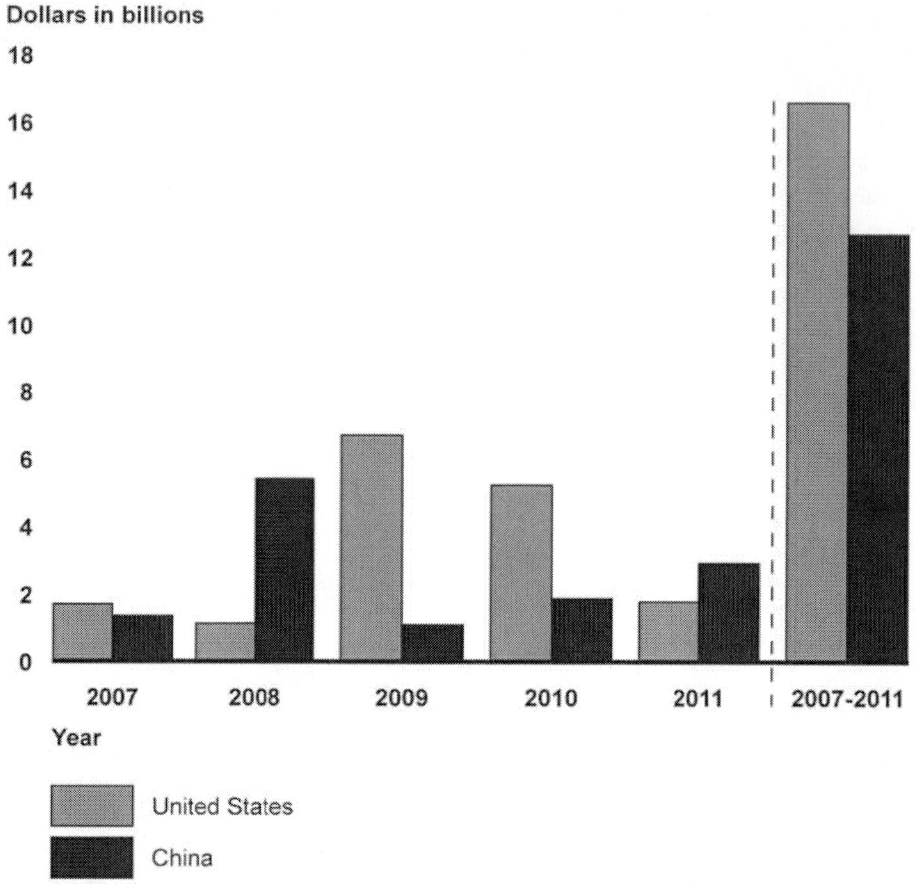

Source: GAO analysis of data from BEA, China's Ministry of Commerce, China's National Bureau of Statistics, and Haver Analytics.

Notes: Although China has reported investment data since 2003, China did not include financial investment in its total investment data prior to 2007. According to experts, China's foreign direct investment flows are likely underreported and have other limitations. U.S. foreign direct investment flows shown are less than actual flows, in part because data for some countries in some years are confidential and have not been released. Foreign direct investment values are shown in nominal dollars.

Figure 12. Reported Flows of Foreign Direct Investment from the United States and China to Sub-Saharan Africa, 2007-2011.

As figure 12 shows, reported foreign direct investment flows to sub-Saharan Africa for the United States and China varied substantially during this period. For example, China's foreign direct investment flows increased significantly in 2008, in part because of the Industrial and Commercial Bank of China's purchase of 20 percent of South Africa's Standard Bank for about $4.8 billion. Also, U.S. foreign direct investment flows increased significantly in 2009, reflecting about $5 billion in flows to Nigeria.

For both the United States and China, the top sector for foreign direct investment was mining. According to the BEA, from 2006 through 2011, the largest share of U.S. foreign direct investment stock was in mining, with a significant portion tied to crude-oil extraction; other major sectors included finance and insurance, nonbank holding companies,[69] and manufacturing.[70] China does not publish data on foreign direct investment in sub-Saharan Africa by sector. However, according to the information office of China's State Council, the top three sectors of China's foreign direct investment stock in all of Africa by the end of 2009 were mining (29 percent), manufacturing (22 percent), and construction (16 percent).[71]

According to experts, China's data on foreign direct investment have several limitations that affect the reliability of these data.

- China's foreign direct investments in sub-Saharan Africa are likely underreported, according to experts. Chinese firms set up subsidiaries, in places such as Hong Kong and the British Virgin Islands, that can be used to make investments in sub-Saharan Africa. Such investments are not captured by China's data on foreign direct investment and may be a significant source of underreporting. In addition, many small and medium-sized enterprises may not register their foreign direct investments, which therefore may not be reflected in China's data.
  The flow data reported for China's foreign direct investment are inconsistent with changes in the stock data, for reasons that are difficult to determine. For example, in 2008, China's foreign direct investment flow to sub-Saharan Africa was reported to be $5.4 billion; however, the change in foreign direct investment stock from the end of 2007 to the end of 2008 was reported to be -$1.6 billion, suggesting a difference of $7 billion between the flow and stock data. According to an IMF working paper, these variations between flows and stock are difficult to explain solely as a result of annual variation in the valuation of the foreign direct investment stock.[72]
- China does not define foreign direct investment when reporting its data. However, the types of data China reports for its foreign direct investments (e.g., equity investment data, reinvested earnings data) are similar to data reported for U.S. foreign direct investment, which the United States defines on the basis of OECD's definition of foreign direct investment.

Although data on U.S. foreign investments are not complete, these data are generally considered reliable. Because of confidentiality, BEA has not released data on certain U.S. foreign direct investments in some countries for certain years. Additionally, according to BEA, U.S. firms, like Chinese firms, may use subsidiaries in other locations to make investments in sub-Saharan Africa that are not captured in the U.S. data on foreign direct investments to sub-Saharan Africa. In addition, the U.S. data may not include smaller firms. According to BEA, U.S. foreign investment data are based on a benchmark survey conducted in 2009, covering the value of all U.S. foreign direct investment. Moreover, U.S. foreign direct investment data do not show inconsistencies between flow data and changes in stock data to the same extent as China's data.

Angola, Ghana, and Kenya Illustrate Trends and Goals of U.S. and Chinese Engagement in Sub-Saharan Africa

The United States' and China's patterns of engagement in our three case-study countries reflect, to varying extents, broader trends in U.S. and Chinese engagement in sub-Saharan

Africa as well as the two governments' goals and policies in the region. Similar to patterns for sub-Saharan Africa overall, crude oil imports have dominated both U.S. and Chinese trade in goods in Angola, and U.S. firms' total investments, driven by investments in the oil sector, have exceeded Chinese firms' total investments in Angola and Ghana. Also, Chinese government loans—mostly to facilitate Chinese firms' prominent role in infrastructure construction—have exceeded U.S. government financing in each of the case-study countries. Use of Chinese firms to implement projects funded through China's loans and grants is consistent with China's policy of mutual benefit in assisting African countries. U.S. officials expressed concern that some aspects of Chinese government loans, such as their lower cost and greater flexibility, may advantage Chinese firms over U.S. firms. However, direct competition between U.S. and Chinese firms in the case-study countries appears to be limited, although counterfeits manufactured by Chinese firms adversely affect U.S. firms' sales and reputation, especially in Kenya among our case study countries. Reflecting the U.S. goal of promoting development, and in contrast to the Chinese government providing financing primarily as loans, the U.S. government has provided increasing amounts of grants for health and humanitarian assistance in one country, Kenya, as it has in sub-Saharan Africa broadly. Finally, host-government requirements, such as regulations on hiring local labor, influence Chinese and U.S. firms' engagement in each case-study country.

Oil Imports Dominate U.S. and Chinese Trade with Angola, with U.S. Firms Investing Heavily in the Oil Sector in Angola and Ghana

As in other parts of sub-Saharan Africa, crude oil has accounted for most of U.S. and Chinese imports from Angola. Available data also show that U.S. firms' investments have been concentrated in the oil sector and exceeded Chinese firms' investments in Angola and Ghana, although the general nature of U.S. and Chinese investments in the sector differed. Kenya currently does not export oil, although some offshore and onshore oil exploration is under way.

U.S. and Chinese Imports

Imports of crude oil dominated overall U.S. and Chinese trade in goods with Angola from 2001 through 2011.[73] In 2011, crude oil imports accounted for 86 percent of U.S. trade in goods with Angola and 90 percent of China's goods trade. Figure 13 shows U.S. and Chinese imports of crude oil from Angola, as well as their total respective trade with Angola, in 2001 through 2011.

Consistent with the overall trend for sub-Saharan Africa, oil was Angola's primary export to the United States under AGOA. Since 2004, crude oil has constituted almost 100 percent of Angola's exports to the United States under AGOA.[74]

U.S. and Chinese Investments

U.S. firms' investments in Angola have been predominantly in the oil sector, where they have greatly exceeded reported investments by Chinese firms. Although China does not publish data on its investments in countries by sectors, available data on U.S. and Chinese firms' investments in Ghana show that U.S. firms' investments, primarily in oil and other mining sectors, have also exceeded the total reported for Chinese firms. Figure 14 shows U.S. and Chinese firms' cumulative reported foreign direct investments in Angola and Ghana. For Angola, data shown for both U.S. and Chinese firms' reported foreign direct investments are from 2007 through 2011, the latest period for which comparable data are available. For Ghana, Chinese firms' reported foreign investments are shown for 2007 through 2011; U.S. data are shown for 2010 to 2011, because BEA has not released confidential data on U.S. foreign direct investments in the country from 2007 through 2009.

Available data showing the extent of U.S. and Chinese firms' ownership of oil blocks in Angola and Ghana provide some indication of their respective investments in the oil sector.[75] According to these data, U.S. firms have invested both as operators and as nonoperators in the oil sector in Angola and Ghana, while Chinese firms have invested as nonoperators in Angola.[76] As of 2012, U.S. firms acted as operators for 11 of 49 oil blocks in Angola and for 2 of 17 oil blocks in Ghana.[77] As operators, they may have a minority stake but are primarily responsible for activities including drilling, maintenance, and ensuring compliance with required rules and regulations.[78] In addition, U.S. firms have purchased ownership interests in 5 oil blocks in Angola and 4 oil blocks in Ghana as nonoperators—that is, with a minority stake and no responsibility for operations. In contrast, Chinese firms have purchased ownership interests in 12 oil blocks in Angola as nonoperators. Firms from other countries — including Angola, Brazil, Denmark, France, Italy, Norway, and the United Kingdom, among others—also have operator and nonoperator roles in these oil blocks.[79] Figure 15 presents information on U.S. and Chinese firms' investments in oil blocks in Angola and Ghana.

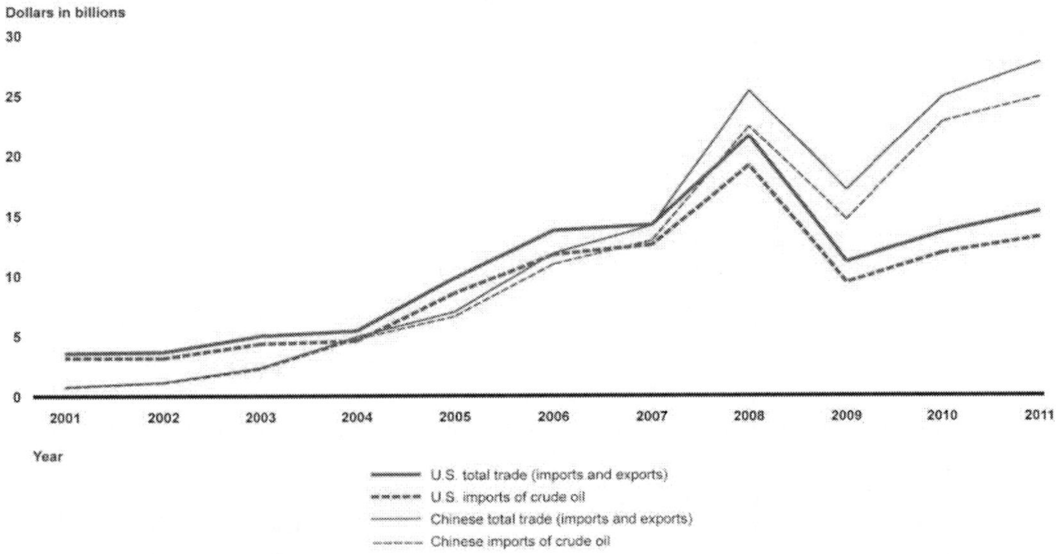

Source: GAO analysis of UN data.

Notes: Total trade is defined as imports plus exports. Trade data are reported in nominal values. Changes in values over time are due in part to changes in the prices of traded goods.

Figure 13. U.S. and Chinese Crude Oil Imports and Total Trade with Angola, 2001-2011.

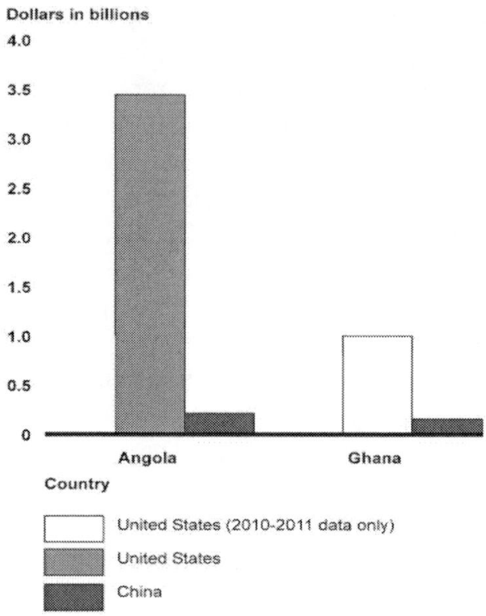

Source: GAO analysis data from BEA and China's Ministry of Commerce.

Notes: BEA did not release U.S. foreign direct investment data for Ghana from 2007 to 2009 for confidentiality reasons. According to experts, China's foreign direct investment data are likely underreported.

Figure 14. U.S. and Chinese Firms' Cumulative Reported Foreign Direct Investments in Angola and Ghana, 2007-2011.

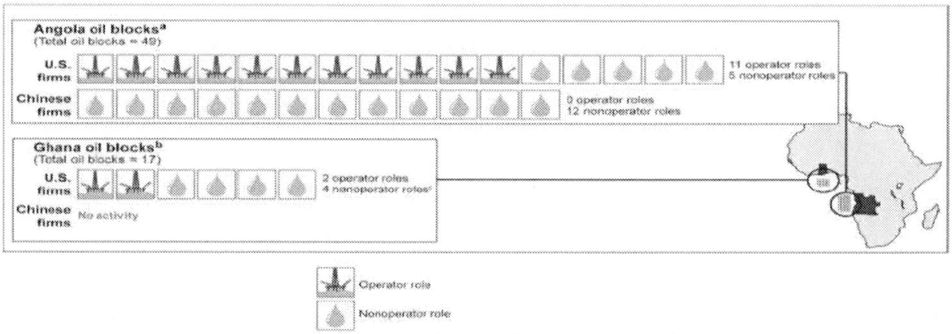

Source: GAO analysis of information from the governments of Angola and Ghana (data); MapInfo (map).

Notes: An operator is generally the oil company that engages in drilling, service, and other operations; an operator has primary responsibility for maintaining well operations and ensuring compliance with required rules and regulations. A nonoperator generally has an ownership stake, similar to a minority and noncontrolling interest.

[a] In addition to U.S. firms, other firms, including firms from Angola, Brazil, France, Denmark, and the United Kingdom, operate Angola's 49 oil blocks.

[b] In addition to U.S. firms, other firms, including firms from Bermuda, Italy, Nigeria, and the United Kingdom, operate Ghana's 17 oil blocks. In one oil block, one U.S. firm had an operator role and another U.S. firm had a nonoperator role.

Figure 15. Numbers and Types of U.S. and Chinese Firms' Investments in Oil Blocks in Angola and Ghana as of 2012.

U.S. oil companies have an operator role in several oil blocks in Angola and Ghana because of the superior technological capability and management expertise required for complex offshore oil exploration and production operations, according to representatives from major oil firms and U.S. agency officials. In contrast, Chinese firms generally lack the technology and capacity to manage offshore oil operations.[80] However, as nonoperators, Chinese firms can acquire project management experience by participating in decision making for oil well operations, according to a representative from another large oil firm.

Chinese firms have been willing to pay high prices to acquire ownership interest as nonoperators in Angola. According to a representative from a large U.S. oil company, in some instances Chinese firms have been willing to pay much higher prices than U.S. firms to purchase ownership interests, in part because Chinese firms are not answerable to shareholders and because they receive support, including financing, from the Chinese government. For example, the representative said, in 2008, no U.S. firm could match a Chinese firm's offer of $1 billion in "bonus" funds to purchase partial ownership in an oil block in Angola.[81] According to a representative from another large U.S. oil firm, Chinese firms do not consider the cost and profitability of their oil sector purchases in the same manner as Western firms, because Chinese state-owned firms may view these purchases as a means of meeting the Chinese government's strategic objective of securing oil supply.[82]

The Chinese Government Has Provided More Loans Than the U.S. Government, Primarily for Construction by Chinese Firms

Available data indicate that Chinese government loans to the governments of all three case-study countries—primarily for infrastructure construction by Chinese firms—have exceeded U.S. government loans. The Chinese government has also provided a small amount of grants, mostly for construction projects. The tying of loans and grants to the use of Chinese firms is consistent with China's policy of seeking mutual benefit in assisting African countries with infrastructure development; however, U.S. officials are concerned that China's loans may disadvantage U.S. firms. In addition to financing from the Chinese government, funding from other donors, including the United States, has supported Chinese firms' infrastructure construction projects.

Chinese Government Loans Exceed U.S. Government Loans and Benefit Chinese Firms

Available data indicate that Chinese government loans and related financing to Angola, Ghana, and Kenya have exceeded U.S. government loans and related financing.[83] As figure 16 shows, Chinese government credit lines to Angola from 2002 through 2011 exceeded U.S. loans and related financing by more than $11 billion, Chinese government loans to Ghana from 2006 through 2011 exceeded U.S. loans and related financing by more than $2.4 billion, and Chinese government loans to Kenya from July 2009 through June 2012 exceeded U.S. government loans and related financing by more than $77 million.[84]

Chinese government loans and related financing were primarily for infrastructure projects, such as construction of roads, rail, hospitals, schools, housing, and water and energy infrastructure, to be implemented by Chinese firms, including state-owned firms.[85] U.S. officials observed that China's infrastructure construction addresses a key need in Africa. In contrast to Chinese loans and related financing, U.S. government loans and related financing generally have supported private-sector and host-government purchases of U.S. exports, including aircraft and machinery, through U.S. Ex-Im, as well as investments in loan portfolios, geothermal energy, and medical equipment through OPIC. U.S. agencies such as U.S. Ex-Im and OPIC offer loans and related financing for specific transactions intended to increase U.S. exports or benefit U.S. firms' investments.

The government of China has generally committed loans and credit lines to support Chinese firms' infrastructure construction in the three case-study countries through high-level agreements with each country's government. For example:

- *Angola.* The Chinese government's commitments of about $12 billion in credit lines to the Angolan government in 2002 through 2011 have driven much of Chinese firms' engagement in the country, according to U.S. and Angolan officials.[86]
- *Ghana.* The Chinese government signed a $3 billion loan agreement with the Ghanaian government in December 2011 for 12 eligible infrastructure projects to be implemented primarily by Chinese firms,[87] according to Ghana's finance ministry.[88]
- *Kenya.* The Chinese government's commitments of about $480 million in loans, mostly for infrastructure construction, between July 2009 and June 2012 were generally provided under agreements between the Chinese and Kenyan governments. According to Kenyan finance ministry officials, these agreements identified Chinese firms that would implement loan-financed projects.

Chinese government loans and related financing for projects in Africa have enabled Chinese firms to establish and expand operations within the region. For example, according to officials from an Angolan nongovernmentalorganization (NGO), Chinese state-owned enterprises and, later, Chinese private-sector firms began operating in Angola after the Chinese government agreed to provide loans to the Angolan government following the conclusion of the country's civil war in 2002.

According to Kenyan officials, China's investments in Kenya have increased, in part because some Chinese firms that initially came to Kenya to work on Chinese government–financed projects have diversified into other sectors.

In addition providing loans, the Chinese government has also provided small amounts of grant assistance, primarily for infrastructure such as hospitals, government buildings, and sports stadiums that were built by Chinese firms. For example, China committed almost $39 million in grant funding to Kenya from July 2009 through June 2012 for construction projects including roads, a sports stadium, and a hospital, according to Kenyan government reports on donor funding. In 2011, China committed $15 million in grants for the construction of Ghana's Ministry of Foreign Affairs' building, according to Ghanaian government budget reports.[89]

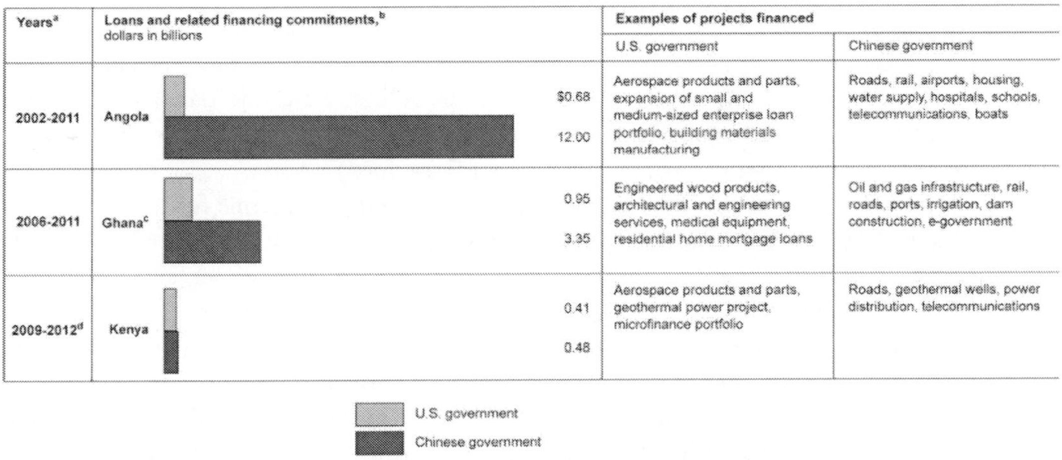

Source: GAO analysis data from OPIC, U.S. Ex-Im, U.S. officials, experts and government of Ghana and Kenya.

[a] Data on Chinese government loans and related financing for each country were available only for the indicated periods. Although data on U.S. government loans and related financing are available for prior years, U.S. government commitments are shown only for the indicated periods.

[b] U.S. government commitments include loans and related financing such as loan guarantees and insurance. Chinese government commitments include credit lines as well as loans. In Angola, China committed credit lines, from which a borrower can draw funds, incurring a loan.

[c] The Ghanaian government published data on China's loan commitments as of September of each year in its annual budget documents for 2006 through 2011. Available budget data did not include China's $3 billion loan to Ghana signed in December 2011. We have included the $3 billion loan with previous loan commitments because this financing represents China's most significant loan package to Ghana.

[d] U.S. government and Chinese government loans and related financing commitments are presented for Kenya's fiscal years, from July 2009 through June 2012, because data for China were only available for this period.

Figure 16. Available Data on U.S. Government and Chinese Government Loans and Related Financing Commitments for Angola, Ghana, and Kenya.

U.S. Officials Are Concerned That Chinese Government Loans May Disadvantage U.S. Firms

U.S. officials from several agencies expressed concerns that some aspects of Chinese government loans—their lower cost, greater flexibility, and lack of transparency—may advantage Chinese firms over U.S. firms.

- *Lower cost.* Our analysis of information on specific Chinese government infrastructure loans to Angola, Ghana, and Kenya showed that borrowers' costs for these loans have generally been less than borrowers' costs for U.S. government loans to Angola and Kenya, and, to a lesser extent, to Ghana (see app. II for more details).[90] The Chinese government loans that we analyzed generally required a lower repayment over time, in terms of net present value, than would a U.S. government loan for a similar project.[91] For example, compared with China Ex-Im's and China Development Bank's November 2009 loans of $6 billion and $1.5 billion, respectively, to Angola, the repayment required for a hypothetical U.S. Ex-Im loan to

Angola at the same time and of the same size would be greater because of factors such as higher fees (7.62 percent up-front fees for the U.S. Ex-Im loan vs. 0.25 percent fees for the China Ex-Im and China Development Bank loans) and a shorter repayment period (5 years for the U.S. Ex-Im loan vs. 15 years for the China Ex-Im loan and 8 years for the China Development Bank loan).[92]

- *Greater flexibility.* China's loans may provide more flexible terms for the use of local content such as labor and materials, making them more attractive to host-country governments. U.S. Ex-Im finances the purchase of goods originated and shipped from the United States and also finances U.S.-provided services. In addition to financing U.S. exports, U.S. Ex-Im may in some cases provide financing for local costs, such as local labor and materials, up to 30 percent of the contract value of the export.[93] U.S. Ex-Im authorized more than $70 million for local costs in Ghana between 2001 and 2011, equal to about 10 percent of its export financing for Ghana. Under its recent $3 billion loan agreement with Ghana, China agreed to finance 60 percent Chinese content and up to 40 percent Ghanaian content, according to a senior Ghanaian government official.[94]
- *Lack of transparency.* U.S. officials and others noted that, in general, the Chinese government's engagement with African countries lacks transparency. According to U.S. officials, in some cases the lack of transparency regarding aspects of Chinese government loans, such as their amount, terms, and purpose, may limit the U.S. government's ability to provide competitive loans to support the purchase of U.S. exports, thus affecting U.S. firms' ability to compete with Chinese firms' costs of products and services. For instance, according to U.S. Ex-Im officials, absence of information on the cost of China's loans may prevent U.S. Ex-Im from offering competitive loans for U.S. exports and may thus disadvantage U.S. firms interested in exporting their goods and services. According to agency officials, U.S. Ex-Im adheres to OECD rules, which in rare cases allow a participant export credit agency to match a non-OECD participant's financing terms and conditions, if there is evidence or specific information about the non-OECD country's financing offer. However, according to U.S. Ex-Im, such information is typically difficult to obtain from the borrower, who is the potential beneficiary of the better terms. Moreover, because the Chinese government is generally not transparent in its lending practices, according to U.S. Ex-Im officials, it is difficult to obtain specific information on China's financing terms and U.S. Ex-Im can rarely use this OECD provision.[95]

Other Donors Have Also Financed Construction by Chinese Firms

Funding provided by other donors, such as the World Bank and the United States through MCC, has supported construction projects for which Chinese firms have competed in the case-study countries.[96] For example, according to data on World Bank-funded contracts in the three case-study countries, Chinese firms won about $455 million in contracts for construction projects.[97] In Ghana, the only one of our three case-study countries to qualify for an MCC compact, Chinese firms won about $112 million in contracts (22 percent of overall MCC-Ghana contract dollars) for construction projects. Chinese firms are also heavily engaged in construction contracts for the African Development Bank in Kenya, according to one donor official.[98] Figure 17 shows examples of Chinese firms' construction projects in Angola, Ghana, and Kenya.

Source: GAO.
Housing units near Luanda, Angola, being constructed by Chinese firms, according to a U.S. official.

Source: GAO.
Accra Sports Stadium, the primary soccer arena in Accra, Ghana, renovated by a Chinese firm for the 2008 Africa Cup of Nations.

Source: GAO.
Nairobi–Thika Highway, built by three Chinese state-owned firms and funded by the African Development Bank and the Chinese government in Kenya.

Figure 17. Examples of Construction Projects Implemented by Chinese Firms in Angola, Ghana, and Kenya.

Chinese firms are competitive in the construction sector in part because their business practices keep construction costs low, according to officials from U.S. and host-country governments and other donor organizations. For example, Chinese firms house workers near project sites and maintain long work days. According to some host-government officials, because Chinese firms are engaged in infrastructure development in other parts of Africa, their cost of moving materials and equipment to new project sites may be lower than that of other firms. An official from a donor organization in Kenya noted that Chinese firms have bid below estimates developed by independent engineers who assessed costs for donor-funded projects.

Competition between U.S. and Chinese Firms and Products Has Been Limited

U.S. and Chinese firms and products largely operate in different, noncompeting sectors in the three case-study countries, aside from their operations in the information and technology sector. U.S. and Chinese firms also face limited competition in part because U.S. firms are less willing to conduct business in some areas of sub-Saharan Africa, citing factors such as business risk and market size. In addition, counterfeits manufactured by Chinese firms adversely affect U.S. firms' sales and reputation in Kenya.

U.S. and Chinese Firms Generally Operate in Different Sectors

U.S. and Chinese firms and products generally operate in different sectors, with the exception of the information and communications sector, according to officials from U.S. agencies and U.S. firms in the three case-study countries. For example, U.S. officials in Angola noted that U.S. firms are active primarily in the oil and gas sector, while Chinese firms are active in the construction sector.[99] Similarly, U.S. officials and host-government officials in Ghana stated that U.S. firms are generally more engaged in higher-technology sectors, while Chinese firms are most active in infrastructure construction. Moreover, according to Commerce officials, anecdotal evidence suggests that U.S. firms are choosing not to compete for projects such as major infrastructure construction for which they perceive competition with Chinese firms to be extremely difficult.

Data on World Bank– and MCC-funded contracts illustrate U.S. and Chinese firms' operations in noncompeting sectors. In all three case-study countries, U.S. firms won a small share of the combined value of these donor-funded contracts, primarily for consulting services, while Chinese firms won a much larger share of these contracts' combined value, primarily for construction services. In Ghana, the only case-study country to qualify for an MCC compact, no U.S. firms bid on MCC contracts for construction projects, according to officials who oversaw MCC contracts in Ghana, while Chinese firms won about $112 million in contracts (22 percent of overall MCC contract dollars), all for construction projects.[100] Similarly, in all three countries, Chinese firms won a large share of World Bank–financed construction contracts but won a very small share of consulting contracts.[101] Figure 18 shows World Bank–financed contracts won by U.S. and Chinese firms, as well as firms from other countries, in Angola, Ghana, and Kenya from 2001 to 2011.

Data from Commerce provide some evidence that European firms have been U.S. firms' primary competitors for host-country government contracts in our case-study countries. From August 2002 to February 2012, U.S. firms requested assistance from Commerce's Advocacy Center in competing for 47 host-government contracts for goods and services in Angola, Ghana, and Kenya. Chinese firms competed for 9 of these contracts, mostly in Ghana and Kenya, for telecommunications, computers and information technology, and transportation services (see figure 19). French, German, and British firms competed with U.S. firms for more of the contracts and in more sectors, including oil and gas, energy and power, aerospace, and telecommunications, than did Chinese firms.

U.S. and Chinese firms' competition in information technology and telecommunications was particularly noted by U.S. officials and U.S. firms in Kenya, although it is unclear whether this competition directly affects U.S.-made exports to these countries. For instance, a senior official at a large U.S. information and communications technology firm noted that Chinese firms are innovating and adapting quickly to local markets, such as in Kenya, where a Chinese firm in this sector has established one of Kenya's largest training centers.[102] In addition, trade data indicate that China's exports of telecommunications equipment to Kenya rose from $0.5 million in 2001 to $122 million in 2011. However, the extent to which direct competition from Chinese firms affects U.S.-made exports is unclear, in part because multinational corporations headquartered in the United States operate and export globally. For example, according to a representative of a U.S. firm that manufactures telecommunications equipment, because most of its products are manufactured outside the United States, competition from Chinese telecommunications firms does not affect its U.S.-made exports.

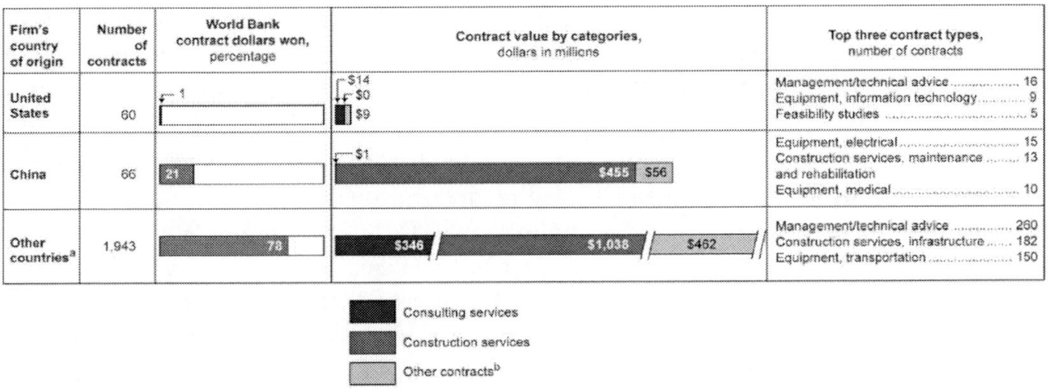

Source: GAO analysis of World Bank data.

Notes: According to the World Bank, the data shown include only contracts reviewed by World Bank staff prior to award. In general, these types of contracts constitute about 40 percent of total World Bank investment lending. The nationality of a firm reflects the country where it is registered, although the firm's parent may be headquartered in another country.

[a] Firms from at least 52 other countries won World Bank contracts, with firms from Angola, Ghana, and Kenya winning the most contracts.

[b] Other contracts primarily include contracts to provide goods such as transportation equipment, medical equipment and products, and information technology equipment.

Figure 18. World Bank–Financed Contracts with U.S., Chinese, and Other Firms in Angola, Ghana, and Kenya, 2001-2011.

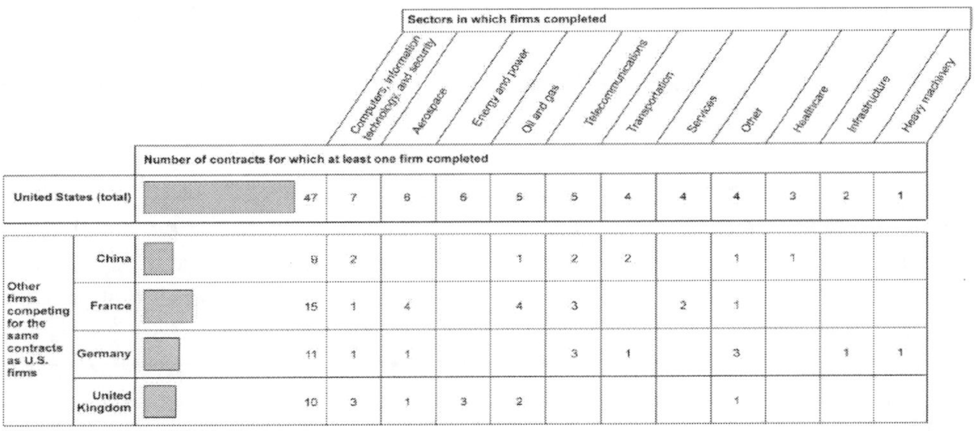

Source: GAO analysis of Department of Commerce data.

Notes: Data shown are for 47 contracts for which U.S. firms requested Department of Commerce advocacy assistance in August 2002 through February 2012. Firms from France, Germany, and the United Kingdom competed with U.S. firms for the largest numbers of contracts.

Figure 19. Nationality of Firms Competing for 47 Angolan, Ghanaian, and Kenyan Government Contracts, 2002-2012.

Business Risk and Market Size Limit U.S.-Chinese Competition

Competition between U.S. and Chinese firms may be limited in part by U.S. firms' hesitation to conduct business in parts of sub-Saharan Africa, owing to factors such as business risk and market size. According to U.S. and host-country officials, U.S. firms are less willing than Chinese firms to risk investments in sectors other than oil and gas because U.S. firms are concerned about risks associated with conducting business in the region, such as corruption and a lack of economic and political stability. For example, according to a senior representative from a U.S. firm in Kenya, the business environment in Kenya, and in East Africa broadly, lacks the regulatory and structural framework to which U.S. firms are accustomed. U.S. firms prefer limited risk and moderate growth, whereas Africa overall is a higher-risk and higher-growth market, according to the U.S. firm representative. In addition, U.S. and Ghanaian officials stated that markets such as Ghana are often too small to be cost-effective for U.S. firms' operations and that these firms are therefore unwilling to invest. In contrast to U.S. firms, Chinese firms are more willing to be flexible in commercial dealings—for example, collaborating with local businesses—and to take on business risk, according to business representatives and U.S. officials in Kenya and Ghana. Some officials stated that this willingness results in part from Chinese government financing, which helps offset risks that other firms must face independently and which eases decision making in the absence of accountability to shareholders.

Chinese Counterfeits Have Negatively Affected U.S. Firms

Counterfeit goods and related products from China have adversely affected U.S. firms' sales and reputation, especially in Kenya among our case-study countries.[103] According to a 2012 study by the Kenyan Association of Manufacturers, counterfeit goods primarily from China, especially in the energy, electronic, and electrical components sectors, have negatively affected the sales and reputation of U.S. firms and others with operations in Kenya.[104] For example, a representative of a U.S. firm that manufactures batteries in Kenya noted that an influx of counterfeit and substandard products, mainly from China, caused the U.S. firm's business to decline and that over time the firm has decreased the number of its employees in Kenya from 800 to 300.[105] In some cases, Chinese products, although of poorer quality, also mimicked the U.S. firm's product branding and color schemes, according to a former senior executive of this U.S. firm. The former executive noted that although the U.S. firm successfully litigated in Kenyan courts against this trademark infraction, the penalty was too lenient to have a deterrent effect on the Chinese manufacturers. In another instance, a representative of a large U.S. firm with regional headquarters in Kenya stated that the Chinese theft of intellectual property, in general, is one of the biggest challenges that U.S. firms face in Africa.[106] To combat Chinese counterfeits, the U.S. embassy in Kenya has sponsored several public-education programs, and the U.S. government is providing technical assistance to Kenya's Anti-Counterfeit Agency, established in 2010.

U.S. Government Engagement in Kenya Illustrates Strong Focus on Aid

Similar to overall U.S. aid trends for sub-Saharan Africa, and in keeping with the U.S. goal to support development in the region, the U.S. government has provided generally increasing amounts of development assistance, predominantly grants, to Kenya, primarily driven by health and humanitarian assistance (see figure 20).[107] From 2001 to 2010, the United States committed almost $4 billion in development assistance to Kenya.[108]

U.S. aid to Kenya also included assistance for building trade capacity. From 2001 to 2011, about 96 percent of U.S. imports from Kenya under AGOA consisted of apparel, textiles, leather, and footwear (see figure 21). AGOA's "third-country fabric" provision has enabled Kenya to increase its apparel exports generally, according to U.S. and Kenyan officials, and Kenya has become one of the largest sub-Saharan African exporters of nonpetroleum goods to the United States under AGOA. U.S. and Kenyan officials pointed to the positive employment effects in Kenya associated with apparel exports under AGOA. However, they also noted AGOA's limited success in enabling Kenya and other sub-Saharan African countries to manufacture the textiles and fabrics that form the input for apparel manufacturing. Kenya and Ghana obtain fabrics mostly from China and other Asian countries to manufacture apparel for export to the United States, according to U.S. officials in these countries.109 Chinese exports of textile and fabrics to Kenya grew during this period from $40 million in 2001 to $347 million in 2011.

Limited available data suggest that, in contrast to U.S. aid, China's aid as grants to Kenya was relatively small.[110] Moreover, U.S. officials stated that projects supported by China's grants—primarily infrastructure projects—are different from those supported by the United States in Kenya. Nevertheless, according to USAID officials, China's funding of infrastructure projects, through loans and grants, complements the U.S. government's focus on aid for poverty reduction. U.S. officials and other donors further observed that although China is invited to donor meetings, it does not actively coordinate its projects with other donors, preferring instead to work with host-country officials directly.

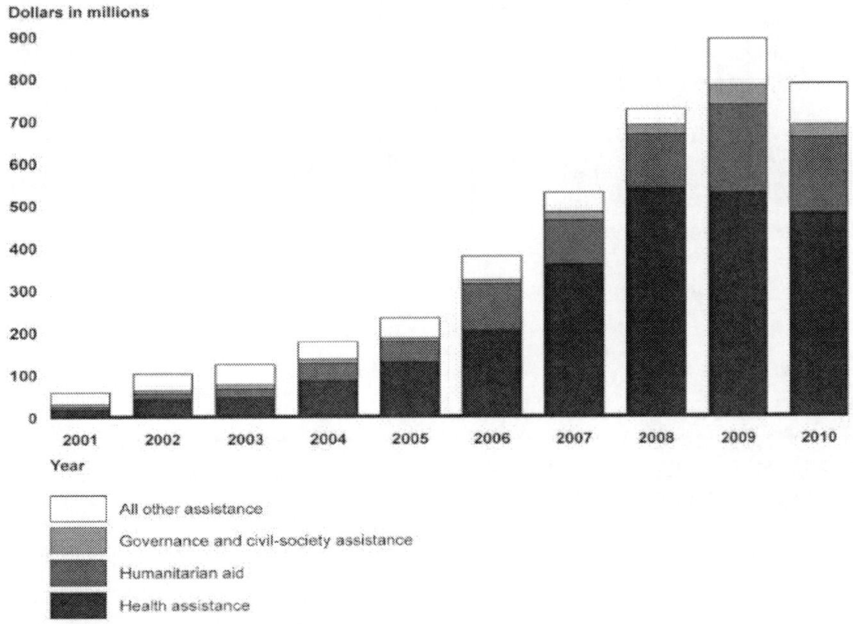

Source: GAO analysis of data from USAID.

Note: Data are reported in nominal dollars.

Figure 20. U.S. Development Assistance Committed to Kenya, 2001-2010.

Host Governments Have Influenced U.S. and Chinese Engagement

Host-government requirements regarding foreign firms' use of local content—including employment of local workers—and expectations of foreign firms' exercising corporate social responsibility have influenced the United States' and China's respective engagement in the case-study countries.

Local content. Host-governments' local content requirements—which include employing local workers, partnering with domestic firms, and using local materials—have influenced U.S. and Chinese firms' engagement in these countries. For example, the Angolan government's requirement that foreign firms take local firms as partners has posed some challenges for U.S. firms, while the Ghanaian and Kenyan governments' strict requirements that foreign firms hire local workers have resulted in Chinese firms' hiring more local workers for construction projects in these countries.

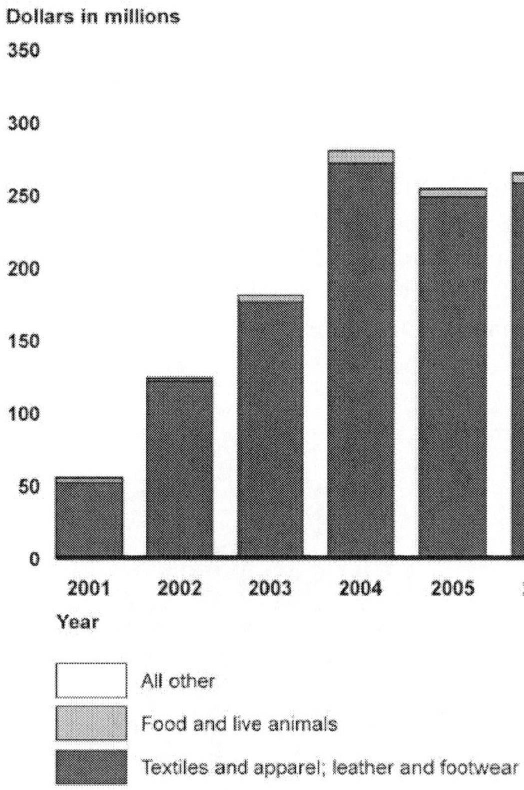

Source: GAO analysis of Department of Commerce data.
Note: Data are reported in nominal dollars.

Figure 21. U.S. Imports from Kenya under AGOA, 2001-2011.

- *Angola.* According to a 2012 report from State, for companies set up by national or foreign investors, the Angolan government limits the number of foreign employees to 30 percent of the workforce, effectively requiring that Angolans constitute 70 percent of the workforce.[111] In the petroleum sector, in addition to hiring local workers or sourcing local products, oil service companies may meet Angola's local-content requirements by partnering with local Angolan firms.[112] According to U.S. officials, Angola's local-content requirements impede U.S. firms' ability to voluntarily choose their business partners. U.S. officials also noted that Angola's local-content requirements have raised concerns for some U.S. firms related to their responsibilities under the U.S. Foreign Corrupt Practices Act, which outlaws payments to foreign government officials to assist in securing or retaining business opportunities. According to U.S. officials, given the intertwining of Angolan private and government interests, complying with Angola's local content requirements could put U.S. companies in a position of having to partner with unknown, and potentially corrupt, entities. For instance, in one case a U.S. firm reported its partnership with an Angolan firm to U.S. officials after the U.S. firm became aware of links between the local firm and a senior Angolan government official, according to a U.S. official and information released by this firm. The Chinese government negotiated a lower local content requirement for Chinese firms implementing Chinese government–funded infrastructure projects, according to an Angolan NGO and reported statements by the former Chinese ambassador to Angola. According to these sources, the Chinese government's agreements with the Angolan government allow Chinese firms to use up to 70 percent foreign labor, and no less than 30 percent Angolan labor. However, these sources stated that Chinese firms generally were unable to meet the requirement to hire 30 percent of the workforce locally, in part because of a lack of skilled local workers in the years following Angola's civil war.

- *Ghana.* According to a 2012 report from State, Ghana's local content rules consist of a local-employment requirement for the retail sector. However, Ghana issues work permits for foreign workers in proportion to the size of the foreign firm's investment.[113] Moreover, according to U.S. officials, strong unions and greater public sensitivity to hiring practices limit the hiring of non-Ghanaian workers. Data from Ghana's Ministry of Roads indicate that Ghanaian workers constitute the majority of workers hired by Chinese firms for construction projects.
- *Kenya.* Although the Kenyan government does not directly specify a minimum requirement for local employment, it encourages investments in sectors that create local employment, according to a 2012 report from State.[114] Additionally, the Kenyan government restricts the number of work permits for expatriate workers in foreign firms, according to officials from the Kenyan Private Investment Authority. As a result of these requirements, Kenya has restricted the number of Chinese workers, which has led to Chinese firms' hiring more local workers, according to U.S. and Kenyan government officials.

Corporate social responsibility. The Ghanaian and Angolan governments require firms in extractive industries, such as oil and other mining, to exercise corporate social responsibility by supporting philanthropic activities in the communities where they operate. For example, in the oil and diamond sectors, contracts with the Angolan government spell out the commitments companies must make to invest in infrastructure and social services to benefit local communities, such as building schools, equipping hospitals, or funding microcredit programs, according to State's investment climate report. Despite differences in U.S. and Chinese firms' roles in Angola's oil sector, where U.S. firms are mostly operators of oil blocks and Chinese firms are nonoperators, both contribute funds for community projects.

Specifically, while U.S. and other oil companies in operator roles are held responsible for these activities, oil companies in nonoperator roles, such as Chinese firms in Angola, also contribute funds toward these philanthropic activities, according to a representative from a large western oil firm.

In addition to influencing U.S. and Chinese engagement, the governments of Ghana and Kenya have enhanced the transparency of Chinese government financing in their countries by publishing information In addition to influencing U.S. and Chinese engagement, the governments of Ghana and Kenya have enhanced the transparency of Chinese government financing in their countries by publishing information about the scale, terms, and use of Chinese loans and grants.[115] Specifically, the Ghanaian government published the terms, such as the interest rate and fees, of its $3 billion loan agreement with China Development Bank and publishes annual budget reports that include information on the amount of Chinese government loans and grants for specific projects. Similarly, the Kenyan government annually publishes data on specific projects funded by the Chinese government.[116] In contrast, the Angolan government has published limited information on Chinese government loans. Specifically, the Angolan Ministry of Finance website lists projects as of 2008 that were funded through Chinese government credit lines issued in 2004 and 2007, but it has not published data on the terms of Chinese government credit lines and loans.

CONCLUSION

Assessing the implications of China's economic engagement in sub-Saharan Africa involves considerable challenges for U.S. policymakers. One such challenge is the limited availability of reliable information. While it is clear that China's economic engagement in the region has grown rapidly over the past decade, with China surpassing the United States as sub-Saharan Africa's leading trading partner, information on key aspects of that engagement is lacking. For example, unlike most global economic powers, China does not publish comprehensive data on its foreign assistance, or government-sponsored loans to the region. Our case-study analysis shows that additional information can, to some degree, be obtained by collecting available data on specific countries, but these data do not fully eliminate information gaps. The information we obtained shows that, while both the United States and China are substantial oil importers from sub-Saharan Africa, their involvement across the region has differed in other respects. For example, the United States' emphasis on providing development assistance has been in contrast to China's active pursuit of increasing economic engagement through large-scale loans to governments for infrastructure projects, often involving the use of Chinese contractors. Available information from Angola, Ghana, and Kenya suggests that U.S. and Chinese firms generally operate in different and noncompeting sectors: U.S. firms are more concentrated in higher-technology areas, including petroleum exploration and production, and Chinese firms more concentrated in infrastructure. Increases in Chinese technological capacity could affect U.S. and Chinese commercial engagement in some sectors of sub-Saharan Africa in ways that are not easily known at this time. Although not in direct response to China's engagement, the United States has recently elevated the importance of U.S. commercial engagement in its sub-Saharan Africa strategy, calling for increased trade and investment in the region. This reprioritization of U.S. goals reflects this region's prospects for economic growth as well as the perspective that advancing U.S. interests can benefit from a stronger integration of commercial goals with diplomatic engagement. Any increases in U.S. commercial engagement will take place in the context of policies that govern the ways in which the U.S. government can work to promote commercial interests, during a period of tight government budgets, and—as viewed by many U.S. firms—in the high-risk and high-cost business environments of many sub-Saharan African countries.

Agency and Third-Party Comments

We sent a draft of this report for review and comment to the Departments of Commerce, Defense, Energy, State, and the Treasury and to MCC, OPIC, USAID, U.S. Ex-Im, the U.S. Trade and Development Agency, and USTR. We received technical comments from Commerce, Energy, State, Treasury, OPIC, U.S. Ex-Im, and USTR, which we incorporated as appropriate. In addition, we sent relevant sections of the draft report to the World Bank, which also provided technical comments that we incorporated as appropriate.

David B. Gootnick, Director,
International Affairs and Trade

Appendix I. Objectives, Scope, and Methodology

Our objectives were to (1) examine U.S. and Chinese goals and policies for sub-Saharan Africa; (2) examine the United States' and China's trade, grants and loans, and investment activities for sub-Saharan Africa;[117] and (3) compare aspects of the United States' and China's engagement in selected case-study countries—Angola, Ghana, and Kenya. To review U.S. and Chinese goals and policies with respect to sub-Saharan Africa, we reviewed U.S. government policies, plans, and legislation; publicly available Chinese government policies; and statements from U.S. government officials. To examine the United States' and China's engagement with sub-Saharan Africa, including our case-study countries, we analyzed available data on U.S. and Chinese trade, grants and loans, and investments from 2001 through 2010 or 2011. To the extent that data were unavailable for this period, we used data for the most recent 3- to 5-year period available. To identify the best available data sources and any data limitations, we interviewed U.S. government officials and experts in Washington, D.C. We met with officials from the U.S. Agency for International Development (USAID); Departments of Commerce, Defense, Energy, State, and the Treasury; Export-Import Bank of the United States (U.S. Ex-Im); Millennium Challenge Corporation (MCC); Office of the U.S. Trade Representative (USTR); Overseas Private Investment Corporation (OPIC); and U.S. Trade and Development Agency. We also met with host-government officials, the World Bank, nongovernmental organizations (NGO), U.S. firms, business associations such as the Corporate Council on Africa and U.S.-Angola Chamber of Commerce, and experts from think tanks and academic institutions. We analyzed information on U.S. programs and funding from Commerce, MCC, OPIC, U.S. Ex-Im, and USAID. To describe China's engagement, we also assessed publicly available information from Chinese ministries, such as the Ministry of Commerce; the World Bank; the International Monetary Fund (IMF); the World Trade Organization; and scholarly literature. The information on foreign laws in this report is not a product of our original analysis but is derived from interviews and secondary sources. To compare in greater depth aspects of the United States' and China's engagement in sub-Saharan Africa, we conducted case studies of Angola, Ghana, and Kenya. We selected these countries on the basis of an assessment of the levels, types, and intersection of the United States' and China's engagement in trade, grants and loans, and investment activity in each country; the three countries' geographic diversity; and input from U.S. government officials and relevant experts. These case studies are meant to be illustrative and are not generalizable.

- To obtain data on the United States' and China's trade in goods, we accessed the United Nations (UN) Commodity Trade database by means of the Department of Commerce's Trade Policy Information System. This database provides data for comparable categories of exports and imports of goods for the United States and China. For data on U.S. imports under the African Growth and Opportunity Act, we used Commerce's Trade Policy Information System. Although comparable data for trade in services were not systematically available for the United States and China, we cite relevant examples for services provided by U.S. and Chinese firms, using World Bank and MCC data on contracts for projects funded by these organizations in sub-Saharan Africa and using available data for U.S., Chinese, and other firms' bids for host-government contracts from Commerce's Advocacy Center. We also present our estimates of U.S. trade in services, based on tabulations from Commerce's Bureau of Economic Analysis (BEA) and other sources, including the Census Bureau. BEA's trade-in-services data for several categories of service—travel and passenger fares, transportation, education, and "other" private services—are based on data from various sources.[118] We used data on the number of Chinese laborers in Angola, from China's Ministry of Commerce and from a news report citing the former Chinese ambassador to Angola, as an indicator of China's service exports.
- To obtain data on the United States' grants and loans, we used data from USAID, U.S. Ex-Im, and OPIC. To obtain data on China's grants and aid, we used data from China's foreign aid policy and China scholar Deborah Brautigam. For country-specific data on China's grants and loans, we used data provided by U.S. government officials and academic scholars and data published by host governments.
- For data on U.S. firms' investments, we used BEA data that we obtained directly from BEA. For Chinese firms' investments, we used data from China's Ministry of Commerce, China's National Bureau of Statistics, the information office of China's State Council, and Haver Analytics, as well as information on China's data from the IMF and academic experts. For U.S. and Chinese firms' investments in the oil sector in Angola and Ghana, we used data published by the governments of Angola and Ghana, with updates from the U.S. Department of Energy.

  To ensure comparability, and given challenges in determining appropriate deflators for some data, we used nominal rather than inflation-adjusted values for U.S. and Chinese trade, grants and loans, and investments in sub-Saharan Africa. All of our information sources reported nominal data in U.S. dollars. All percentages noted in this document are rounded to the nearest number. We have noted data limitations as appropriate, such as limits in the availability of data on China's grants and loans and likely underreporting of its investment data. Overall, we determined that the data presented in this study are generally reliable for the purposes for which they are used. To assess the reliability of data, where possible, we cross-checked the data with other sources, conducted checks on the data for internal consistency, and consulted with U.S. officials and experts.

- We determined that trade-in-goods data for the United States and China were generally reliable for comparing trends over time as well as composition of trade. U.S. trade-in-services data represent broad estimates rather than precise values: values for certain services are extrapolated at the country level from broader data (e.g., travel service data are based on multiplying the number of travelers for a country with data on average expenditures for travelers and average passenger fees for the region), while values for other services (e.g., business, professional, and technical services) are calculated from a range of estimates based on survey data. In instances where the volume of trade for that service was presented as a range, we used the highest value to estimate the volume of trade for that service. China's trade-in-services data comprise data for Chinese imports and exports to the world, are not disaggregated by region or country, and cannot be compared with the U.S. data for sub-Saharan Africa and case-study countries. China's data also include data on the number of Chinese laborers in Africa and a few African countries, including Angola. The United States does not have comparable data on U.S. workers in Africa and in countries like Angola.
- In the absence of comparable U.S. and Chinese trade-in-services data, we analyzed data for contracts funded by the World Bank and MCC as well as data from Commerce's Advocacy Center on host-government contracts. Although these data represent a small share of services activity in the region, they provide insights into the degree of competition between U.S. and Chinese firms for the projects represented. We found that the data for contracts funded by the World Bank are generally reliable. We utilized data from MCC largely to provide information on the nature and extent of U.S. and Chinese firms' engagement in Ghana, and found the data to be generally reliable for that purpose. Commerce's Advocacy Center data were for a limited number of cases (47) where U.S. firms requested the agency's assistance in bidding for host-government contracts. Because these data included the nationality of other firms bidding on a host-government contract, we used this information to determine the extent to which Chinese firms or firms of other nationalities were competing with U.S. firms on these contracts. We did not use these data to determine the nationality of the winner for these contracts, because the data generally did not identify the nationality of the bidder.
- We determined that U.S. development assistance data are generally reliable for showing the trend and composition of aid to sub-Saharan African countries over time. We also determined that data from U.S. Ex-Im and OPIC are generally reliable to present trends and aggregate amounts by year, and we present these data with appropriate caveats. Since China does not publish aid data, we used the best available estimates of China's aid to Africa, produced by expert Deborah Brautigam. We did not independently verify Dr. Brautigam's data but obtained an understanding of the methodology she used to construct her estimates. We were unable to verify the

reliability of data published by host-government ministries, but where possible, we asked for input from knowledgeable U.S. government officials. We have attributed to the appropriate sources information on Chinese government loans to the case-study countries and, to the extent possible, checked this information for consistency among the sources.

- To compare borrowers' costs for loans from the Chinese government with borrowers' costs for loans from other lenders, we analyzed data on loans provided by the Chinese government, the U.S. government, and the World Bank for similar sectors to the same countries for comparable periods. We obtained information on specific loans from U.S. officials, host-government officials and documents, the World Bank, the Organization for Economic Cooperation and Development (OECD), an online source for the London Interbank Offered Rate (see www.fedprimerates.com), and an expert on China-Angola relations.[119] We collected publicly available information from the World Bank and verified loan terms with World Bank officials. To compare loans by U.S. and Chinese government agencies and the World Bank to the governments of Angola, Ghana, and Kenya, we collected and analyzed information on the terms of the loans (i.e., date of the loan agreement, face value of the loan, interest rate, repayment period, grace period, disbursement pattern, and fees). Chinese government loans included loans by the Export-Import Bank of China (China Ex-Im) and the China Development Bank supporting Chinese exports of goods and services. For these loans, we identified the borrowing country, the date of the loan agreement, the sector (primarily construction), and the face value, as benchmarks for collecting similar information for U.S. and World Bank loans. For U.S. government loans, we used information on U.S. Ex-Im loans that support U.S. exports of goods and services. Because U.S. Ex-Im did not provide loans for the construction sector to host governments during a similar period as the Chinese loans, we asked U.S. Ex-Im to provide hypothetical loan terms for loans that it might have offered for the construction sector on the same date and of the same magnitude as the Chinese government loans. We also collected information on the only two loans that U.S. Ex-Im provided to the government of one of our case-study countries, both of them to the government of Ghana, since 2001. For World Bank loans, when possible, we selected loans with publicly available information from the World Bank on loan terms and that were given for the construction sector during a similar period as the Chinese government loans. Because we could not find World Bank loans for the construction sector given in a similar period in Angola and Ghana, we used loans for the agriculture sector in Angola that included an infrastructure construction component and for the oil and gas sector in Ghana. To calculate the present value of the loan and repayment, we collected historical data on OECD's differentiated discount rate. Using this information, we calculated the loan's present value—that is the present value of future disbursements to the borrower, and we calculated the present value of future repayments to the lender for the life of the loan. We then used the ratio of the present value of repayment to the present value of the loan to calculate the loan's grant element—that is, the loan's concessionality.[120] Where necessary, we made assumptions to complete the calculations. For example, we assumed a disbursement period of 8 and a half years for China Ex-Im's November 2009 loan to Angola. We based this assumption on information from Angola's

Ministry of Finance regarding a 2004 loan from China, which indicated that almost 50 percent of the loan had been disbursed as of 2008, about 4 and a quarter years after the loan agreement. Extrapolating this rate, we assumed that the loan would be fully disbursed 8 and a half years after the loan agreement. The IMF provides an online tool to calculate the grant element of the loan; however, we used a different methodology that allowed us to directly incorporate factors including the date of the loan, which affects the discount rate used to calculate the grant element. Using the IMF calculation tool could result in different calculations of the loans' grant elements.

- To identify patterns in, and to compare, U.S. and Chinese foreign direct investment, we report U.S. and Chinese data on foreign direct investments while noting their limitations. First, data on U.S. foreign direct investments in several countries were unavailable because of confidentiality concerns. Second, while both the United States' and China's foreign direct investment to sub-Saharan Africa may be underreported, experts have expressed particular concern regarding China's data. U.S. and Chinese firms set up subsidiaries in places such as Netherlands and the British Virgin Islands, which can be used to make investments in sub-Saharan Africa that are not captured by U.S. and Chinese data on foreign direct investment. Experts state that this could be a significant source of underreporting for China's data. In addition, U.S. and China's data may not include foreign direct investments from all firms. An IMF working paper expressed particular concern regarding foreign direct investments from China's small and medium-sized firms that are not captured in China's data.[121] For U.S. data, according to BEA, U.S. data on foreign direct investments are based on a benchmark survey conducted in 2009, BEA's most comprehensive survey of U.S. foreign direct investment; this survey covers the value of all U.S. foreign direct investment and is the basis on which data for other years are compiled. Third, the flow data reported for China's foreign direct investment are inconsistent with changes in the stock data; according to the IMF working paper, these variations between flows and stock are difficult to explain.[122] U.S. foreign direct investment data do not show such levels of inconsistencies between the flow data and changes in the stock data. Fourth, China does not define foreign direct investment when reporting its data. However, the types of data included by China in its foreign direct investments (e.g., equity investment data, reinvested earnings data) appear similar to data reported for U.S. foreign direct investment, which the United States defines on the basis of OECD's definition of foreign direct investment.[123] Despite these limitations, various reports, including those published by international organizations such as the IMF, government agencies, academic experts, and other research institutions, use China's reported investment data to describe China's foreign direct investment activities in Africa. And despite U.S. foreign direct investment data being suppressed for some countries and some potential underreporting, we determined the U.S. foreign direct investment data to be reliable for reporting general patterns, when limitations are noted. Data on China's foreign direct investment by sector are reported by an official Chinese government source, and we have attributed these data as such. We have appropriately attributed data on U.S. and Chinese firms' investments in the oil sector in Angola and Ghana and have checked these data for consistency across sources to the extent available.

We conducted meetings in Washington, D.C., and fieldwork in Angola, Ghana, and Kenya, including meetings with officials from U.S. agencies; host-government ministries (e.g., those responsible for finance, foreign affairs, roads and urban development, energy, trade, and investment); U.S. businesses (representing sectors such as transportation, telecommunications, oil and gas, financial services, and agriculture); other donors; and nongovernmental organizations (e.g., think tanks, academic institutions, and advocacy organizations). We were unable to meet with Chinese government officials, despite our requests in Africa and in Washington, D.C. We conducted this performance audit from November 2011 to February 2013 in accordance with generally accepted government auditing standards. Those standards require that we plan and perform the audit to obtain sufficient, appropriate evidence to provide a reasonable basis for our findings and conclusions based on our audit objectives. We believe that the evidence obtained provides a reasonable basis for our findings and conclusions based on our audit objectives.

APPENDIX II. U.S. AND CHINESE GOVERNMENT LOANS TO ANGOLA, GHANA, AND KENYA

Our analysis of information on specific Chinese government loans to Angola, Kenya, and Ghana showed that these loans are generally less costly and more concessional than U.S. government loans to Angola, Kenya, and, to a lesser extent, Ghana. Our analysis also shows that these Chinese government loans are more costly than specific World Bank loans to Ghana and Kenya.[124] To compare Chinese government loans with U.S. government and World Bank loans, we identified U.S. government and World Bank loans that were similar in agreement date, size, sector, and borrowing country. These factors affect a loan's interest rate, other associated fees, and duration. Because U.S. Ex-Im did not offer loans for the construction sector to the host government during a similar time period as the Chinese government loans, we obtained loan terms from U.S. Ex-Im for hypothetical loans for the construction sector on the same date and of the same magnitude as the Chinese government loans.[125] In instances where we could not obtain information about specific terms, we made assumptions based on the terms of comparable loans. We then compared Chinese government loans with those of the U.S. government and the World Bank based on the terms of the loans, such as their face value, interest rate, upfront fee, and repayment period, to calculate the loan's degree of concessionality or grant element, defined as the present value of future disbursements less the present value of future repayment (see table 3).[126] A positive difference between these two values indicates a grant element—a percentage of the loan that does not have to be repaid—and a negative difference indicates a negative grant element—a percentage of the loan that must be repaid in addition to the present value of the loan. The IMF provides an online tool to calculate the grant element of the loan; however, we used a different methodology that allowed us to directly incorporate factors including the date of the loan, which affects the discount rate used to calculate the grant element. Using the IMF calculation tool could result in different calculations of the loans' grant elements than those shown in table 3.

Table 3. Comparison of Selected Chinese Government Loans with U.S. Government and World Bank Loans to Angola, Ghana, and Kenya

Lender	Agreement date	Face value, dollars in millions	Interest rate, percent	Up-front fee, percent	Maturity, years (Repayment period, years)	Present value of loan,[a] dollars in millions	Present value of repayment,[a] dollars in millions	Difference between present and repayment values, dollars inmillions (Grant element, percent[b])
Angola								
China	November 2009	$6,000	3.22%	0.25%	28.5 (15)	$4,879	$4,064	$815 (17%)
China	November 2009	1,500	2.52	0.25	13 (8)	1,432	1,236	196 (14)
United States [c,d]	*November 2009*	*6,000*	*2.48*	*7.62*	*5.5 (5)*	*5,930*	*6,022*	*-91 (-2)*
World Bank[e]	November 2009	30	3.20[f]	None	34 (25)	24	21	3.2 (13)
Ghana								
China	December 2011	1,500	3.74	0.25	28.5 (15)	1,262	1,240	22 (2)
China	December 2011	1,500	3.64	0.25	21.5 (10)	1,262	1,244	18 (1)
United States[c]	*December 2011*	*1,500*	*2.45*	*10.15*	*15 (10)*	*1,356*	*1,360*	*-4 (-0.3)*
World Bank[e]	April 2011	38	0[f]	none	35 (25)	34	18	16 (48)
Kenya								
China	July 2011	45	2.00	0.25	35.5 (20)	38	27	10 (27)
United States[c]	*July 2011*	*45*	*3.51*	*17.37*	*15 (10)*	*41*	*46*	*-6 (-14)*
World Bank[e]	May 2011	300	0[f]	none	40 (30)	263	131	132 (50)

Source: GAO analysis of information obtained from U.S. officials, host governments, the World Bank, OECD, www.fedprimerates.com, and Lucy Corkin.

Notes: Italics indicate loans with a negative grant element—that is, loans whose present value of repayment exceeds their present value. While not listed in the table, each loan's commitment fee and disbursement period were used in the calculations of present loan value, present repayment value, and grant element. Face value, present loan value, and present repayment value are reported in nominal values. London Interbank Offered Rates are drawn from www.fedprimerates.com. Lucy Corkin is an expert in China-Angola relations. See Lucy Corkin, "Angolan Political Elites' Management of Chinese Credit Lines," in Marcus Power and Ana C. Alves, eds., China and Angola: A Marriage of Convenience? (Capetown, South Africa: Pambazuka Press, 2012), 45-67.

[a] U.S. Ex-Im did not make any loans to the Angolan government during this period, according to U.S. Ex-Im officials, and therefore U.S. Ex-Im did not provide terms for hypothetical loans that could be compared with Chinese government loans.

[b] The present value of the loan reflects the present value of future disbursements of the loan. The loan is generally disbursed in increments over time.

[c] The grant element measures a loan's degree of concessionality.

[d] These U.S. government loans to Ghanaian government represent the only two loans that U.S. Ex-Im has provided to a government of one of our case-study countries since 2001.

[e] According to U.S. Ex-Im, this loan was part of a tied-aid transaction in which U.S. Ex-Im provided a $7.8 million grant in addition to the loan shown. The terms shown represent only the loan component of this transaction. According to U.S. Ex-Im, this tied-aid transaction represented the only such transaction with a sub-Saharan African country since 2001.

Table 4. Additional U.S. and Chinese Government Loans to Angola and Ghana

Lender	Agreement date	Face value, dollars in millions	Interest rate, percent	Upfront fee, percent	Maturity, years (Repayment period, years)	Present value of loan,[b] dollars in millions	Present value of repayment,[b] dollars in millions	Difference between present and repayment values, dollars in millions(Grant element, percent[c])
Angola[a]								
China	March 2004	$2,000	2.61%	0.25%	25.5 (12)	$1,585	$1,149	$436 (27%)
China	*July 2007*	*500*	*6.61*	*0.25*	*13 (7)*	*485*	*492*	*-7 (-1)*
	September 2007	*2,000*	*6.74*	*0.25*	*28.5 (15)*	*1,529*	*1,583*	*-54 (-4)*
Ghana[d]								
United States[e]	October 2006	15	4.44	5.94	15 (15)	15	15	1 (4)
United States	*June 2008*	*358*	*4.45*	*20.26*	*16 (10)*	*300*	*331*	*-32 (-11)*

Source: GAO analysis of information obtained from U.S. officials, host governments, the World Bank, OECD, www.fedprimerates.com, and Lucy Corkin.

Notes: Italics indicate loans with a negative grant element—that is, loans whose present value of repayment exceeds their present value. While not listed in the table, each loan's commitment fee and disbursement period were used in the calculations of present loan value, present repayment value, and grant element. Face value, present loan value, and present repayment value are reported in nominal values. London Interbank Offered Rates are drawn from www.fedprimerates.com. Lucy Corkin is an expert in China-Angola relations. See Lucy Corkin, "Angolan Political Elites' Management of Chinese Credit Lines," in Marcus Power and Ana C. Alves, eds., China and Angola: A Marriage of Convenience? (Capetown, South Africa: Pambazuka Press, 2012), 45-67.

[a] U.S. Ex-Im did not make any loans to the Angolan government during this period, according to U.S. Ex-Im officials, and therefore U.S. Ex-Im did not provide terms for hypothetical loans that could be compared with Chinese government loans.

[b] The present value of the loan reflects the present value of future disbursements of the loan. The loan is generally disbursed in increments over time.

[c] The grant element measures a loan's degree of concessionality.

[d] These U.S. government loans to Ghanaian government represent the only two loans that U.S. Ex-Im has provided to a government of one of our case-study countries since 2001.

[e] According to U.S. Ex-Im, this loan was part of a tied-aid transaction in which U.S. Ex-Im provided a $7.8 million grant in addition to the loan shown. The terms shown represent only the loan component of this transaction. According to U.S. Ex-Im, this tied-aid transaction represented the only such transaction with a sub-Saharan African country since 2001.

Our analysis indicates that the Chinese government loans to Angola, Ghana, and Kenya that we analyzed were generally more concessional than were hypothetical loans that U.S. Ex-Im might have offered. For example, two Chinese government loans to Angola in November 2009, for $6 billion and $1.5 billion, had estimated grant elements of 17 and 14 percent, respectively. In contrast, a loan that U.S. Ex-Im might have extended for the same time period would have had an estimated grant element of -2 percent, given U.S. Ex-Im terms that would apply to Angola. Because of higher upfront fees and a shorter repayment period, the repayment on the U.S. Ex-Im loan would have been higher than the repayment on the Chinese government loan.[127] By comparison, a World Bank loan to Angola in November 2009 had an estimated grant element of 13 percent, less concessional than the Chinese government loan but more concessional than the U.S. Ex-Im loan.[128] Two December 2011 Chinese government loans to Ghana and a July 2011 Chinese government loan to Kenya also had higher degrees of concessionality than hypothetical U.S. government loans to those countries. Table 4 shows the terms, present values of the loan and repayment, and grant element for additional U.S. and Chinese government loans to Angola and Ghana.

Differences in each loan's interest rate; upfront fee; maturity, which includes the repayment, grace, and disbursement periods; and commitment fee drive the differences in the grant elements.

- *Interest rate.* For loans of similar time periods, the Chinese government loans charged higher interest rates than the U.S. government loans. Moreover, except in Angola, the World Bank charged much lower interest rates than both the U.S. government and the Chinese government. Higher interest rates increase repayments, decreasing the loan's grant element. Interest rates can vary depending on the borrowing country, sector, repayment period, and economic and political conditions, and other factors. For example, U.S. Ex-Im sets its interest rates on the basis of a minimum interest rate required by OECD that, in turn, is based on the U.S. Treasury bond rate, the loan repayment period, and the sector. According to U.S. Ex-Im officials, the Chinese government loans' interest rates reflect the risk of the borrower's defaulting on the loan and the cost of the funds, whereas the U.S. government loans' interest rates reflect only the cost of the funds.
- *Up-front fee.* U.S. Ex-Im loans follow the OECD rules for minimum exposure fees and carry substantially higher up-front fees than the Chinese government and the World Bank's loans.[129] Higher up-front fees increase repayments, decreasing the loan's grant element. According to U.S. Ex-Im officials, the up-front fee reflects the risk of the borrower's defaulting on the loan and is based on country risk, the terms of the loan, and the disbursement period. U.S. Ex-Im officials stated that, in contrast, the Chinese government loans' up-front fees do not include the risk of the borrower's defaulting on the loan and are similar to a transaction fee; instead, the loans' interest rates reflect the risk of the borrower's defaulting. According to U.S. Ex-Im officials, U.S. Ex-Im generally allows the borrower to pay the up-front fee as the loan is disbursed and generally provides a loan for the up-front fee that allows the borrower to repay the fee over a period of time.
- *Maturity.* A loan's maturity includes the repayment, grace, and disbursement periods. Only interest payments are made during the grace and disbursement periods, whereas both interest and principal repayments are made during the repayment period. The

Chinese government loans have longer repayment periods than the hypothetical U.S. government loans; the World Bank's loans have the longest repayment periods by far. Moreover, the Chinese government's and World Bank's loans offer grace periods, whereas the U.S. government loans do not. Longer repayment and grace periods allow for deeper discounting of future repayments, increasing the loan's grant element. Longer repayment and grace periods, which increase the loan's maturity, may also increase the discount rate used to calculate the present value of the loan and repayment, generally increasing the grant element. The disbursement period varies by loan, with longer disbursement periods decreasing both the loan and repayment value but generally increasing the grant element. Almost all of the loans in tables 3 and 4 are not disbursed fully at the onset of the loan but instead are disbursed over a period of time, sometimes over many years. U.S. government loans are disbursed as goods and services are delivered. Most of the Chinese government loans are used to fund infrastructure projects. According to experts, like U.S. government loans, the loans are disbursed as the Chinese firm implements the infrastructure project. In addition, the Chinese government loans are disbursed to the project's contractor, almost always a Chinese firm, keeping the loans' funds between the Chinese bank and the Chinese contractor.

- *Commitment fee.* The commitment fee for Chinese government loans is 1 percent, while the commitment fee for U.S. government and World Bank loans is .5 percent.[130] Commitment fees, which are charged on the amount of the loan that is not disbursed, increase the repayments, decreasing the loan's grant element. The impact of commitment fees grows with longer disbursement periods.

End Notes

[1] This review was conducted in response to a request from Representative Jack Kingston and Senator James Inhofe—then Ranking Member, Senate Foreign Relations Subcommittee on East Asian and Pacific Affairs—to review U.S. and Chinese engagement in sub-Saharan Africa.

[2] The data sources we identified include trade data from the United Nations (UN) Commodity Trade database, the U.S. Department of Commerce's (Commerce) Trade Policy Information System, and Commerce's Bureau of Economic Analysis (BEA); aid data from the U.S. Agency for International Development (USAID) and scholars; loan and other financing data from the Export-Import Bank of the United States (U.S. Ex-Im) and Overseas Private Investment Corporation (OPIC); and investment data from BEA and China's Ministry of Commerce.

[3] When data were unavailable for this period, we used data for shorter periods. For comparability, and given challenges in determining appropriate deflators for some data, we used nominal rather than inflation-adjusted values for data on trade, grants and loans, and investments. All information sources reported nominal data in U.S. dollars. All of the data we report are for calendar years, except where noted otherwise.

[4] Data in this report generally do not include South Sudan, which gained independence in July 2011.

[5] The four countries are Angola, Chad, Equatorial Guinea, and Sierra Leone. Analysis of economic growth was based on the World Bank's data on annual gross domestic product (GDP) growth from 2001 through 2011.

[6] Transparency International, *Corruption Perceptions Index 2011* (Berlin, Germany: 2011), 4-5.

[7] According to a report by the Center for Global Development, Ghana was able to achieve this change in income status relatively quickly as a result of rebasing its GDP in 2009. The GDP rebasing—a statistical adjustment to correct for some underreporting in national accounts—put Ghana in a new income category. Although the World Bank calculates income status on the basis of gross national income, the Center for Global Development report states that gross national income and GDP amounts do not differ significantly. Todd Moss and Stephanie Majerowicz, *No Longer Poor: Ghana's New Income Status and Implications of Graduation from IDA* (Washington, D.C.: Center for Global Development, 2012).

[8] In 2011, U.S. GDP, based on purchasing power parity, was $15 trillion and U.S. per-capita GDP was approximately $48,400.

[9] OECD is an organization of 34 industrialized countries, operating by consensus, that fosters dialogue among members to discuss, develop, and refine economic and social policies and provides an arena for establishing multilateral agreements.

[10] See World Bank and People's Republic of China Development Research Center of the State Council, *China 2030: Building a Modern, Harmonious, and Creative High-Income Society* (Washington, D.C.: 2012). China's State Council is the highest executive and administrative entity in the Chinese government and oversees all major central government ministries, commissions, and other key state entities.

[11] In 2011, China's GDP, based on purchasing power parity, was $11.4 trillion, or about three-quarters of U.S. GDP; China's per-capita GDP was approximately $8,500, or one-sixth of U.S. per-capita GDP.

[12] See World Bank and People's Republic of China Development Research Center of the State Council, China 2030. After 15 years of negotiations to join the World Trade Organization, on December 11, 2001, China bound itself to open and liberalize its economy and offer a more predictable environment for trade and foreign investment in accordance with the organization's rules.

[13] World Bank and People's Republic of China Development Research Center of the State Council, *China 2030*.

[14] For example, state-owned enterprises in China will accept informal guidance from government officials and, in return, are more likely to receive preferential access to bank finance, privileged access to business opportunities, and even protection against competition. However, the study notes that more than one in four state-owned enterprises in China incurs a loss, and state-owned enterprises have exhibited lower growth in productivity than have private enterprises.

[15] Pub. L. No. 95-213, as amended (codified at 15 U.S.C. §§78dd-1 *et seq*).

[16] The OECD Anti-Bribery Convention establishes legally binding standards to criminalize bribery of foreign public officials in international business transactions. Five nonmember countries have adopted the OECD convention: Argentina, Brazil, Bulgaria, Russia, and South Africa.

[17] The UN Convention against Corruption calls for participating countries to criminalize acts of corruption and to agree to cooperate with one another to fight against and prevent corruption. Angola, Ghana, and Kenya, our case-study countries, are also signatories to this convention.

[18] Transparency International's 2011 Bribe Payers Index ranks 28 of the world's largest economies according to the perceived likelihood that companies from these countries would pay bribes abroad, based on the views of business executives as captured by Transparency International's 2011 Bribe Payers Survey. In the index, lower rankings indicate lower perceived likelihood of paying bribes abroad. The index ranks only Russian firms higher than Chinese firms.

[19] For example, China's State-owned Assets Supervision and Administration Commission of the State Council supervises and manages state-owned enterprises, and oversees related outbound investment.

[20] The white paper was published on the Chinese state-run news agency's website. See Information Office of the State Council, People's Republic of China, "White Paper: China's Foreign Aid" (April 2011), accessed Oct. 17, 2011, http://news.xinhuanet.com/ english2010/china/2011-04/21/c_13839683.htm.

[21] According to scholar Deborah Brautigam, China's Ministries of Commerce and Foreign Affairs have an uneasy division of labor and sharing of authorities over foreign aid. See Deborah Brautigam, *The Dragon's Gift: The Real Story of China in Africa* (New York, N.Y.: Oxford University Press, 2009), 111.

[22] Pub. L. No. 106-200, as amended (codified at 19 U.S.C. §§ 3701 *et seq*).

[23] State's fiscal year 2013 bureau plan for sub-Saharan Africa identified additional goals related to adapting to climate change, enhancing food security and sustainable agricultural development, building public support for a mutually beneficial U.S.-Africa partnership, and increasing U.S. diplomatic effectiveness.

[24] White House, "U.S. Strategy Toward Sub-Saharan Africa" (June 2012), accessed June 14, 2012, http://www.whitehouse.gov/sites/default/files/docs/africa_strategy_2.pdf.

[25] Commerce officials noted that, pursuant to the 2012 strategy, Commerce is leading the development of an initiative called "Doing Business in Africa" that combines the tools of U.S. trade promotion agencies to assist U.S. firms in exploring commercial opportunities in sub-Saharan Africa.

[26] Office of the United States Trade Representative, "2011 Trade Policy Agenda and 2010 Annual Report," accessed January 12, 2012, http://www.ustr.gov/webfm_send/2597.

[27] AGOA authorizes the President to designate countries as eligible to receive AGOA benefits if they are determined to have established, or are making continual progress toward establishing, the following: market-based economies; the rule of law and political pluralism; elimination of barriers to U.S. trade and investment; protection of intellectual property; efforts to combat corruption; policies to reduce poverty and increase availability of health care and educational opportunities; protection of human rights and worker rights; and elimination of certain child labor practices.

[28] The United States also offers tariff reductions for goods from most sub-Saharan African countries under the Generalized System of Preferences (GSP). The Africa Investment Incentive Act of 2006, Pub. L. No. 109-432, div. D, Title VI, expanded the list of products that eligible sub-Saharan African countries may export to the

United States duty free under GSP, which covers approximately 4,600 items. GSP and AGOA eligibility criteria overlap, and countries must be GSP eligible to take advantage of trade benefits under AGOA.

[29] This subset includes "lesser developed beneficiary countries" as defined by AGOA, which include countries, such as Ghana and Kenya, that the UN does not classify as least developed countries. In August 2012, Congress voted to extend the third-country fabric provision, which was set to expire the following month. See Pub. L. No. 112-163.

[30] For example, the U.S. government has Trade and Investment Framework Agreements in sub-Saharan Africa with Angola, Ghana, Liberia, Mauritius, Mozambique, Nigeria, Rwanda, and South Africa as well as with the Common Market for Eastern and Southern Africa, the East African Community, and the West African Economic and Monetary Union. The U.S. government also has a Trade, Investment, and Development Cooperative Agreement with the Southern African Customs Union. In addition, according to Commerce officials, the U.S. Department of Commerce recently established the U.S.–East African Community Commercial Dialogue, the first such effort in Africa, to enable the United States and East African Community governments to work with their respective private sectors to increase two-way trade and investment.

[31] The U.S. government has bilateral investment treaties with Cameroon, the Democratic Republic of the Congo, Mozambique, the Republic of the Congo, Rwanda, and Senegal.

[32] In addition to providing bilateral assistance to countries in sub-Saharan Africa, the United States assists the region through its membership in, and contributions to, multilateral organizations. According to U.S. officials, the U.S. government's position as the largest shareholder at the World Bank and the largest nonregional shareholder at the African Development Bank enables it to advance U.S. priorities in sub-Saharan Africa through these institutions.

[33] In sub-Saharan Africa, Ghana and Tanzania participate in the Partnership for Growth Initiative.

[34] Ministry of Foreign Affairs, People's Republic of China, "China's African Policy," accessed October 11, 2011, http://www.fmprc.gov.cn/eng/zxxx/t230615.htm.

[35] The policy is stated in a white paper published on the Chinese state-run news agency's website. See Information Office of the State Council, People's Republic of China, "White Paper: China's Foreign Aid," accessed October 11, 2011, http://news.xinhuanet.com/english2010/ china/2011-04/21/c_13839683.htm.

[36] This report did not include an analysis of U.S. or Chinese security-related goals in sub-Saharan Africa. We did not obtain information on China's security goals or policies in the region.

[37] China's trade activities in Africa are also partly driven by its "Going Global" policy, initiated in 1999, which encouraged Chinese firms to seek trade and investment opportunities globally, and as part of which large, generally state-supported Chinese firms make investments to boost China's long-term national growth.

[38] China is a participant in the 2005 Paris Declaration on Aid Effectiveness, in which donor and partner countries agreed to improve aid effectiveness through results-oriented assistance and donor coordination, among other principles. However, U.S. officials noted that China had a nonbinding role in the Paris Declaration and therefore cannot be held accountable to other donors.

[39] M. McDonald, "After FOCAC: Have China-Africa Relations Finally Turned a Corner, or Was FOCAC V Simply More of the Same?" *African East-Asian Affairs/China Monitor* (2012).

[40] According to OECD, foreign direct investment is the ownership by a foreign person or business of 10 percent or more of the voting equity of a firm located in the host country. Foreign direct investment flows provide information for foreign direct investment activity within a given period of time, while foreign direct investment stock indicates the level of foreign direct investment at a given *point* in time.

[41] Petroleum includes oil (crude and refined) and petroleum products (e.g., jelly and waxes).

[42] Total trade in goods is defined as imports plus exports. In 2011, trade with the United States and China represented an estimated 31 percent of sub-Saharan Africa's total trade, while sub-Saharan Africa represented 3 percent of total trade for both the United States and China.

[43] Examples of U.S. imports of ores, metals, and minerals are platinum and diamonds. Examples of Chinese imports of ores, metals, and minerals include iron ore and copper.

[44] For example, in 2001, 68 percent of U.S. imports of goods from sub-Saharan Africa were petroleum and petroleum products and 14 percent were ores, metals, and minerals. In 2001, 61 percent of Chinese imports were petroleum and petroleum products and 19 percent was ores, metals, and minerals.

[45] In 2011, an additional 3 percent received duty-free treatment under GSP. According to USTR, goods from certain countries can also enter duty free under other U.S. trade provisions.

[46] Transportation equipment represented nearly 4 percent, and textiles, apparel, leather, and footwear represented nearly 2 percent of imports under AGOA in 2011. From 2001 to 2011, the value of nonpetroleum U.S. imports under AGOA increased 322 percent, from about $1 billion to $4.3 billion.

[47] In contrast to the list of sub-Saharan African countries eligible for AGOA trade preferences, China's list of eligible countries includes only least developed countries. For example, in 2012, 40 sub-Saharan African countries were eligible for AGOA while 30 sub-Saharan African countries were eligible for China's trade preferences.

[48] See World Trade Organization, Trade Policy Review Body, *Trade Policy Review: Report by the Secretariat—China*, WT/TPR/S/199 (2008).

[49] South Africa is sub-Saharan Africa's largest economy and represented 13 percent of U.S. imports in goods from sub-Saharan Africa and 23 percent of China's imports in 2011.

[50] South Africa received 34 percent of U.S. exports of goods to sub-Saharan Africa and 24 percent of Chinese exports to the region in 2011.

[51] Trade in services refers to the buying and selling of intangible products and activities; examples of trade-in-services sectors include tourism, financial services, and telecommunications. Contracted activities, such as construction and consulting services, are also examples of trade-in-services activities. United States does not publish trade-in-services data for sub-Saharan Africa. However, BEA provided underlying tabulations from BEA and other sources that we used to estimate U.S. trade in services with sub-Saharan Africa. When BEA provided ranges of estimates for sectors of services such as business, professional, and technical services, we used the higher values to calculate estimates of total trade in services, including imports and exports of services. Therefore, the averages we report represent the higher values in underlying tabulations from BEA and other sources and our analysis of BEA's survey data. See appendix I for examples of these other sources.

[52] Our estimate of U.S. imports of services from sub-Saharan Africa does not include imports of travel and passenger fares, because regional sub-Saharan Africa data were not available for this category. However, U.S. imports of travel and passenger fares averaged $3.2 billion per year for 2006 through 2011 for all of Africa and averaged $1.2 billion for Angola, Ghana, and South Africa.

[53] From 2006 through 2011, annual U.S. imports averaged at least $1 billion for business, professional, and technical services; at least $1.2 billion for travel and passenger fares; and $250 million to $400 million for financial services. Because data on U.S. imports of travel and passenger fares were unavailable for sub-Saharan Africa, the $1.2 billion includes only data for Angola, Ghana, and South Africa as a minimum level of U.S. imports for travel and passenger fares. During the same period, annual U.S. exports averaged at least $2.7 billion for business, professional, and technical services and $1.7 billion for travel and passenger fares.

[54] Services provided by U.S. firms under World Bank–funded contracts represent a small fraction (less than 1 percent) of annual U.S. trade in service exports to sub-Saharan Africa. However, World Bank contracts represent one of the few instances in which data are available for examination of potential competition between U.S. and Chinese firms. According to the World Bank, the contract data include only contracts reviewed by World Bank staff prior to award, which constitute about 40 percent of total World Bank investment lending. In addition, the nationality of a firm reflects the country in which it is registered, although the firm's parent may be headquartered in another country.

[55] China's Ministry of Commerce publishes data on trade in services and also provides data on trade in services to the UN Service Trade database. These data include exports and imports globally and by sector but not by country. The Ministry of Commerce's data also include the number of Chinese workers abroad for all of Africa, Angola, Nigeria, and Sudan, providing an indicator of the magnitude of service exports to Africa and these countries (see supplemental report GAO-13-280SP for a discussion of the number of Chinese workers in Angola). The United States does not publish comparable data for American workers abroad.

[56] Construction contracts represented 55 percent and consulting contracts represented 21 percent of the total value of World Bank contracts for sub-Saharan Africa.

[57] OECD defines official development assistance as those flows to countries and territories on the OECD's list of official development assistance recipients and to multilateral development institutions that are provided by official agencies, have the promotion of economic development and welfare of developing countries as their main objective, and are concessional and convey a grant element of at least 25 percent. According to U.S. aid data reported to OECD, U.S. development assistance to sub-Saharan Africa since 2008 has consisted of grants only. Between 2001 and 2010, less than 1 percent of annual U.S. development assistance to sub-Saharan Africa consisted of concessional loans for developmental purposes.

[58] Pub. L. No. 108-105. Through this program, the U.S. government has supported global HIV/AIDS prevention, treatment, and care.

[59] The United States and other developed countries that are members of the OECD report aid data annually to the OECD, which makes this information publicly available. China is not an OECD member and does not report such data, although some nonmember countries, such as certain countries in the Persian Gulf, do report aid data to the OECD.

[60] Information Office of the State Council, People's Republic of China, "White Paper: China's Foreign Aid."

[61] To support Chinese-made products and firms' investments, the Chinese government also provides sub-Saharan African countries commercial loans that do not meet OECD's definition of development assistance.

[62] See Deborah Brautigam, *The Dragon's Gift*, app. 6. Dr. Brautigam calculated the Chinese government's estimated foreign aid using information from Chinese government sources, interviews, and extrapolations based on these sources.

[63] From 2001 to 2011, U.S. Ex-Im authorized about $ 7.2 billion in financing, including 72 percent for loan guarantees and loans, 23 percent for insurance, and 5 percent for working capital. During the same period, OPIC authorized approximately $3.3 billion in financing, including 70 percent for project financing, such as loans and loan guarantees, and 30 percent for insurance.

[64] In providing such guarantees, U.S. Ex-Im promises to pay the lender if the buyer defaults.

[65] China is not a participant in the OECD Arrangement on Officially Supported Export Credits, an international agreement that governs various aspects of United States and other member countries' officially supported export credits. The agreement seeks to increase transparency among participants. Major industrialized countries are participants in this agreement. However, some countries with substantial export credit activity—including China and India—are not participants in the agreement. For more information, see GAO, *U.S. Export-Import Bank: Actions Needed to Promote Competitiveness and International Cooperation*, GAO-12-294 (Washington, D.C.: Feb. 7, 2012).

[66] See Vivien Foster et al. *Building Bridges: China's Growing Role as Infrastructure Financier for Africa* (Washington, D.C.: International Bank for Reconstruction and Development/World Bank, 2008).

[67] According to OECD, foreign direct investment is the ownership by a foreign person or business of 10 percent or more of the voting equity of a firm located in the host country. Foreign direct investment flows provide information for foreign direct investment activity within a given period of time, while foreign direct investment stock indicates the level of foreign direct investment at a given point in time.

[68] China's reported foreign direct investment data represent official information published by the Chinese government and, despite their limitations, have been used in various reports, including those published by international organizations (such as IMF), government agencies, academic experts, and other research institutions, to describe China's foreign direct investment activities in Africa. The data appear to capture, for example, the Industrial and Commercial Bank of China's 2008 purchase of a 20 percent stake in South Africa's Standard Bank for about $4.8 billion.

[69] According to BEA, these nonbank holding companies generally had U.S. parent companies in mining, utilities, manufacturing (primarily petroleum related), and nonbank finance and insurance. A holding company typically does not produce goods or services itself but instead exists to own assets of other companies, which may be located in countries other than the holding company's.

[70] These sectors, with the exception of finance and insurance, also dominated U.S. foreign direct investment from 2001 through 2005.

[71] According to data from China's Ministry of Commerce, by the end of 2009, 88 percent of China's total foreign direct investment stock in Africa was in sub-Saharan Africa.

[72] See Montfort Mlachila and Misa Takebe, "FDI from BRICs to LICs: Emerging Growth Driver?" *IMF Working Paper*, WP/11/178 (2011), 11.

[73] In 2011, oil was also among the top categories of U.S. and Chinese imports from Ghana, although much smaller in magnitude than their imports from Angola. The absence of crude oil imports from Ghana prior to 2010 reflects the recent discovery and commercial production of crude oil in the country.

[74] From 2004, when Angola became eligible to export goods to the United States under AGOA, through 2011, more than half of U.S. oil imports from Angola received duty-free treatment under that program. During the same period, approximately 41 percent of U.S. oil imports from Angola received duty-free treatment under GSP. In 2011, nearly 87 percent of U.S. imports of oil from Angola received duty-free treatment under AGOA, while less than 3 percent of oil from Angola was imported under GSP.

[75] An oil block is a geographic area delineated by licensing authorities for oil exploration and production. The licensing authority grants exploration, production rights, or both, to an oil company or joint venture within the boundaries of the block, usually on an exclusive basis.

[76] According to a report by the U.S. Department of Energy's Energy Information Administration, Angola's national oil company, Sonangol, is the sole concessionaire and majority shareholder for oil and gas exploration and production in Angola and controls all petroleum industry activities. Sonangol works with foreign companies through joint ventures and production-sharing agreements. The Angolan government has plans under way to create a national oil agency that would act as regulator and concessionaire in place of Sonangol. Energy Information Administration, *Country Analysis Briefs: Angola* (Washington D.C.: 2011).

[77] Information on ownership of oil wells is as of September 2012 for Angola and as of August 2012 for Ghana.

[78] Angola has been a large oil producer for decades and is a member of the Organization of Petroleum Exporting Countries, while Ghana has been an oil producer since 2011. Additionally, in Angola, large international oil companies generally operate the country's oil wells; in Ghana, smaller independent oil firms operate the wells.

[79] No single foreign firm dominates Angola's oil sector, because the Angolan government generally distributes ownership stakes among multiple companies.

[80] According to the Department of Energy, one Chinese national oil company recently launched its first deepwater drilling rig in the South China Sea. Additionally, Chinese national oil companies are gaining deepwater management experience as nonoperators and operators in other sub-Saharan African countries including Nigeria, Gabon, Equatorial Guinea, and Cameron, according to the Department of Energy.

[81] Oil companies typically offer "bonuses" in addition to royalty fees to acquire ownership rights in oil blocks.

[82] China's national interest in securing oil supplies has led the Chinese national oil companies to invest throughout the world, according to the Department of Energy.

[83] In addition to loans, China has committed credit lines in some cases. A borrower draws funds from a credit line, incurring a loan. U.S. government agencies such as U.S. Ex-Im and OPIC provide loans as well as loan guarantees and insurance.

[84] We obtained data on China's loans to Angola from information published by the Angolan Ministry of Finance and from a U.S. official. Other sources corroborated data on China's total lending and provided some additional information about its loans to Angola. Additionally, we obtained information about China's loans and grants to Ghana and Kenya from documents published by the Ghanaian and Kenyan governments. Data on China's loans were available for different time periods in each of the case-study countries. China does not publish country-specific data on its loans and grants.

[85] A joint study by the World Bank and the Chinese government states that China's state-owned enterprises and government are closely connected and that Chinese state-owned enterprises are more likely to receive preferential access to bank finance, privileged access to business opportunities, and even protection against competition. See World Bank and Development Research Center of the State Council, People's Republic of China, *China 2030: Building a Modern, Harmonious, and Creative High-Income Society*.

[86] Comprehensive information on disbursement of China's credit lines and loans to Angola is not available. However, data published by the Angolan Ministry of Finance indicates that as of June 2008 about 30 percent China's credit lines of $2 billion in 2004 and $2.5 billion in 2007 were disbursed.

[87] U.S. officials said that they questioned how much of China's $3 billion loan commitment to Ghana in December 2011 will be disbursed. Although disbursement information for this loan is not yet available, data published by Ghana's Ministry of Finance and Economic Planning for the construction of the Bui hydroelectric dam indicate that as of September 2011, almost $129 million (70 percent) of the nearly $185 million committed by the Chinese government had been disbursed since 2008.

[88] In 2006 and 2011, the Chinese government also committed about $353 million to the Ghanaian government for several projects, including dam construction, communication infrastructure and systems, and electrification.

[89] No published information is available regarding China's grants to Angola.

[90] In addition, our analysis of information on specific Chinese government infrastructure loans to Angola, Ghana, and Kenya showed that these loans are more costly than World Bank loans to Ghana and Kenya, but not to Angola.

[91] Because U.S. Ex-Im did not offer loans for the construction sector during a similar period as the Chinese loans, U.S. Ex-Im provided us terms for hypothetical loans for the construction sector for the same country, on the same date, and of the same magnitude as the Chinese government loans.

[92] We obtained information about loans such as the amount, interest rate, maturity, and repayment period. When we could not obtain information about specific loan terms, such as the disbursement periods and the commitment fees for China's loans to Angola and Kenya, we made assumptions on the basis of comparable loans' terms or as appropriate. The repayment value of loans can differ on the basis of each loan's interest rate, maturity, and other fees. According to U.S. Ex-Im officials, U.S. Ex-Im's fees reflect risk of the borrower's defaulting on the loan and are based on country risk, the risk classification of the borrower, the terms of the loan, and the disbursement period.

[93] Under OECD rules, U.S. Ex-Im can provide up to 30 percent financing for local costs for medium- and long-term transactions if these expenses are related to the U.S. exporter's scope of work and if the U.S. exporter has demonstrated that local cost support is available from a competitor export credit agency or that private market financing of local costs was difficult to obtain for the transaction. Between 2001 and 2011, U.S. Ex-Im committed more than $70 million for financing local costs in Ghana and committed an additional $1.2 million in Nigeria. Information on large Chinese government loans indicates that China requires between 60 and 70 percent Chinese content.

[94] Chinese content includes materials made in China as well as Chinese labor to implement projects in the host country.

[95] In one instance, according to U.S. Ex-Im, it was able to obtain information to match China's loan offer for a rail project in Pakistan in 2010.

[96] MCC signed a 5-year, $547 million agreement or compact with Ghana that began in 2007. The MCC compact provided grants to fund agriculture, transportation, and rural services projects, including the construction of postharvest infrastructure such as a cargo center and packhouses, upgrades to a major highway and other roads, and improvements to the rural electrification infrastructure.

[97] Construction projects accounted for 89 percent of overall contract dollars won by Chinese firms for World Bank-funded projects.

[98] According to a report published by the World Bank in 2008, Chinese firms won more than 30 percent, by value, of construction contracts financed by the World Bank and African Development Bank in Africa from 2004 through 2006, making Chinese firms more successful than contractors of any other nationality. Furthermore, since 1999, China's construction sector has seen annual growth of 20 percent, making China the largest construction market in the global economy. See Vivian Foster et al., *Building Bridges: China's Growing Role as Infrastructure Financier for Africa* (Washington, D.C.: International Bank for Reconstruction and Development/World Bank, 2008).

[99] Although Chinese firms have invested in Angola's oil sector, they have done so in a nonoperator role. In contrast, U.S. firms have an operator role in several oil blocks in Angola.

[100] Portuguese firms won the highest amount of MCC construction contracts in Ghana, by nationality, with a total of almost $114 million in contracts. Ghanaian firms were the top contractor by nationality overall, with a total of $192 million in contracts.

[101] Services provided by U.S. firms under World Bank-funded contracts represent a small fraction (less than 1 percent) of annual U.S. trade in service exports to Angola, Ghana, and Kenya. However, World Bank contracts represent one of the few instances where data are available for examination of potential competition between U.S. and Chinese firms. According to the World Bank, the data include only contracts reviewed by World Bank staff prior to award, which comprise about 40 percent of total World Bank investment lending. The nationality of a firm reflects the country where it is registered, although the firm's parent may be headquartered in another country.

[102] In addition, according to the U.S. firm official, both the Chinese government and European governments are more active than the U.S. government in combining government and business interests to take advantage of large telecommunications projects in countries such as Kenya.

[103] According to a March 2012 draft report by the Kenyan Association of Manufacturers, counterfeiting includes the violation of trademarks, industrial designs, geographical indications, copyright, and related rights. Kenyan Association of Manufacturers, *The Study to Determine Severity of the Counterfeit Problem In Kenya as It Affects Industries and Impact of Proliferation of Counterfeit Products from Other EAC Partner States And Far East Countries Into the Kenyan Market*, draft report (March 2012).

[104] The Kenyan Association of Manufacturers report on counterfeits notes that counterfeit products result in a loss of revenue for manufacturers in Kenya as well as for the Kenyan government. The report cited a senior Kenyan official's statement that Kenyan manufacturers incur a net loss of more than $40 million and that the Kenyan government loses about $80 million in tax revenue annually as a result of counterfeit products. According to manufacturers interviewed for that report, about 30 percent of electrical components and electronics (e.g., motors, generators, switchgears, and batteries) are counterfeits and are primarily from China. See Kenyan Association of Manufacturers, *The Study to Determine Severity of the Counterfeit Problem*.

[105] Trade data indicate that China's exports of batteries (including rechargeable batteries and parts) increased from $15 million in 2001 to $48 million in 2011.

[106] Although China and African countries have initiated efforts to combat counterfeits and protect intellectual property rights, the success of these efforts is unclear, according to Commerce officials.

[107] According to U.S. aid data reported to OECD, concessional loans constituted less than 0.1 percent of U.S. aid to Kenya from 2001 through 2010. The United States has not committed any loans as aid to Kenya since 2008.

[108] During the same period, the United States committed about $1.6 billion in development assistance to Ghana as part of an MCC compact starting in 2007. This assistance differed from U.S. assistance to Kenya in its focus on infrastructure and agriculture projects. For more information on MCC-funded projects in Ghana see the supplemental report GAO-13-280SP. Compared to Kenya and Ghana, the United States committed a smaller amount of aid to Angola—about $804 million—during the same period because the United States discontinued humanitarian assistance to Angola.

[109] According to U.S. officials in Kenya, about 90 percent of Kenya's apparel exports are made of imported fabric. Specifically, about half of the imported fabric is from China (mostly woven fabrics) and Taiwan (mostly higher-end fabrics), and the remainder is from India and Pakistan (mostly knits from both countries).

[110] Comprehensive data on China's grants to Angola, Ghana, and Kenya are not available, in part because China does not publish country-specific aid data. The United States and other developed countries that are members of OECD are required to report aid data annually to OECD, which makes this information publicly available. China is not an OECD member and does not report such data.

[111] U.S. Department of State, *2012 Investment Climate Statement–Angola* (Washington D.C.: 2012).

[112] The petroleum sector in Angola is subject to revised local content regulation, according to State. A 2008 decree by the Angolan government requires oil companies to first seek Angolan employees to fill any vacant position prior to seeking expatriate appointment, which must first be authorized by the Ministry of Petroleum.

[113] U.S. Department of State, *2012 Investment Climate Statement—Ghana* (Washington D.C.: 2012). This report also notes that Ghana requires foreign investors to have local partners in only a few sectors—fishing, insurance, and the extractive industries.

[114] U.S. Department of State, 2012 Investment Climate Statement—Kenya (Washington D.C.: 2012).

[115] As a member of OECD's Development Assistance Committee, the U.S. government annually reports its data in disaggregated format for public reporting. Additionally, the OECD Arrangement on Export Credits requires participants such as U.S. Ex-Im to notify, consult with, and share information with other participants if U.S. Ex-Im offers loans on terms more generous than what the agreement specifies.

[116] The Kenyan government annually publishes reports on donor funding committed for the upcoming fiscal year. We were able to obtain these reports published from 2009 through 2011.

[117] We did not include security issues within the scope of this study.

[118] For example, to estimate travel and passenger fares, BEA uses data on passenger numbers collected by the Department of Homeland Security and tabulated by Commerce's International Trade Administration. To estimate numbers of students from sub-Saharan Africa countries who are studying in the United States and

numbers of U.S. students studying in these countries, BEA uses data based an annual survey of accredited U.S. institutions conducted by the Institute for International Education.

[119] See Lucy Corkin, "Angolan Political Elites' Management of Chinese Credit Lines," in Marcus Power and Ana C. Alves, eds., *China and Angola: A Marriage of Convenience?* (Capetown, South Africa: Pambazuka Press, 2012), 45-67.

[120] The higher the grant element, the more concessional the loan and the less the borrower has to repay relative to the amount borrowed. As a reference, donors who are OECD members define official development assistance to include loans for developmental purposes with a grant element of at least 25 percent.

[121] See Montfort Mlachila and Misa Takebe, "FDI from BRICs to LICs: Emerging Growth Driver?" *IMF Working Paper,* WP/11/178 (2011), 12.

[122] Mlachila and Takebe, "FDI from BRICs to LICs: Emerging Growth Driver?"

[123] According to the OECD, foreign direct investment is the ownership by a foreign person or business of 10 percent or more of the voting equity of a firm located in the host country.

[124] The World Bank offers different types of loans to Angola compared to Ghana and Kenya.

[125] For the World Bank loans, we were unable to find loans of similar magnitude to the Chinese government loans. We were also unable to find loans that contained construction projects for Ghana with publicly available terms.

[126] In addition, we used information and assumptions regarding the disbursement period, disbursement pattern, grace period, the discount rate, commitment fees, repayment pattern, and agreement date to calculate the present value of the loan and of future repayment. For example, to discount future disbursement and repayment, we use the OECD's differentiated discount rate. This rate, recommended by the OECD to calculate the concessionality of loans for determining tied aid, is based on the official lending rates of OECD export credit agencies and a specified margin.

[127] Higher fees would not always result in a less concessional loan, if offset by other factors including lower interest rates.

[128] As a reference, according to the OECD, official development assistance includes loans for developmental purposes with a grant element of at least 25 percent. To determine whether a loan qualifies as official development assistance, a 10 percent discount rate is used to calculate the concessionality of the loan.

[129] U.S. Ex-Im also calls the upfront fee the exposure fee.

[130] World Bank officials review and approve the level of the commitment fee annually.

In: Sub-Saharan Africa
Editor: Jacqueline S. Santiago

ISBN: 978-1-62618-433-6

Chapter 2

SUB-SAHARAN AFRICA: CASE STUDIES OF U.S. AND CHINESE ECONOMIC ENGAGEMENT IN ANGOLA, GHANA, AND KENYA*

United States Government Accountability Office

ABBREVIATIONS

AGOA	African Growth and Opportunity Act
BEA	Bureau of Economic Analysis
Commerce	Department of Commerce
GSP	Generalized System of Preferences
IMF	International Monetary Fund
MCC	Millennium Challenge Corporation
NGO	nongovernmental organization
OECD	Organization for Economic Cooperation and Development
OPIC	Overseas Private Investment Corporation
UN	United Nations
USAID	U.S. Agency for International Development
U.S. Ex-Im	Export-Import Bank of the United States

February 7, 2013

The Honorable James M. Inhofe
United States Senate

The Honorable Jack Kingston
House of Representatives

---

* This is an edited, reformatted and augmented version of the United States Government Accountability Office, GAO-13-280SP, dated February, 2013.

This supplemental report is a companion to *Sub-Saharan Africa: Trends in U.S. and Chinese Economic Engagement* (GAO-13-199).[1] This supplement presents the results of our case studies of U.S. and Chinese economic engagement in three sub-Saharan African countries— Angola, Ghana, and Kenya.[2] We conducted these case studies to compare the United States' and China's trade, grants and loans, and investment activities in sub-Saharan Africa. For contextual information about the three countries and additional information on U.S. and Chinese engagement in sub-Saharan Africa broadly, see GAO-13-199.

We selected the three countries on the basis of our assessment of the levels, types, and intersection of the United States' and China's engagement in trade, grants and loans, and investment activity in each country; the three countries' geographic diversity; and input from U.S. government officials and relevant experts. The case studies are meant to be illustrative and are not generalizable. We conducted work in Washington, D.C., and in Angola, Ghana, and Kenya, including meetings with officials from U.S. agencies, host-government ministries, U.S. businesses, other donors, and nongovernmental organizations (NGO). We were unable to meet with Chinese government officials, despite our requests, in Africa or Washington, D.C. We have noted data limitations as appropriate, such as lack of available data on China's grants and loans and likely underreporting of its investment data. Overall, we determined that the data presented in these case studies are generally reliable for the purposes for which the data are used. For a more detailed discussion of our scope and methodology, see GAO-13-199. We conducted this workfrom November 2011 to February 2013 in accordance with generally accepted government auditing standards.

David B. Gootnick,
Director, International Affairs and Trade

CASE STUDY OF U.S. AND CHINESE ECONOMIC ENGAGEMENT IN ANGOLA

U.S. and Chinese Trade with Angola

China's Total Trade in Goods in Angola Surpassed U.S. Trade in 2008, and Oil Imports Dominated Both

U.S. and Chinese trade in goods with Angola has risen dramatically, dominated by oil imports, with China's trade surpassing the United States'.[3] From 2001 through 2011, China's and the United States' total trade with Angola rose rapidly, reflecting a similarly rapid increase in imports of crude oil; China's total trade surpassed the United States' in 2008, and China's imports of crude oil exceeded the United States' in 2004 and in 2007 through 2011 (see figure 1). Imports accounted for 90 percent of the United States' total trade with Angola, and crude oil made up 96 percent of those imports. Imports represented 90 percent of China's total trade, and almost all of its imports were crude oil.[4]

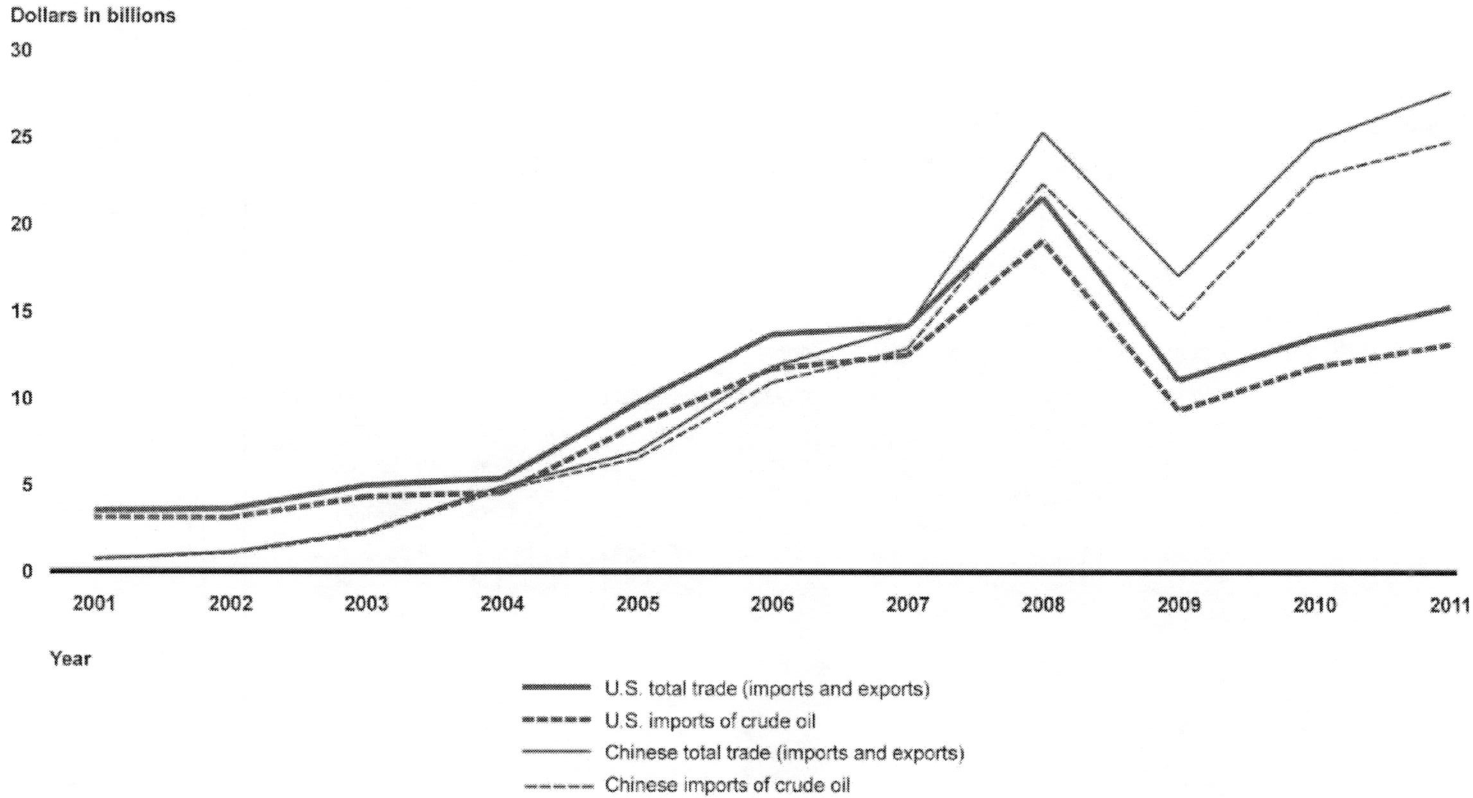

Source: GAO analysis of UN data.

Notes: Total trade is defined as imports plus exports. Trade data are reported in nominal values. Changes in value over time are due in part to changes in the prices of traded goods, such as substantial increases in the price of oil.

Figure 1. U.S. and Chinese Total Trade in Goods with Angola, Including Crude Oil Imports, 2001-2011.

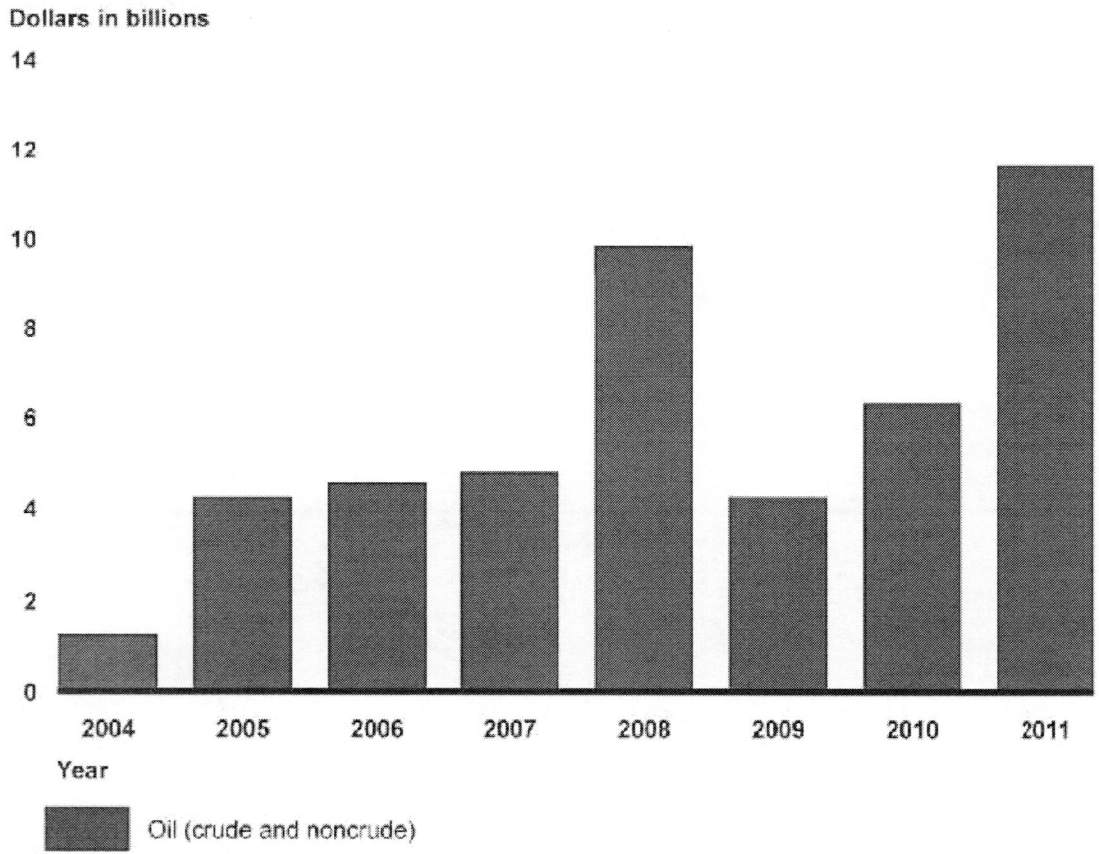

Source: GAO analysis of Department of Commerce data.

Notes: All U.S. imports under AGOA from Angola during this period consisted of oil. Angola became eligible to export goods under AGOA in 2004. Data are shown in nominal values.

Figure 2. U.S. Imports of Goods under AGOA from Angola, 2004-2011.

Almost all of U.S. imports from Angola enter the United States without tariffs. Since 2004, after Angola became eligible as a beneficiary of the African Growth and Opportunity Act (AGOA), the U.S. trade-preference program, 52 percent of total U.S. imports, including 53 percent of U.S. oil imports, from Angola have been tariff free under the program's terms. In addition, since 2001, 42 percent of total U.S. imports from Angola, including 43 percent of U.S. oil imports from Angola, have been tariff free under the Generalized System of Preferences (GSP). All imports from Angola under AGOA have consisted of oil, primarily crude oil. Figure 2 shows U.S. imports under AGOA from Angola from 2004 through 2011.

Almost all Chinese imports from least developed countries, which include Angola, enter China without tariffs. In 2003, China announced that some commodities from least developed countries in Africa, which includes Angola, would be given duty-free status. By 2007, according to a report by the World Trade Organization that cited Chinese officials, 98 percent of the total value of Chinese imports from least developed countries, which include Angola, entered China tariff free.

Like its imports, China's exports to Angola exceed U.S. exports. In 2011, China exported just under $2.8 billion in goods to Angola, while the United States exported less than $1.5 billion. Although China exported relatively few goods to Angola in 2001, its exports rapidly increased and surpassed those of the United States in 2008. In 2011, top Chinese exports included manufactured goods (e.g., cement, iron and steel rails) and machinery and transport equipment (e.g., electric generators and motorcycles). Top U.S. exports to Angola included machinery and transport equipment such as civil-engineering equipment, and food such as frozen poultry products. Figure 3 shows the trends and composition of U.S. and Chinese exports to Angola from 2001 through 2011.

U.S. Trade in Services with Angola Is Estimated at About $2.4 Billion per Year, but No Comparable Data Are Available for China's Trade in Services

From 2006 through 2011, total U.S. trade in services with Angola averaged about $2.2 billion annually, with U.S. imports of services averaging about $411 million and U.S. exports of services averaging about $1.8 billion.[5] For U.S. trade in services with Angola, the largest sectors for U.S. imports were transportation services and travel and passenger fares, and the largest sector for exports was business, professional, and technical services.[6] No comparable data are available for China's trade in services with Angola, in part because China does not publish country-specific information on its trade in services.

U.S. Firms Generally Have Not Competed with Chinese Firms on World Bank–Financed and Host-Government Contracts

U.S. and Chinese firms largely have not competed in similar sectors in Angola for donor-funded and host-government contracts, including contracts for provision of goods and services. According to data on World Bank-financed contracts in Angola for which U.S. and Chinese firms won contracts between 2001 and 2011, Chinese firms won fewer contracts but a larger share of contract dollars than U.S. firms and were active in providing construction services.[7] U.S. firms won a smaller share of contract dollars and were primarily active in consulting services, such as management and technical advice, and legal advisory services. Figure 4 shows World Bank contracts in Angola that firms from the United States, China, and other countries won in 2001 through 2011.

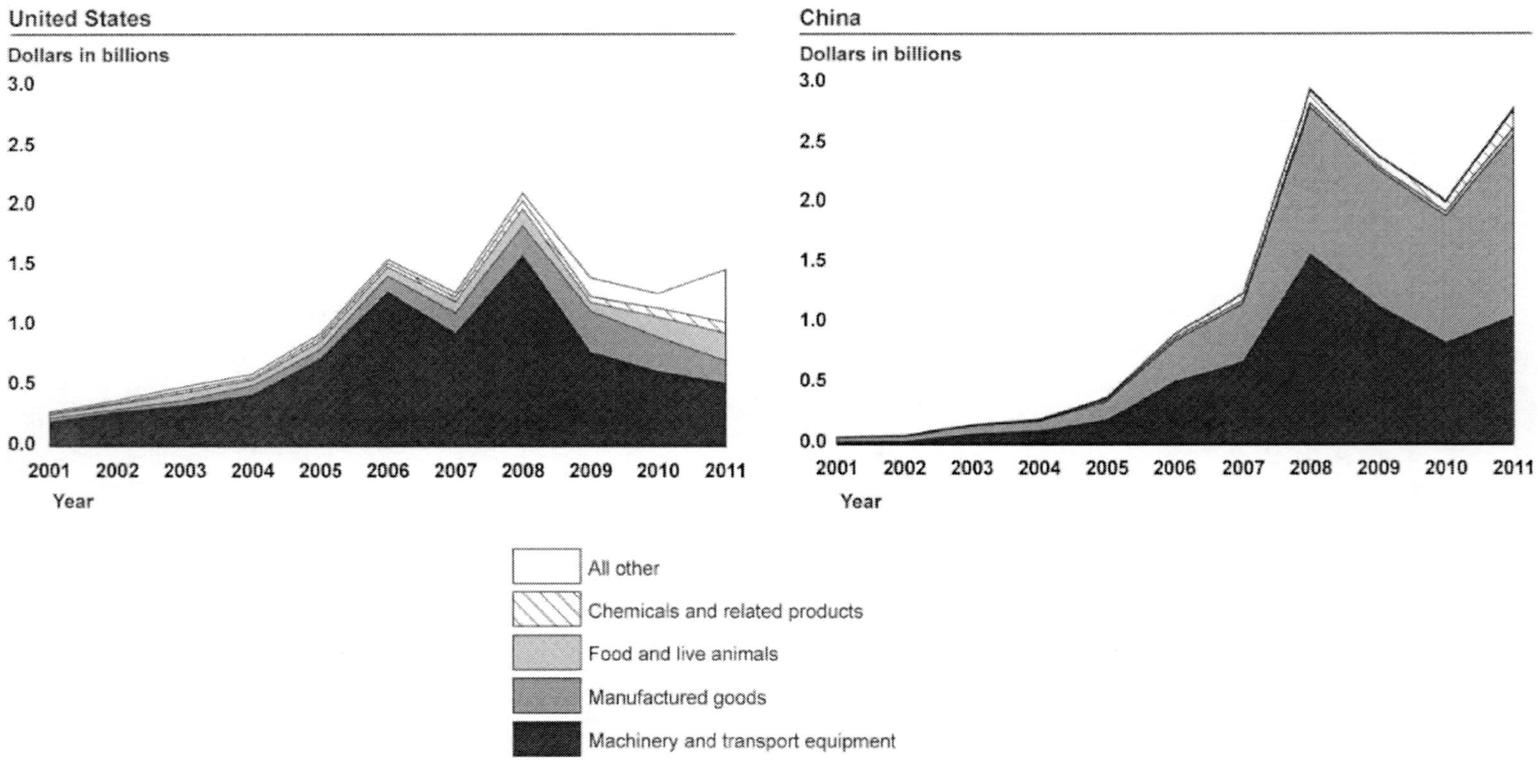

Source: GAO analysis of UN data.

Note: Export data are reported in nominal dollars.

Figure 3. U.S. and Chinese Exports of Goods to Angola, 2001-2011.

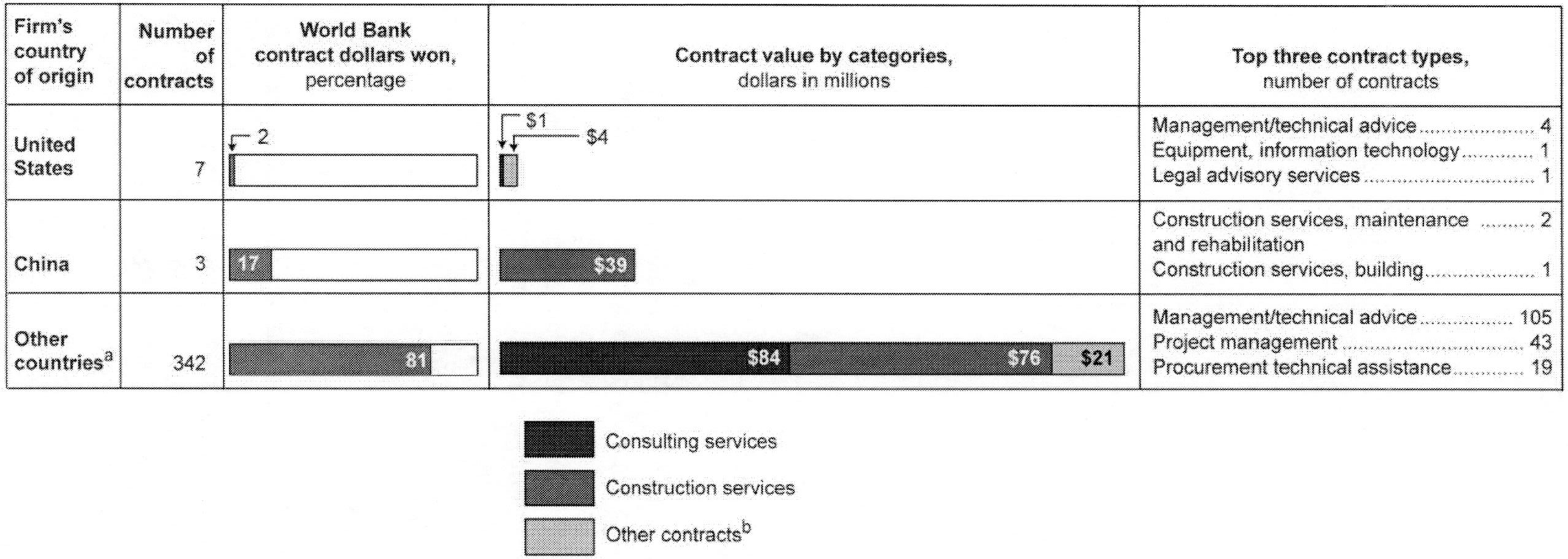

Source: GAO analysis of World Bank data.

Notes: According to the World Bank, the data shown include only contracts reviewed by World Bank staff prior to award. In general, these types of contracts constitute about 40 percent of total World Bank investment lending. The nationality of a firm reflects the country in which it is registered, although the firm's parent may be headquartered in another country.

[a] Firms from at least 26 other countries won World Bank contracts, with Angolan and Portuguese firms winning the most contracts.

[b] Other contracts were primarily for goods such as transportation equipment, information technology equipment, and educational equipment.

Figure 4. World Bank-Financed Contracts Won by Firms from the United States, China, and Other Countries in Angola, 2001-2011.

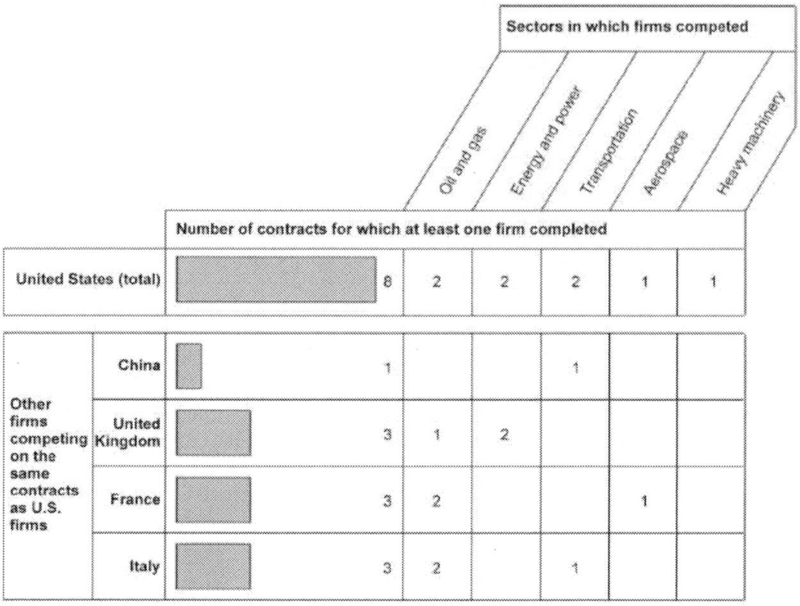

Source: GAO analysis of Department of Commerce data.

Notes: Data shown are for eight Angolan government contracts for which U.S. firms requested Commerce advocacy assistance in August 2002 through February 2012. Firms from the United Kingdom, France, and Italy competed with U.S firms for the largest numbers of contracts.

Figure 5. Nationality of Firms Competing for Eight Angolan Government Contracts for Goods and Services, 2002-2012.

Department of Commerce (Commerce) data on U.S. firms bidding on host-government contracts provide some evidence that U.S. firms primarily competed with European firms for these contracts. From August 2002 to February 2012, U.S. firms requested assistance from Commerce's Advocacy Center in competing for eight Angolan government contracts for goods and services. French, British, and Italian firms competed with U.S. firms for more of these contracts and in more sectors—primarily the oil and gas sector and the energy and power sector—than did Chinese firms (see figure 5). Chinese firms competed for only one of the contracts, for locomotives in the transportation sector.

U.S. and Chinese Grants and Loans to Angola

U.S. Government Committed About $800 Million in Grants to Angola, but Data Are Not Available for China's Grants

From 2001 to 2010, the U.S. government committed $804 million in grants to Angola,[8] primarily for health and humanitarian assistance.[9] As figure 6 shows, the level of U.S. government aid to Angola has varied over time, peaking in 2003 at about $152 million, declining until 2006 as humanitarian assistance was reduced sharply, and increasing again somewhat by 2010. The composition of U.S. aid to Angola has also varied over time, with humanitarian assistance constituting the bulk of assistance between 2002 and 2005 and health assistance generally increasing from 2006 to 2010. In contrast to the United States, China does not publish data on its grants to Angola.

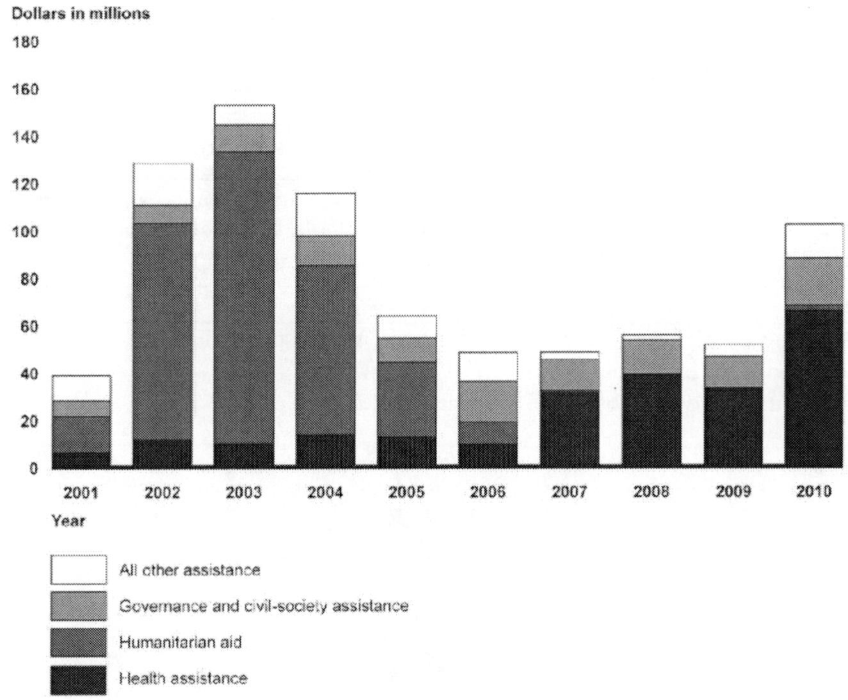

Source: GAO analysis of data from USAID.
Note: Aid data are shown in nominal dollars by calendar year.

Figure 6. U.S. Development Assistance Committed to Angola, 2001-2010.

Chinese Government Loan Commitments to Angola Significantly Exceed U.S. Government Loan Commitments for Trade and Investment

The U.S. government committed about $711 million in loans and related financing, such as loan guarantees and insurance, between 2001 through 2011 to support U.S. exports to, and U.S. firms' investments in, Angola. The Export-Import Bank of the United States (U.S. Ex-Im) committed about $678 million—95 percent of total U.S. government loan commitments— primarily for U.S. aerospace products and parts. Also, through OPIC, the U.S. government committed about $32 million in financing from 2001 through 2011 to support U.S. firms' investments in Angola in sectors such as credit financing, cement and concrete manufacturing, and grain and oilseed milling. Figure 7 shows U.S. government loans and related financing committed for U.S.-made products and U.S. firms' investments in Angola from 2001 through 2011.

As of September 2012, the Chinese government had committed an estimated $12 billion in credit lines to Angola since 2002 through the Export-Import Bank of China and the China Development Bank (see table 1),[10] according to the Angolan Ministry of Finance and a U.S. official.[11] Chinese government loans to Angola are generally guaranteed by Angola's oil in case of default and are repaid through proceeds from the sale of oil, according to officials from the U.S. government and a donor agency in Angola. According to the Angolan Ministry of Finance, U.S. officials, and a donor agency official in Angola, Chinese government loans to Angola have been for infrastructure construction, such as roads, rail, hospitals, schools, housing, water supply, and telecommunications.

Table 1. Chinese Credit Lines to Angola since 2002

Dollars in billions		
Year committed	**Financing committed**	**Types of projects**
2004	$2.0	Roads, rail, airports, housing, watersupply, hospitals, schools, telecommunications, boats
2007	2.5	
2009	7.5	
Total	**$12.0**	

Source: GAO analysis of information from the Angolan Ministry of Finance, U.S. officials, and a donor agency official in Angola.

Note: Data shown are those available as of September 2012.

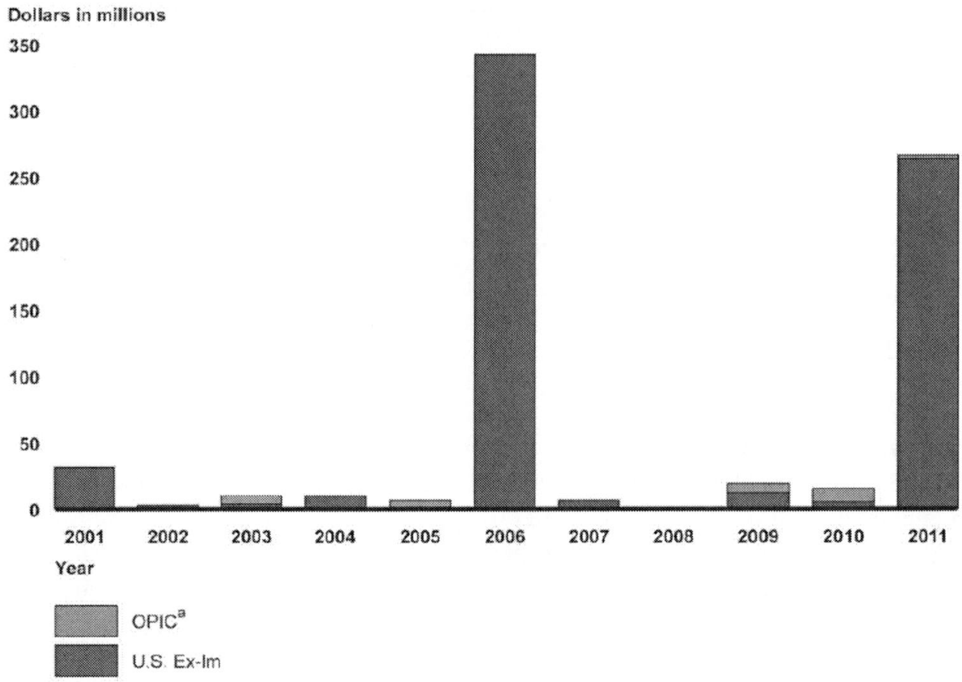

Source: GAO analysis of data from U.S. Ex-Im and OPIC.

Notes: Data are shown in nominal dollars. In addition, these values are shown by calendar year, although U.S. Ex-Im and OPIC typically report data by fiscal year.

[a] OPIC may report data for some financing commitments, such as investment funds, only at the regional level. Data shown do not reflect OPIC investment funds for regional use in sub-Saharan Africa, possibly including Angola. According to OPIC officials, because recipients of OPIC investment assistance may choose to invest in a set of countries, OPIC may initially lack information such as the countries where investments are made. In addition, according to OPIC officials, in countries with limited investment activity, business confidentiality agreements may prevent the disclosure of data that would reveal details of individual transactions.

Figure 7. U.S. Government Loans and Related Financing Committed for U.S.-Made Products and U.S. Firms' Investments in Angola, 2001-2011.

A large number of Chinese laborers work in Angola on projects financed by the Chinese government and implemented by Chinese firms.[12] As part of their loan agreement, the governments of China and Angola agreed that 70 percent of workers implementing construction projects would be Chinese and the remaining 30 percent would be Angolans, according to an Angolan nongovernmental organization (NGO) and reported statements by the former Chinese ambassador to Angola.[13] However, the Angolan NGO and former Chinese ambassador noted that Chinese firms usually did not meet Angola's requirements for local hiring; according to the Angolan NGO, this resulted in part from a lack of skills among Angolans after the country's long civil war.[14] Consequently, a large number of Chinese work in Angola on these projects.[15] For example, data published by China's Ministry of Commerce showed that more than 31,000 Chinese laborers were in Angola by 2009, and the former Chinese ambassador to Angola estimated that between 60,000 and 70,000 Chinese were in Angola in 2011, to implement projects financed through the Chinese credit lines, according to a news report published in March 2011. Figure 8 shows examples of Chinese firms' construction projects in Angola.

The Chinese government's engagement with Angola has been evolving since 2002. According to an expert in China-Africa relations, the Chinese government was one of the first foreign governments to provide relatively cheap financing to Angola after the country's civil war ended in 2002. According to an Angolan NGO, China provided this financing without significant conditions and, partly as a result of this financing, has developed relatively close ties with the Angolan government. After the end of Angola's civil war, the Angolan government emphasized rapid reconstruction, according to an Angolan NGO and officials from U.S. and Angolan firms.[16] However, according to Angolan government officials, the government is now focused on reducing poverty and diversifying the economy.

Source: GAO

Left to right: Signage for a Chinese firm constructing a building in downtown Luanda, Angola. Housing units near Luanda, Angola, being constructed by Chinese firms, according to a U.S. official.

Figure 8. Examples of Construction Projects Implemented by Chinese Firms in Angola.

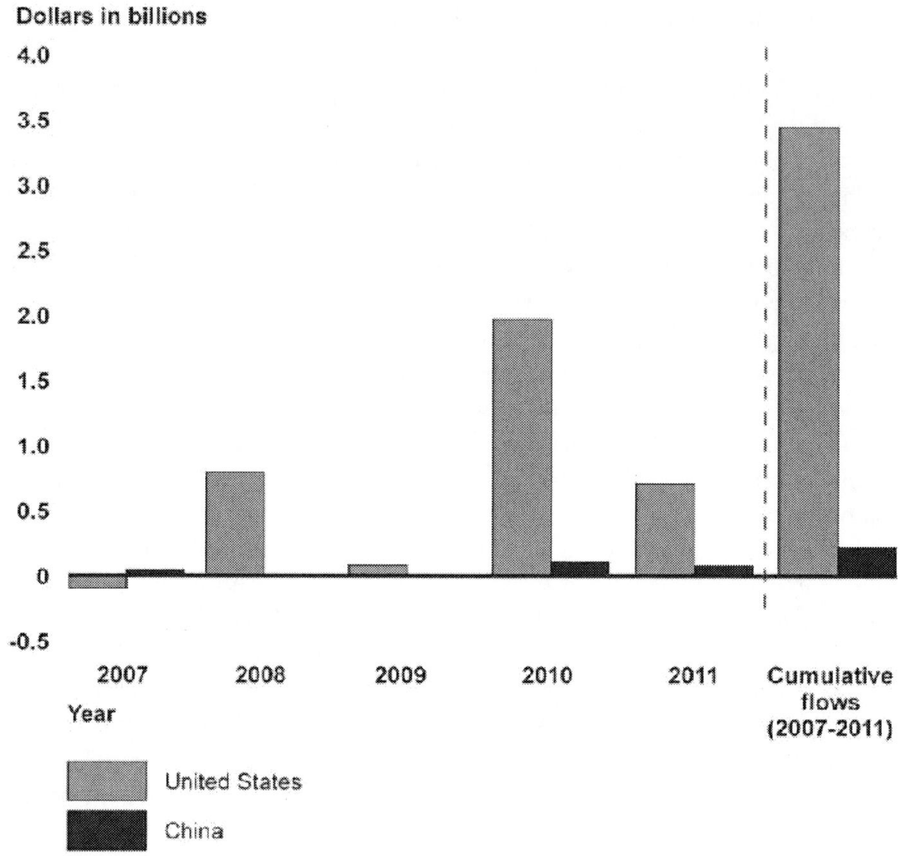

Source: GAO analysis of data from BEA, China's Ministry of Commerce, China's National Bureau of Statistics and Haver Analytics.

Note: Data are shown in nominal values.

Figure 9. Reported Flows of Foreign Direct Investment from the United States and China to Angola, 2007-2011.

U.S. and Chinese Investments in Angola

U.S. firms' investments in Angola, largely in the oil sector, exceed Chinese firms' reported investments. U.S. cumulative foreign direct investment flows from 2007 through 2011 were $3.4 billion,[17] while China's reported investment flows were about $214 million (see figure 9). According to experts, data on China's foreign direct investments are likely under-reported,[18] and according to the Bureau of Economic Analysis (BEA), data on U.S. foreign direct investments may also be underreported,[19] limiting precise comparisons of the United States' and China's investments. BEA reports that in 2011, the top sector of U.S. foreign direct investment stock was mining, predominantly crude-oil extraction, and that from 2006 through 2011, one of the fastest growing sectors was companies related to oil-related manufacturing. Comparable data for China's foreign direct investment in Angola by sector are not available.

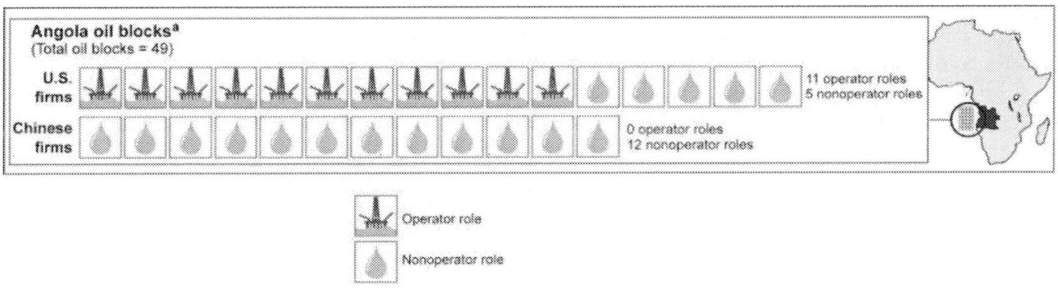

Source: GAO analysis of data from the U.S. Department of Energy and the government of Angola (data): MapInfo (map).

[a] In addition to U.S. firms, firms from Angola, Brazil, Denmark, France, and the United Kingdom, among others, operate Angola's 49 oil blocks.

Figure 10. Numbers and Types of U.S. and Chinese Firms' Investments in Oil Blocks in Angola as of September 2012.

Data on the purchase of ownership interests in oil blocks in Angola indicate that as of September 2012, U.S. firms were active in Angola's petroleum sector (see figure 10).[20] No single foreign firm dominates Angola's oil sector, because the Angolan government tends to distribute ownership stake among multiple companies.

However, U.S. firms act as operators for 11 of 49 oil blocks and have primary responsibility for operations such as drilling, maintenance, and complying with required rules and regulations.[21]

In addition, U.S. firms have purchased ownership interests in 5 oil blocks as nonoperators, generally with a minority stake but no responsibility for operations. Chinese firms, generally lacking the technology and capacity to manage offshore oil operations, have purchased ownership interests as nonoperators in 12 oil blocks in Angola.[22]

Like other nonoperators, Chinese firms' ownership interests help mitigate the operator's financial risks, given the large investments required in oil exploration and production operations.

In addition, through these ownership interests, Chinese firms participate in, and learn management experience through, the decision-making process of oil well operations, according to an official from a major oil firm.

Case Study of U.S. and Chinese Economic Engagement in Ghana

U.S. and Chinese Trade with Ghana

Chinese Trade in Goods Has Exceeded U.S. Trade and Grown More Rapidly

Since 2003, China's total trade in goods with Ghana has surpassed U.S. trade (see figure 11). From 2001 through 2011, the United States' total trade with Ghana grew by a factor of 5, from approximately $384 million to nearly $2 billion, while China's total trade with Ghana grew by a factor of 19, from approximately $182 million to nearly $3.5 billion. Exports to

Ghana made up a significant portion of both the United States' total trade (66 percent) and China's total trade (approximately 92 percent) during that 11-year period.

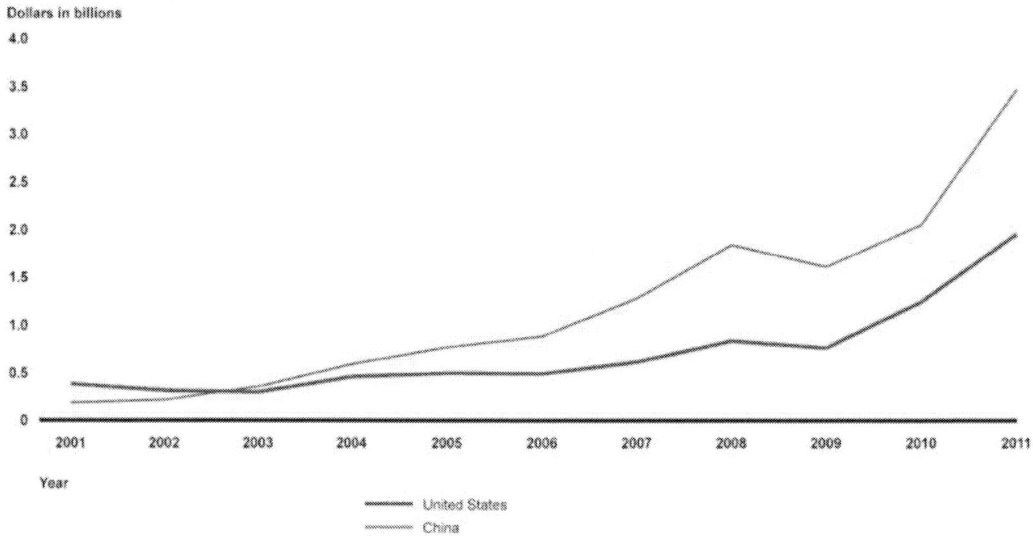

Source: GAO analysis of UN data.

Notes: Total trade is defined as imports plus exports. Trade data are reported in nominal values. Changes in value over time are due in part to changes in the prices of traded goods.

Figure 11. U.S. and Chinese Total Trade in Goods with Ghana, 2001-2011.

In 2001, the United States' and China's exports to Ghana were similar in value—approximately $179 million and nearly $146 million, respectively— but by 2011, Chinese exports had grown more than 20-fold, to $3.1 billion. This growth was largely due to increased exports of manufactured goods, such as footwear and lighting fixtures, and of chemicals such as insecticides.

As figure 12 shows, the United States exported approximately $1.2 billion in goods to Ghana in 2011, six times its exports in 2001. Top U.S. exports in 2011 included machinery and transport equipment, mainly machinery for minerals extraction and motor vehicles, and mineral fuels, primarily refined oil. Figure 12 shows U.S. and Chinese exports to Ghana by key categories.

U.S. imports of goods from Ghana have exceeded Chinese imports. U.S. imports increased nearly fourfold from 2001 to 2011, growing from approximately $200 million in 2001 to $800 million in 2011 (see figure 13). Since 2001, the United States has increased its imports of cocoa from Ghana.

Ghana became an oil-producing nation at the end of 2010 after a U.S. company discovered oil offshore in 2007, and crude oil was the top U.S. import from Ghana in 2011. However, Chinese imports from Ghana grew more rapidly than U.S. imports in the same period, rising 10-fold, from almost $37 million in 2001 to more than $360 million in 2011. China increased its imports of ores from 2001 to 2011 and also began importing crude oil in 2011.

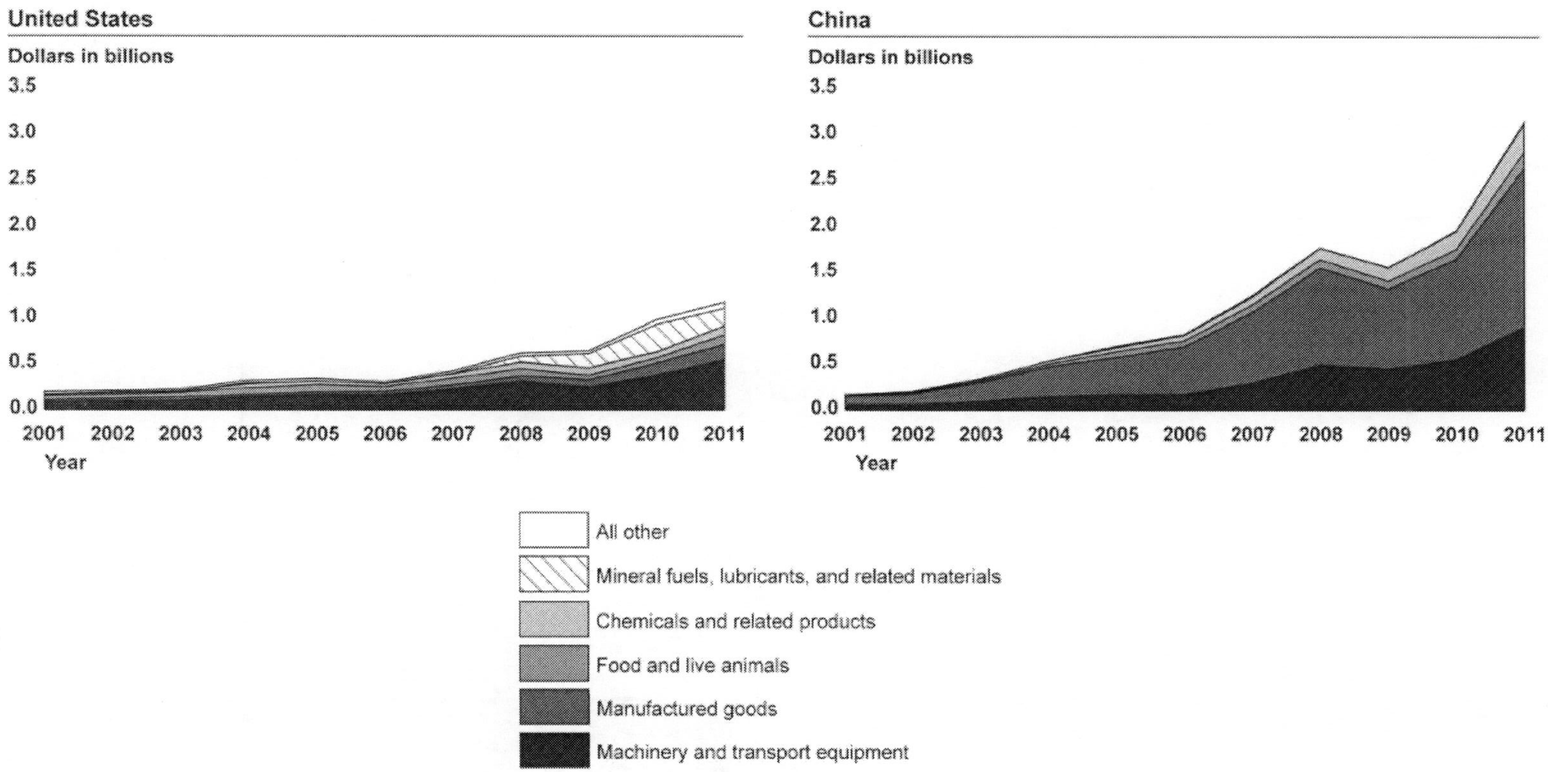

Source: GAO analysis of UN data.
Note: Export values are reported in nominal dollars.

Figure 12. U.S. and Chinese Exports of Goods to Ghana, 2001-2011.

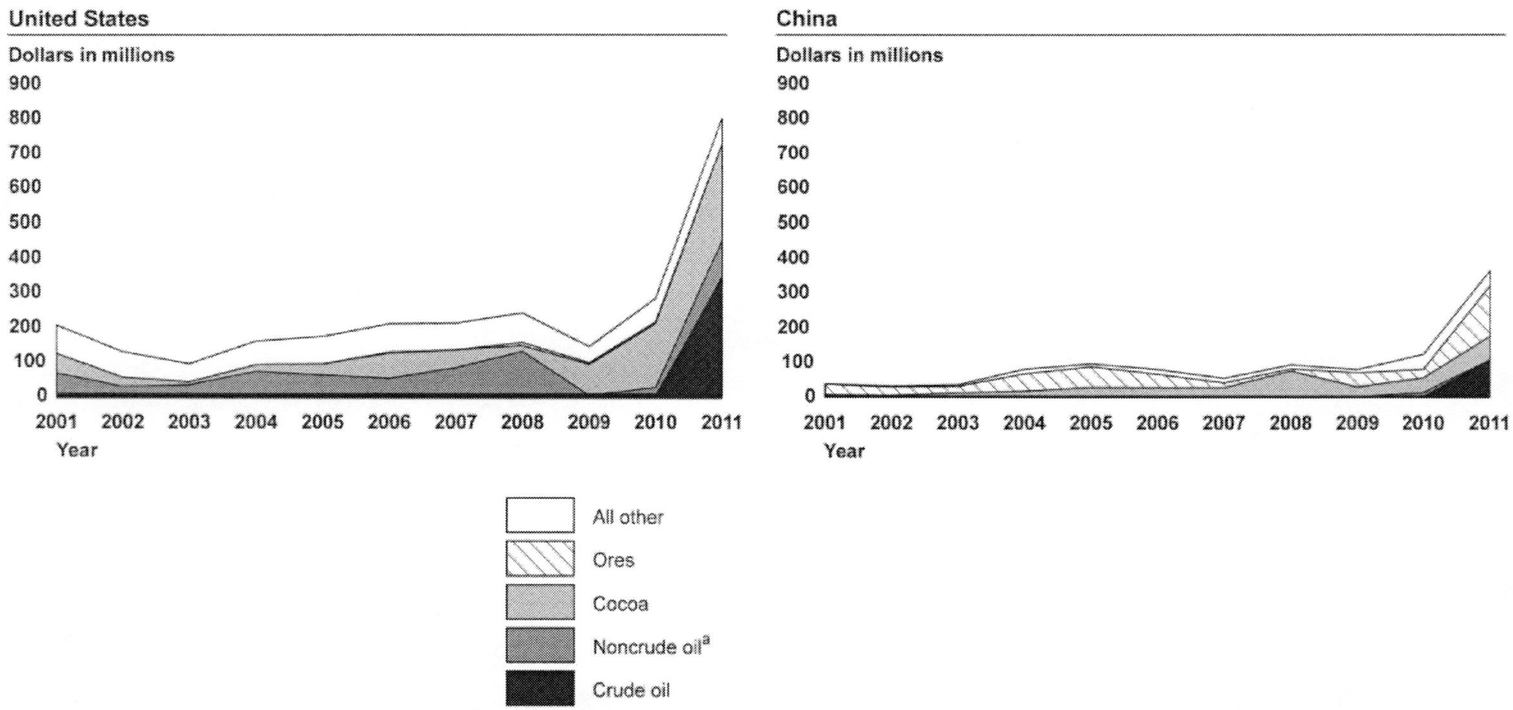

Note: Data are shown in nominal dollars.

[a] Noncrude oil includes refined oil such as gasoline and kerosene.

Figure 13. U.S. and Chinese Imports of Goods from Ghana, 2001-2011.

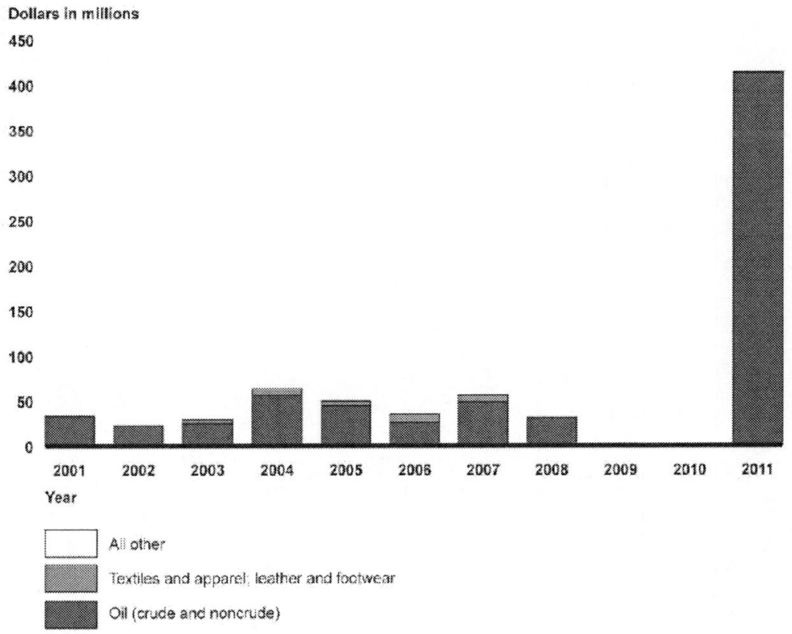

Source: GAO analysis of Department of Commerce data.

Note: Data are shown in nominal dollars. Data represented as "all other"—imports ranging from approximately $6,000 in 2001 to approximately $2 million in 2009—are not visible because of the magnitude of petroleum imports in 2011.

Figure 14. U.S. Imports of Goods under AGOA from Ghana, 2001-2011.

Under AGOA, the U.S. trade preference program, oil constituted 95 percent of U.S. imports from Ghana from 2001 to 2011 (see figure 14). U.S. imports of oil under AGOA, mostly crude oil, grew significantly in 2011, to nearly $413 million, compared with approximately $288 million in imports of oil, all noncrude, for the prior 10 years. The United States imported nearly $739 million in total goods from Ghana under AGOA during that period, including about $36 million of textiles, apparel, leather, and footwear, the second largest category of AGOA imports after oil.[23] Because Ghana is not a least developed country, it does not qualify for duty exemptions under China's trade preferences for least developed countries.

U.S. Trade in Services with Ghana Is Estimated at About $1.4 Billion per Year, but Comparable Data Are Not Available for China's Trade in Services

From 2006 to 2011, total U.S. trade in services with Ghana averaged about $1.2 billion annually, with U.S. imports of services averaging about $644 million per year and U.S. exports of services averaging about $546 million per year.[24] The largest sector for U.S. imports of services was travel and passenger fares. The largest sectors for U.S. exports of services were business, professional, and technical services; and travel and passenger fares. No comparable data are available for China's trade in services, in part because China does not publish country-specific information on its trade in services.

Table 2. U.S., Chinese, and Other Firms' Participation in MCC Contracts for Ghana, 2007-2012

Contractor nationality	Number of projects[a]	MCC contract dollars won, percent of final contract amounts	Contract amount, dollars in millions	Consulting services, percent of contract amount	Construction, percent of contract amount	Goods, percent of contract amount
United States	11	6%	$31.9	100%	0%	0%
China	7	22	111.7	0	100	0
Ghana	>400	37	192.2	29	54	17
Other countries	>200	35	177	28	71	2

Source: GAO analysis of Millennium Challenge Corporation data.

[a] Numbers of projects shown are estimates, particularly for contractors from Ghana and other countries, owing to the size and complexity of MCC's procurement system.

Source: GAO
Left to right: MCC funded N1 Highway in Accra, Ghana, built in part by China Railway Wuju Corporation, MCC signage over N1 Highway.

Figure 15. Photos of MCC-Funded N1 Highway and Signage in Ghana.

U.S. and Chinese Firms' Competition for Donor-Funded and Host-Government Contracts Has Been Limited

U.S. and Chinese firms generally have not competed in similar sectors in Ghana for donor-funded contracts. According to data on Millennium Challenge Corporation (MCC)–funded projects in Ghana for which U.S. and Chinese firms won contracts in 2007 through 2012, all MCC contracts implemented by Chinese firms were for construction projects. Furthermore, officials who oversaw procurement for MCC-funded contracts in Ghana said that U.S. firms did not bid on any MCC construction contracts (see table 2).

Implementation of MCC's 5-year, $547 million compact with Ghana began in 2007, with a focus on reducing poverty through agribusiness development. As table 2 shows, U.S. firms won 11 MCC contracts totaling nearly $32 million (6 percent of the value of MCC contracts in Ghana), all for consulting services.

Chinese firms won 7 contracts totaling approximately $112 million (22 percent of the value of MCC contracts in Ghana), nearly 40 percent of which funded construction of a section of the National "N1" Highway in Accra (see figure 15).[25]

Because of the higher values of construction contracts, Chinese firms' contracts were larger (5 of the 10 largest MCC contracts) than U.S. firms' (1 of the 10 MCC largest contracts). The majority of Chinese-implemented MCC construction projects were transportation projects; the remaining projects were agriculture-related infrastructure, such as irrigation systems.

Data on World Bank–funded contracts in Ghana also illustrate that U.S. and Chinese firms largely do not compete in similar sectors in Ghana.[26] According to available data on World Bank contracts from 2001 through 2011, U.S. and Chinese firms won nearly the same number of contracts, but Chinese firms won significantly more contract dollars (see figure 16).

Chinese and U.S. firms did not appear to overlap in competing for consulting and construction services contracts but overlapped in providing three types of goods: educational, electrical, and transportation equipment.

Although contracts for electrical equipment made up nearly 14 percent of the value of contracts for Chinese firms, the same category constituted less than 2 percent of the value of U.S. firms' contracts. Contracts for educational or transportation equipment did not represent a significant portion of the value of contracts for which both U.S. and Chinese firms competed.

Chinese firms primarily provided electrical equipment and construction services and materials, while U.S. firms primarily provided information technology equipment, management and technical advice, and policy and strategy consulting services.

Commerce data for U.S. firms competing for host-government contracts in Ghana provide some evidence that U.S. firms competed with Chinese firms almost as often as with firms of other nationalities (see figure 17).

From August 2002 until February 2012, U.S. firms requested assistance from Commerce's Advocacy Center in competing for 11 Ghanaian government contracts for goods and services.

U.S. firms competed against Chinese, French, and Israeli firms, respectively, in 4 of the 11 contracts and against German and Ghanaian firms, respectively, for 5 contracts. U.S. and Chinese firms competed for contracts in the telecommunications, computers and information technology, and transportation sectors. U.S. firms competed against firms of other nationalities in sectors that included telecommunications and aerospace.

Chinese firms have reportedly followed Ghanaian hiring requirements and implemented quality construction projects in a timely manner.

According to U.S. and Ghanaian officials, Ghana's local content requirements regarding hiring of local labor limit the hiring of foreign workers, with exceptions made for some high-skilled areas such as engineering.

Data available from Ghana's Ministry of Roads and Highways on certain projects implemented by Chinese firms provide evidence that Ghanaian workers constitute the majority of workers hired by Chinese contractors for construction projects.

Additionally, according to MCC data, Chinese contractors working on MCC-funded projects in Ghana hired seven local workers for every Chinese worker. Ghanaian officials who provided oversight of MCC-funded and other projects in Ghana did not report any concerns with Chinese contractors in regard to hiring local labor.

Furthermore, officials said that large-scale construction projects implemented by Chinese firms were timely and met quality standards, and Chinese contractors were more accommodating of contract changes compared to other contractors.

MCC officials said that the use of an engineering firm to supervise construction projects implemented by a Chinese firm was important to ensuring the quality of work completed.

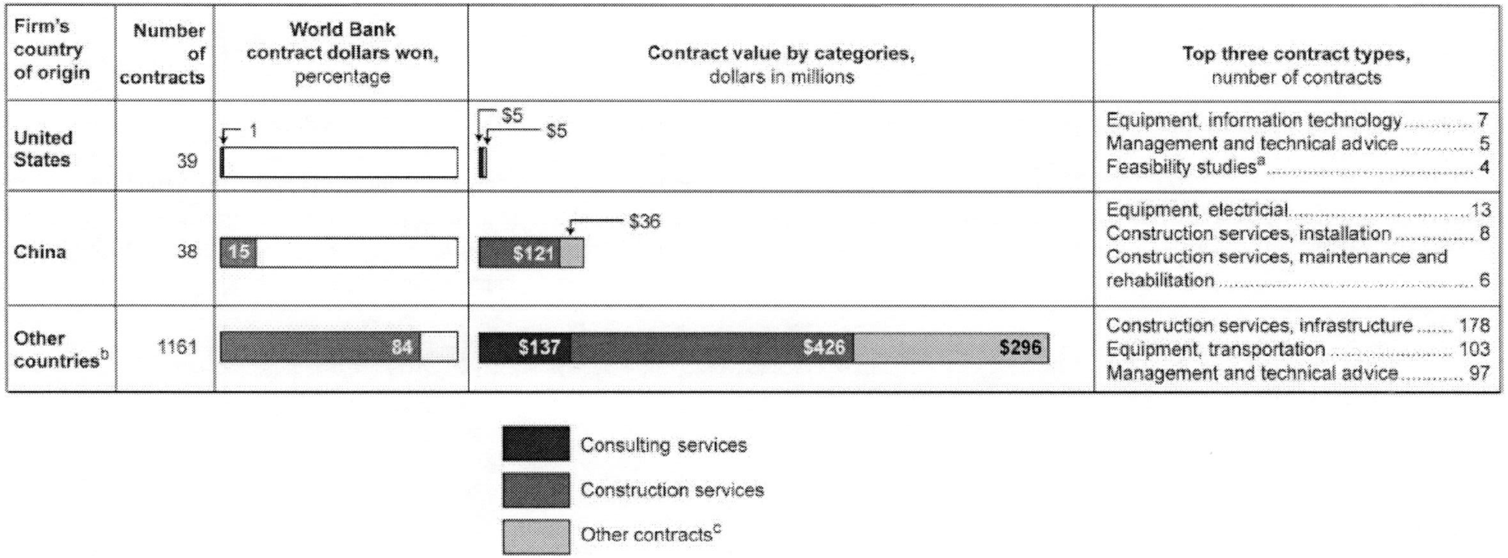

Source: GAO analysis of World Bank data.

Notes: According to the World Bank, the data shown include only contracts reviewed by World Bank staff prior to award. In general, these types of contracts constitute about 40 percent of total World Bank investment lending. The nationality of a firm reflects the country in which it is registered, although the firm's parent may be headquartered in another country.

[a] In addition to winning contracts for feasibility studies, U.S. firms won four contracts for educational equipment and four contracts for policy and strategy services.

[b] Other contracts primarily include goods such as transportation equipment, information technology equipment, and electrical equipment.

[c] Firms from at least 32 other countries won World Bank contracts, with firms from Ghana and the United Kingdom winning the most contracts.

Figure 16. World Bank–Financed Contracts Won by Firms from the United States, China, and Other Countries in Ghana, 2001-2011.

		Number of contracts for which at least one firm competed	Telecommunications	Computers, information technology, and security	Aerospace	Transportation	Healthcare	Infrastructure	Other
United States (total)		11	4	2	1	1	1	1	1
Other firms competing for the same contracts as U.S. firms	China	4	2	1		1			
	Germany	5	3		1				1
	Ghana	5	2		1	1			1
	France	4	2		1				1
	Israel	4	2		1				1

Sectors in which firms competed: Telecommunications; Computers, information technology, and security; Aerospace; Transportation; Healthcare; Infrastructure; Other.

Source: GAO analysis of Department of Commerce data.

Notes: Data shown are for eleven Ghanaian government contracts for which U.S. firms requested Commerce advocacy assistance in August 2002 through February 2012. "Other firms" consists of firms that competed for the largest numbers of contracts. In addition to Chinese firms, firms from Germany, Ghana, France, and Israel competed with U.S. firms for the largest numbers of contracts.

Figure 17. Nationality of Firms Competing for 11 Ghanaian Government Contracts for Goods and Services, 2002-2012.

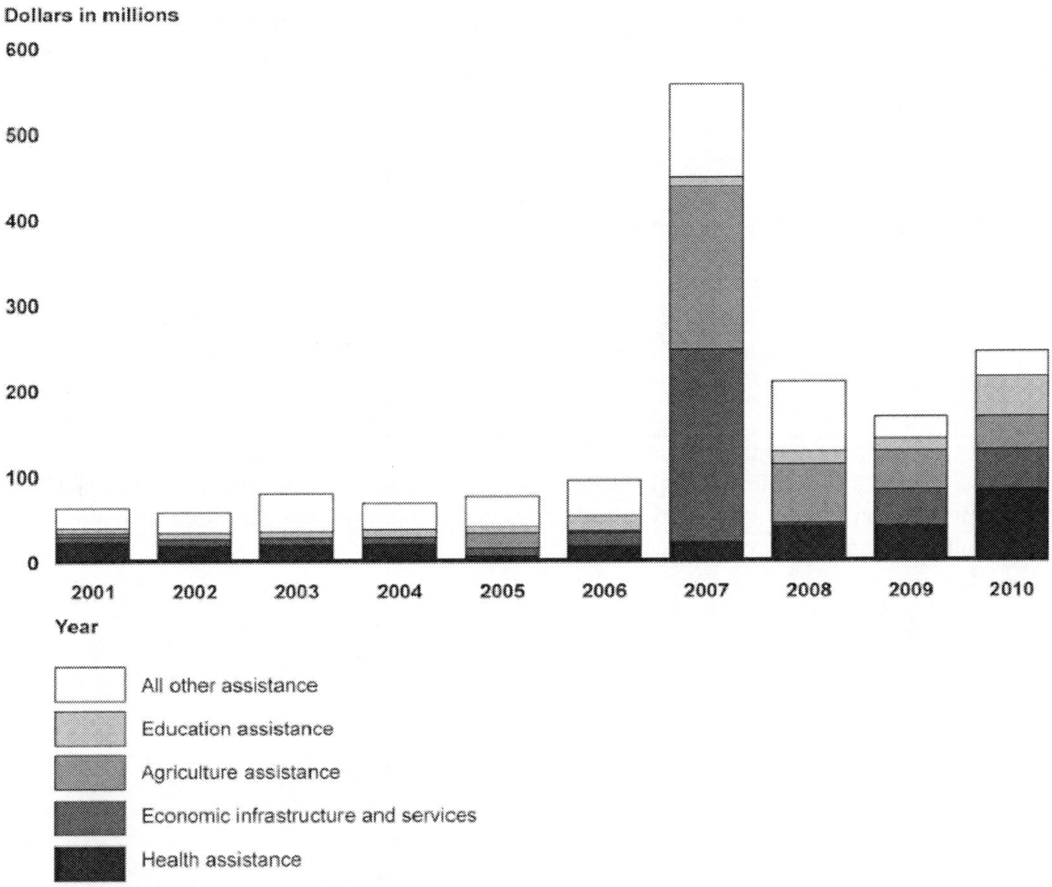

Source: GAO analysis of data from USAID.
Note: Commitments are shown in nominal dollars by calendar year.

Figure 18. U.S. Development Assistance Committed to Ghana, 2001-2010.

U.S. and Chinese Grants and Loans to Ghana

U.S. Government's Grants to Ghana Exceeded China's in Recent Years

The U.S. government's grant commitments to Ghana exceeded China's during the period 2006 through 2010. From 2001 to 2010, the United States committed about $1.6 billion in aid in the form of grants to Ghana, including nearly $1.3 billion beginning in 2006 (see figure 18). The level and composition of U.S. aid has varied, with a sharp 1-year increase in 2007 primarily due to funding from MCC for its $547 million, 5-year compact that focused on agriculture, transportation, and rural services projects.[27] U.S. funding for health assistance generally increased from 2006 to 2010, primarily in the area of antimalaria assistance.

China has not published information on its grant-based aid to Ghana. However, data published by the Ghanaian government indicate that China committed approximately $18 million in grants in 2007, 2008, and 2011, mostly for the construction of Ghana's Ministry of Foreign Affairs complex (see table 3).

Table 3. China's Grant Commitments to Ghana, 2006-2011

Dollars in millions		
Types of projects	**Year committed**	**Grants committed**
Economic and technical cooperation	2007	$2.10
	2008	1.26
Subtotal		**$3.36**
Construction of Ministry of Foreign Affairs complex	2011	15.00
Total		**$18.36**

Source: GAO analysis of data from Ghana's Ministry of Finance and Economic Planning.

Notes: The Ghanaian government published data on China's grant commitments in annual budget documents from 2006 through 2011. According to these documents, the published data are for commitments through the end of September for each year.

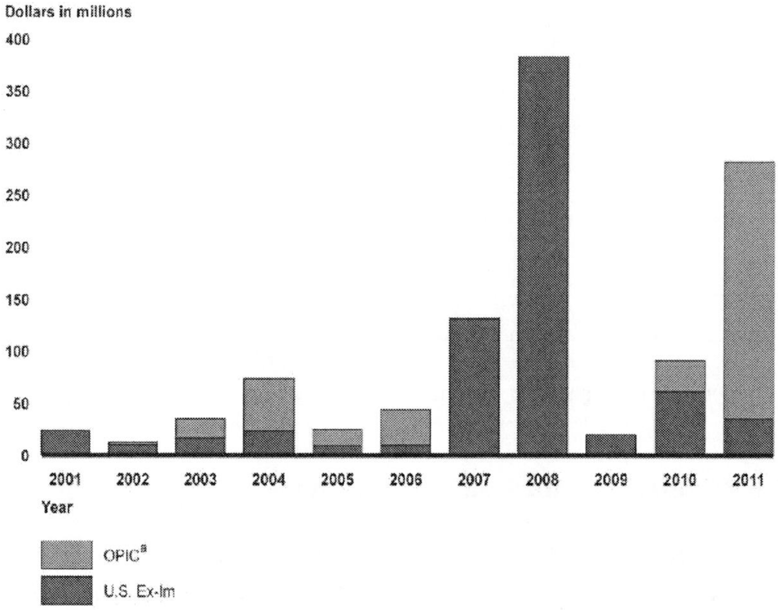

Source: GAO analysis of data from U.S. Ex-Im and OPIC.

Notes: Data shown are for nominal dollars by calendar year. In addition, these values are shown by calendar year, although U.S. Ex-Im and OPIC typically report data by fiscal year.

[a] OPIC may report data for some financing commitments, such as investment funds, only at the regional level. Data shown do not reflect OPIC investment funds for regional use in sub-Saharan Africa, possibly including Ghana. According to OPIC officials, because recipients of OPIC investment assistance may choose to invest in a set of countries, OPIC may initially lack information such as the countries where investments are made. In addition, according to OPIC officials, in countries with limited investment activity, business confidentiality agreements may prevent the disclosure of data that would reveal details of individual transactions.

Figure 19. U.S. Government Loans and Related Financing Committed for U.S-Made Products and U.S. Firms' Investments in Ghana, 2001-2011.

Table 4. China's Loans Committed to Ghana, 2006-2011

Dollars in millions		
Types of projects	**Year committed**	**Loans committed**
Bui hydro electric project	2008	$68.04
	2009	61.83
	2010	54.96
Subtotal		**$184.83**
Communication system for national security	2008	6.29
	2009	5.71
	2010	.74
Subtotal		**$12.74**
Economic and technical cooperation	2007	10.00
	2008	6.00
	2009	5.45
	2010	.96
Subtotal		**$22.41**
E-government project	2010	33.00
Information and communication technology	2010	2.58
National communication infrastructure	2007	3.80
	2008	4.58
	2010	.62
Subtotal		**$9.00**
Supply of Installation of Self-Help Electrification Program	2008	12.30
	2009	11.18
	2010	2.07
Subtotal		**$25.55**
'Support for fisheries sector	2008	18.00
	2009	21.27
	2010	23.40
Subtotal		**$62.67**
Various infrastructure development projects[a]	2011	3,000.00
Total		**$3,352.78**

Source: GAO analysis of data published by Ghana's Ministry of Finance and Economic Planning.

Notes: The Ghanaian government published data on China's loan commitments in annual budget documents from 2006 through 2011. Documents largely state that published data are for commitments through the end of September for that year.

[a] Available budget data did not include China's $3 billion loan to Ghana signed in December 2011; however, we included this loan in our analysis because this financing represents China's most significant loan package to Ghana.

U.S. Government Committed Smaller Amounts of Loans for Ghana Than China Did in Recent Years

From 2001 to 2011, the U.S. government committed approximately $1.1 billion in loans and related financing to support exports of U.S. goods and services and U.S. firms' investments in Ghana, as shown in figure 19.

During this period, U.S. Ex-Im committed about $719 million (64 percent) in loans and other financing for U.S.-made products, including motor vehicles and cars, metal ore mining, and other machinery and equipment. OPIC committed about $399 million (36 percent) in loans and other financing for U.S. firms' investments in areas such as medical equipment, home loans, and the petroleum and minerals sectors.

Comprehensive information on China's loans to Ghana is not available, but according to data published by the government of Ghana, China committed, or agreed to, more than $3 billion in loans to Ghana between 2006 and 2011.

As shown in table 4, China's loans were primarily for infrastructure construction, including a dam and other energy infrastructure; the installation of an electrification system; and communications technology.

China committed its largest loan to Ghana in 2011, when the China Development Bank signed an agreement with the Ghanaian government to provide $3 billion, largely for oil and gas infrastructure and transportation infrastructure, including a railway, ports, and harbors. Chinese firms and materials are to make up about 60 percent of the content used under this agreement, which will be bid competitively among Chinese firms, according to a Ghanaian official. Repayment of some Chinese loans is tied to natural resources, such as oil and cocoa.[28]

U.S. and Chinese Investments in Ghana

Data on the United States' foreign direct investments in Ghana suggest that U.S. foreign direct investment flows exceeded China's reported foreign direct investment flows in the most recent years for which comparable data are available.[29] In the 2-year period 2010 through 2011, U.S. cumulative foreign direct investment was $808 million; in the 5-year period 2007 through 2011, China's reported cumulative foreign direct investment was $158 million (see figure 20).

According to experts, data on China's foreign direct investment are likely underreported,[30] and according to BEA, data on U.S. foreign direct investment may also be underreported,[31] limiting precise comparisons of the United States' and China's investments. According to information from BEA, from 2006 through 2011, the vast majority of U.S. foreign direct investment stock was in mining and activities related to the mining sector, with an average annual growth rate of 25 percent in mining investments during that period. This growth was a turnaround from the decline in U.S. foreign direct investment stock in mining from 2001 through 2005.

Comparable information on China's foreign direct investment in Ghana by sector is not available.

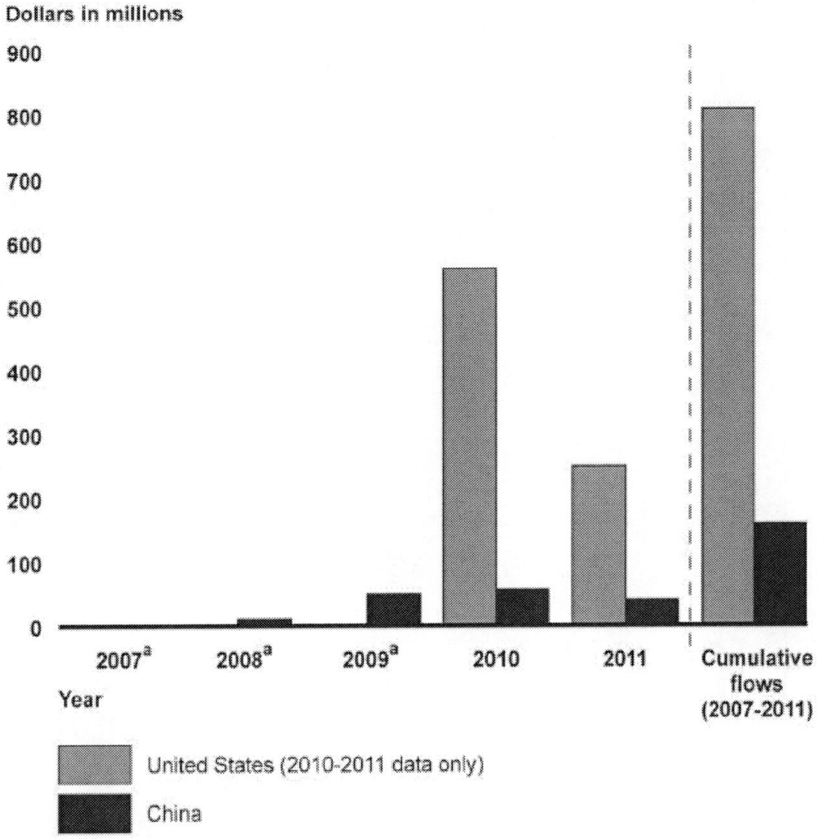

Source: GAO analysis of data from BEA, China's Ministry of Commerce, China's National Bureau of Statistics, and Haver Analytics.

Notes: Data are shown in nominal values.

[a] Data on U.S. foreign direct investment flows from 2007 through 2009 are confidential and have not been released.

Figure 20. Reported Flows of Foreign Direct Investment from the United States and China to Ghana, 2007-2011.

Data on the purchase of ownership interests in oil blocks in Ghana as of August 2012 indicate that U.S. firms are active in the petroleum sector but that Chinese firms are not (see figure 21).

Following a U.S. firm's discovery of oil offshore in Ghana in 2007, commercial production began in late 2010, and Ghana became an oil-exporting country in 2011. U.S. companies have operator roles in 2 of Ghana's 17 oil blocks, with primary responsibility for operations such as drilling, maintenance, and complying with required rules and regulations. In addition, U.S. firms have purchased ownership interests in 4 oil blocks as nonoperators, where these firms have a minority stake and are not responsible for operations.[32]

Chinese firms do not operate or own any shares of Ghana's oil blocks. European and African firms operate the majority of the remaining oil blocks.

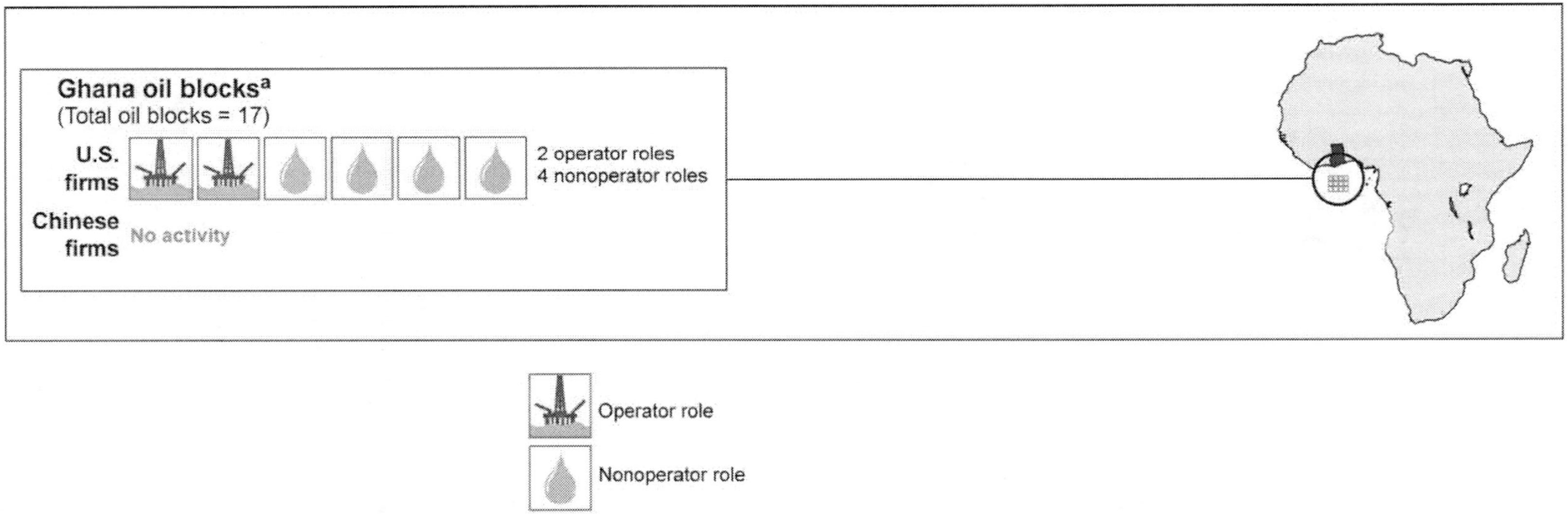

Source: GAO analysis of data from the U.S. Department of Energy and the government of Ghana (data); MapInfo (map).

[a] In addition to U.S. firms, firms from Bermuda, Italy, Nigeria, and the United Kingdom, among others, operate Ghana's 17 oil blocks. In one oil block, a U.S. firm had an operator role and another U.S. firm had a nonoperator role.

Figure 21. Numbers and Types of U.S. and Chinese Firms' Investments in Oil Blocks in Ghana, August 2012.

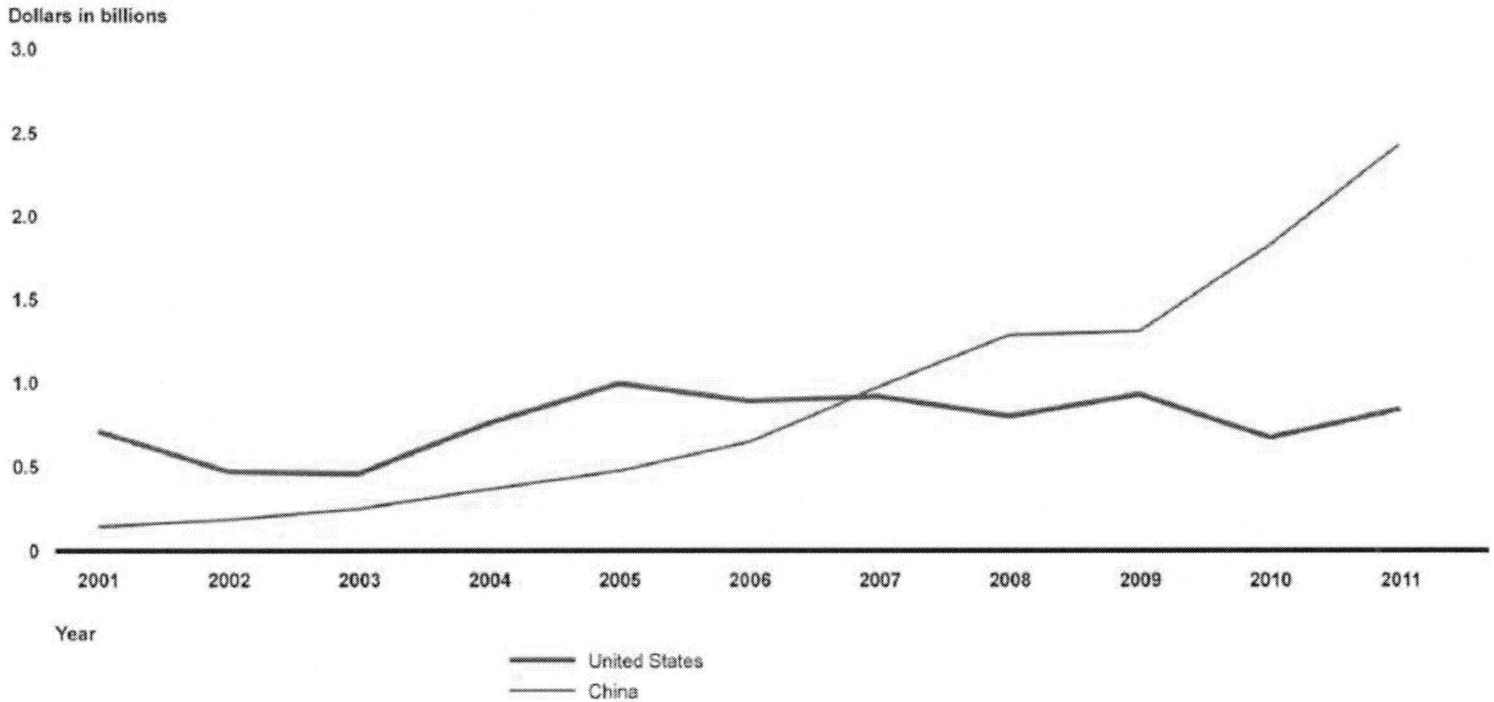

Source: GAO analysis of UN data.

Notes: Total trade is defined as imports plus exports. Trade data are shown in nominal dollars. Changes in value over time are due in part to changes in the prices of traded goods. For consistency with data reported by the IMF's Direction of Trade Statistics and the World Trade Atlas, data for Chinese imports have been adjusted to exclude imports of a category of goods labeled "special transactions."

Figure 22. U.S. and Chinese Total Trade in Goods with Kenya, 2001-2011.

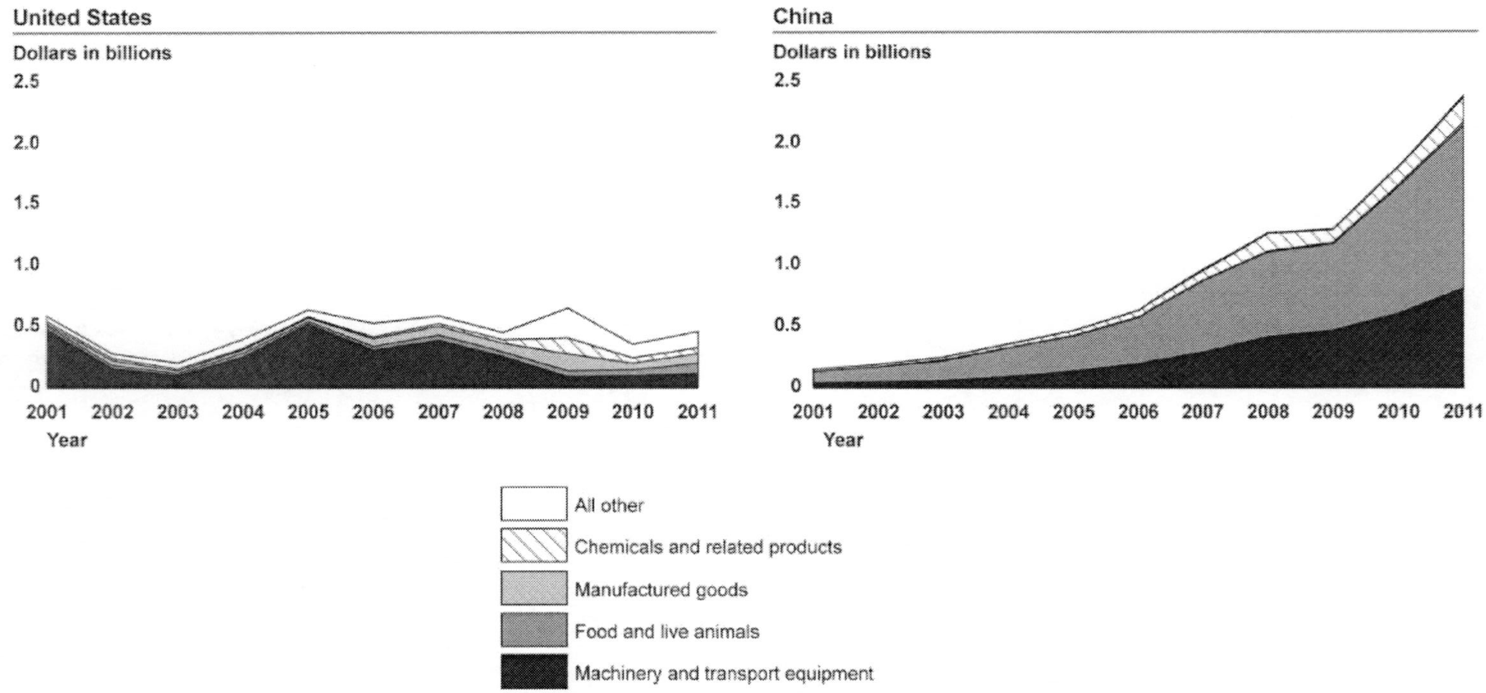

Source: GAO analysis of UN data.

Note: Export data are shown in nominal dollars.

Figure 23. U.S. and Chinese Exports of Goods to Kenya, 2001- 2011.

CASE STUDY OF U.S. AND CHINESE ENGAGEMENT IN KENYA

U.S. and Chinese Trade with Kenya

China's Trade in Goods with Kenya Has Increased

China's total trade in goods with Kenya has increased since 2001 and has exceeded U.S. total trade since 2007 (see figure 22). From 2001 to 2011, total U.S. trade in goods fluctuated but changed relatively little overall, rising from nearly $711 million in 2001 to $844 million in 2011; although U.S. imports nearly tripled, U.S. exports declined by about 20 percent. China's total trade grew by a factor of 17 during this period, from nearly $145 million to approximately $2.4 billion, primarily because of the increase in Chinese exports to Kenya.

From 2001 through 2011, U.S. exports to Kenya decreased while Chinese exports rose, as shown in figure 23. Specifically, U.S. exports to Kenya dropped from $574 million in 2001 to $447 million in 2011, primarily owing to a decline in U.S exports of machinery and transport equipment.[33] Meanwhile, Chinese exports to Kenya in 2011 greatly exceeded the United States', growing from nearly $139 million in 2001 to $2.4 billion in 2011. In 2011, China's top exports included manufactured goods (e.g., woven fabrics and footwear), and machinery and transport equipment (e.g., transmission equipment and motorcycles).

In contrast to exports, U.S. imports of goods from Kenya exceeded Chinese imports in 2001 through 2011. U.S. and Chinese imports of goods differed in size and composition, as shown in figure 24. U.S. imports nearly tripled from 2001 to 2011, from $137 million to $397 million, in part because of an increase in imports of apparel and clothing from $69 million in 2001 to $272 million in 2011.

Under AGOA, the U.S. trade preference program, textiles, apparel, leather, and footwear constituted nearly 96 percent of U.S. imports from Kenya from 2001 to 2011 (see figure 25).[34] AGOA's "third-country fabric provision" has enabled Kenya to generally increase its apparel exports, according to U.S. and Kenyan officials, and Kenya has become one of the largest exporters of nonpetroleum goods to the United States. U.S. and Kenyan officials pointed to the positive employment effects in Kenya associated with apparel exports under AGOA.

However, they also noted AGOA's limited success in enabling Kenya and other sub-Saharan African countries to manufacture textiles and fabrics, which form the input for apparel manufacturing.

Kenya and Ghana obtain fabrics mostly from China and other Asian countries to manufacture apparel for export to the United States, according to U.S. officials in these countries. As a result, Chinese exports of textile and fabrics to Kenya also increased during this period, from $40 million in 2001 to $347 million in 2011. Meanwhile, Chinese imports from Kenya were less than U.S. imports but grew at a faster rate, from nearly $6 million in 2001 to almost $60 million in 2011. Top Chinese imports in 2011 included iron ore, leather, scrap metal, and tea.

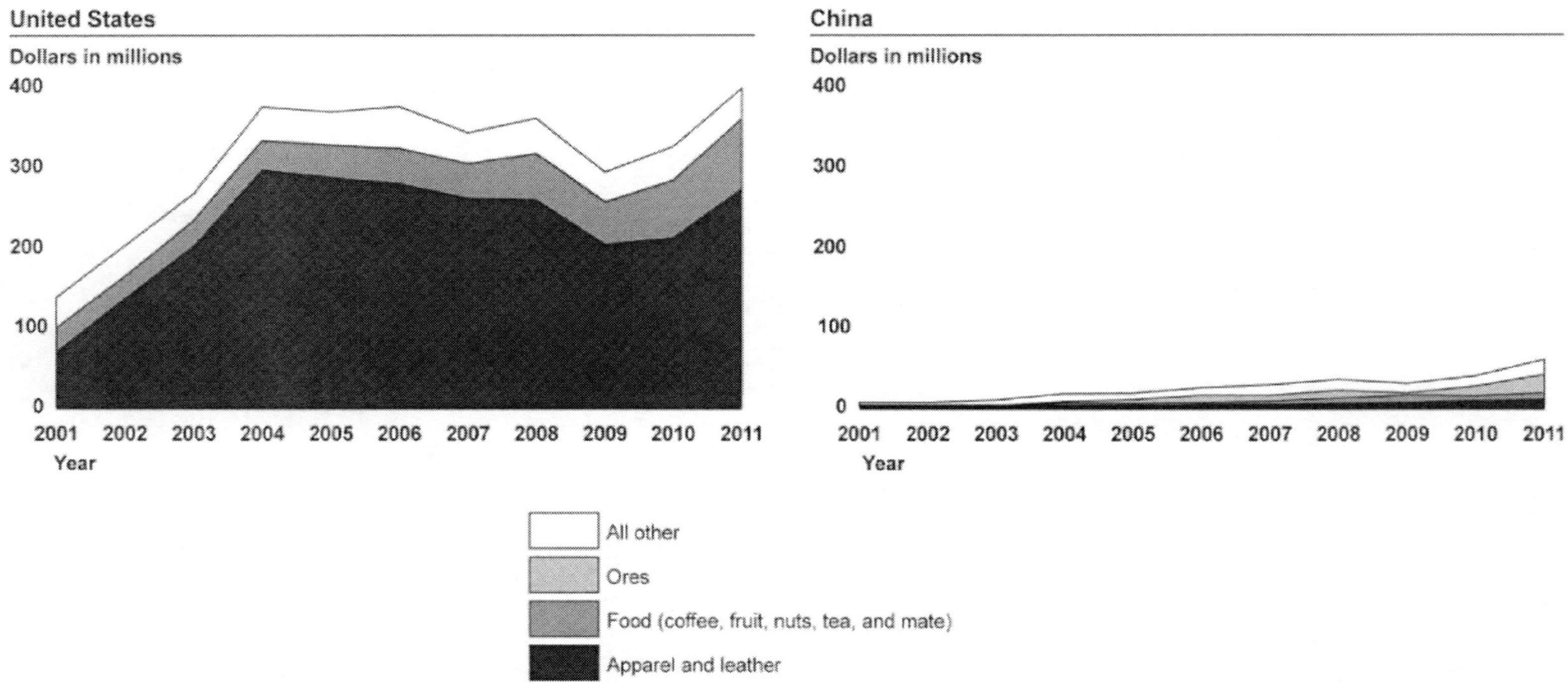

Source: GAO analysis of UN data.
Note: Import data are shown in nominal dollars.

Figure 24. U.S. and Chinese Imports of Goods from Kenya, 2001-2011.

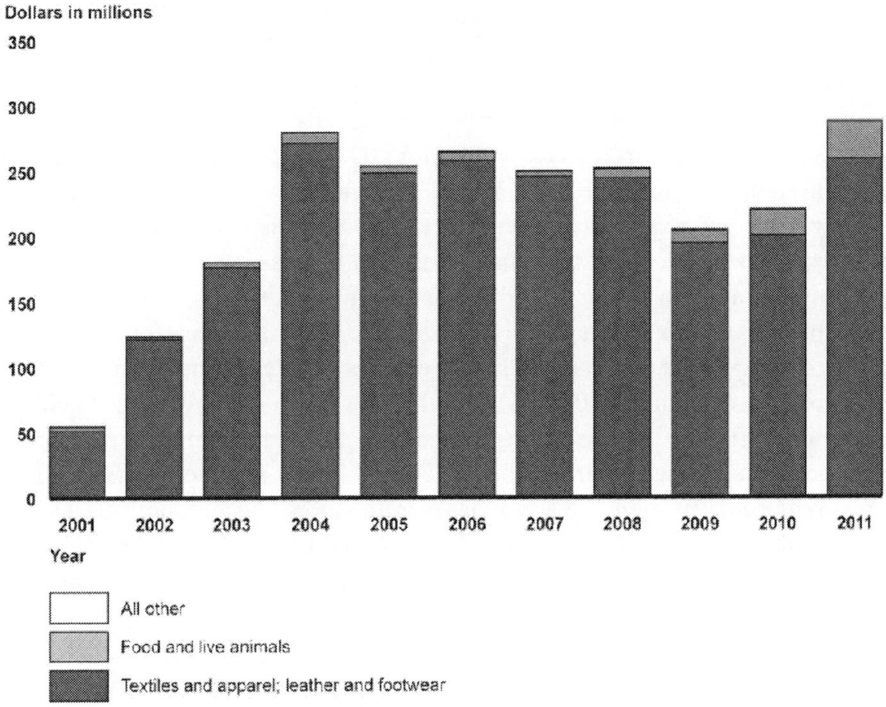

Source: GAO analysis of Department of Commerce data.

Notes: Data are shown in nominal dollars. U.S. imports of goods represented as "all other," ranging from a low of approximately $35,000 in 2003 to a high of nearly $1.13 million in 2011, are not visible.

Figure 25. U.S. Imports of Goods from Kenya under AGOA, 2001-2011.

U.S. Trade in Services with Kenya Is Estimated at Nearly $1 Billion Annually, but Comparable Data on China's Trade in Services Are Not Available

From 2006 through 2011, total U.S. trade in services with Kenya averaged about $899 million annually. U.S. imports of services, not including travel and passenger fares, averaged about $281 million per year, and U.S. exports of services averaged about $618 million per year.[35] The largest sector for U.S. imports of services was business, professional, and technical services. The largest sectors for U.S. exports of services were business, professional, and technical services; education; and travel and passenger fares. Comparable country-level data on China's trade in services in Kenya are not available.

U.S. and Chinese Firms Compete in Some Sectors but Generally Not for Donor-Funded and Host-Government Contracts

Chinese firms are competing with U.S. firms in Kenya's information-and communication-technology sector. Additionally, counterfeits manufactured by Chinese firms adversely affect U.S. firms' sales and reputation in Kenya. However, U.S. and Chinese firms largely do not compete in similar sectors in Kenya for donor-funded and host-government contracts.

Competition in Information and Communication-Technology Sector

Chinese firms are competing with U.S. firms in Kenya's information-and communication-technology sector, but it is not clear whether this competition directly affects U.S.-made exports to these countries, according to officials of U.S. agencies and U.S. firms operating in Kenya. A senior official at a large U.S. information-and communication-technology firm noted that Chinese firms are innovating and adapting quickly to local markets. For example, a Chinese firm in this sector has established one of the largest training centers in Kenya. Moreover, this official noted that in contrast to the U.S. government, the Chinese government and European governments are more active in combining government and business interests to take advantage of large telecommunications projects in countries such as Kenya. Trade data indicate that China's exports of telecommunications equipment to Kenya rose from $0.5 million in 2001 to $122 million in 2011. However, it is unclear whether direct competition from Chinese firms affects U.S.-made exports, in part because multinational corporations headquartered in the United States operate globally. For example, according to a representative of a U.S. firm that manufactures telecommunications equipment, most of its products are manufactured outside the United States and therefore competition from Chinese telecommunications firms in Kenya does not affect U.S.-made exports.

Impact of Counterfeits from China

Counterfeit goods and related products from China have adversely affected U.S. firms' sales and reputation in Kenya.[36] According to a 2012 study by the Kenyan Association of Manufacturers, counterfeit goods primarily from China, especially in the energy, electronic, and electrical components sector, have negatively affected the sales and reputation of U.S. firms and others with operations in Kenya.[37] For example, according to a representative of a U.S. firm that manufactures dry-cell batteries in Kenya, the influx of counterfeit and substandard products, mainly from China, caused the U.S. firm's business to decline, and over time the firm has decreased the number of its employees in Kenya from 800 to 300. Furthermore, according to the former head of the U.S. firm's East Africa division, prior to competition from Chinese products, the U.S. firm's market share of carbon zinc batteries was about 80 percent. However, by May 2011, Chinese products controlled 60 percent of the market. This official also noted that in some cases, Chinese products, although of poorer quality, mimicked the U.S. firm's product branding and color schemes. Although the U.S. firm successfully litigated in Kenyan courts against this trademark infraction, according to this official the penalty was too lenient to have a deterrent effect on the Chinese manufacturers of counterfeits. Trade data indicate that China's exports of batteries (including rechargeable batteries and parts) increased from $15 million in 2001 to $48 million in 2011. To combat Chinese counterfeits, the U.S. embassy in Kenya has sponsored several public-education programs, and the U.S. government is providing technical assistance to Kenya's Anti-Counterfeit Agency, established in 2010. However, corruption in Kenya, as well as the Kenyan government's lack of willingness to take appropriate actions, have significantly impeded the fight against counterfeits, according to U.S. firms and the Kenyan private sector.[38]

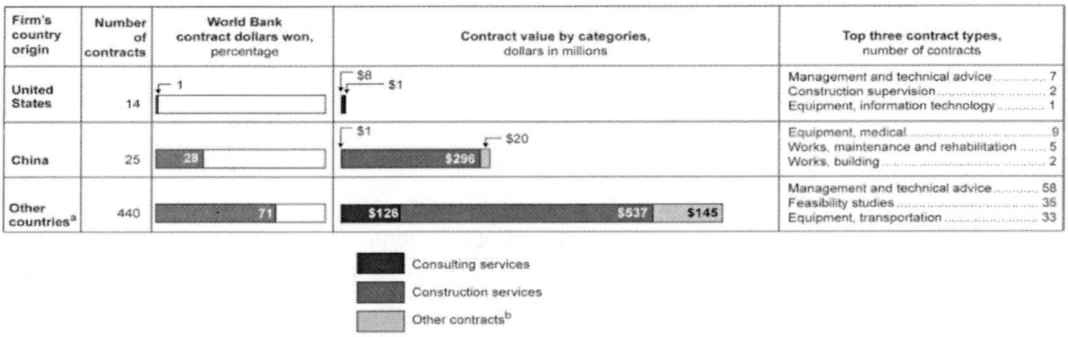

Source: GAO analysis of World Bank data.

Notes: According to the World Bank, the data shown include only contracts reviewed by World Bank staff prior to award. In general, these types of contracts constitute about 40 percent of total World Bank investment lending. In addition, the nationality of a firm reflects the country in which it is registered, although the firm's parent may be headquartered in another country.

[a] Other contracts primarily include goods such as medical equipment and products, transportation equipment, and water supply and sewerage equipment.

[b] Firms from at least 27 other countries won World Bank contracts, with firms from Kenya and the United Kingdom winning the most contracts.

Figure 26. World Bank–Funded Contracts Won by Firms from the United States, China, and Other Countries in Kenya, 2001-2011.

General Absence of Competition for Donor-Funded and Host-Government Contracts

U.S. and Chinese firms largely do not compete with each other in similar sectors in Kenya for donor-funded and Kenyan government contracts, including contracts for the provision of goods and services. According to data on World Bank-funded projects in Kenya for which U.S. and Chinese firms won contracts between 2001 and 2011, Chinese firms won a larger share of contract dollars and were primarily active in providing medical equipment and construction services and materials.[39] In contrast, U.S. firms won a significantly smaller share of overall contract dollars for World Bank–funded projects in Kenya and were primarily active in consulting services, such as providing management and technical advice and supervising construction. Figure 26 compares World Bank-funded contracts won by firms from the United States, China, and other countries. Officials from the Kenyan government and NGOs generally viewed Chinese firms' implementation of construction projects positively, because their projects were completed in a timely manner and were of better quality than those implemented by local Kenyan companies. According to Kenyan Ministry of Roads officials, Chinese contractors generally met standards for road construction, in part because the contracts included adequate supervision by third parties. Moreover, strong application of local-content rules in Kenya has restricted the number of Chinese workers and led to Chinese contractors' hiring more local workers, according to U.S. and Kenyan government officials. In addition, according to U.S. officials and other donors, Chinese firms' business practices, such as housing workers near project sites and maintaining long work days, contribute to keeping construction costs low. Finally, the presence of Chinese firms, even on projects funded by other donors, has helped create a positive image for China in Kenya, according to U.S. and Kenyan officials. By contrast, the United States may get less publicity despite its large aid commitment, because it does not fund infrastructure projects in

Kenya, according to a U.S. official. Figure 27 shows a newly built highway and signage for the Chinese state-owned firm that constructed the road in Nairobi, Kenya. Commerce data on U.S. firms bidding on host-government contracts provide some evidence that European firms were U.S. firms' primary competitors for host-government contracts. From August 2002 to February 2012, U.S. firms requested assistance from Commerce's Advocacy Center in competing for 28 Kenyan government contracts for goods and services. Chinese firms competed on 4 of these contracts, for oil and gas, medical equipment, healthcare, and computers and information technology equipment (see figure 28). French, British, and Dutch firms competed with U.S. firms for more contracts and in more sectors, including aerospace, oil and gas, energy and power, and services, than did Chinese firms.

Source: GAO.

Left to right: Chinese firms won contracts for the newly built Nairobi-Thika Highway, funded by the African Development Bank and the Chinese government. Signage of Sinohydro Corporation Limited, one of the three contractors that build the Nairobi-Thika Highway.

Figure 27. Photos of Newly Built Road and Signage for Chinese Contractor That Built Road Section in Nairobi, Kenya.

Table 5. China's Grants Committed to Kenya, July 2009–June 2012

Types of projects	Year committed[a]	Grants committed
Renovation of Kasarani sports center	2009/2010	$2,927,970
	2010/2011	12,016,970
Subtotal		**$14,944,940**
Construction of hospital in Eastlands	2009/2010	7,092,419
	2010/2011	1,037,388
Subtotal		**$8,129,807**
Gambogi-Serem road	2009/2010	651,877
	2010/2011	606,305
	2011/2012	4,505,242
Subtotal		**$5,763,424**
Rehabilitation of Nairobi roads and street lighting project	2009/2010	3,259,384
Social economic recovery and reconstruction	2009/2010	2,933,445
Emergency food aid	2009/2010	3,146,609
Maize flour processing project	2009/2010	749,111
Total		**$38,926,720**

Source: GAO analysis of Government of Kenya data.

[a] Grant commitments are shown for Kenyan fiscal years (July-June).

		Number of contracts for which at least one firm competed	Computers, information technology, and security	Aerospace	Energy and power	Services	Oil and gas	Other	Healthcare	Telecommunications	Infrastructure	Transportation
United States (total)		28	5	4	4	4	3	3	2	1	1	1
Other firms competing for the same contracts as U.S. firms	China	4	1				1	1	1			
	France	8	1	2		2	2			1		
	United Kingdom	7	3	1	1		1	1				
	Netherlands	6	1			1	3				1	
	South Africa	5	2	1		1	1					
	Germany	5	1					1		1	1	1

(Column group heading: Sectors in which firms competed)

Source: GAO analysis of department of Commerce data.

Note: Data shown are for 28 Kenyan government contracts for which U.S. firms requested Commerce advocacy assistance in August 2002 through February 2012. Firms from France, the United Kingdom, the Netherlands, South Africa, and Germany competed with U.S. firms for the largest numbers of contracts.

Figure 28. Nationality of Firms Competing for 28 Kenyan Government Contracts for Goods and Services, 2002–2012.

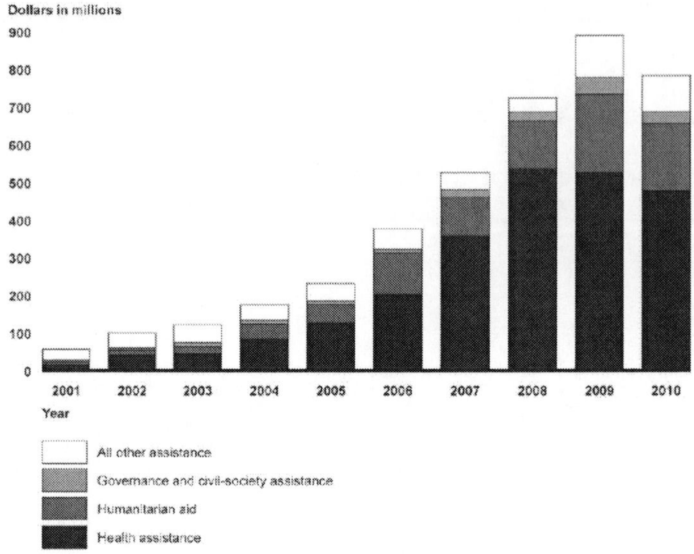

Source: GAO analysis of data from USAID.
Note: Import data are reported in nominal dollars.

Figure 29. U.S. Development Assistance Committed to Kenya, 2001-2010.

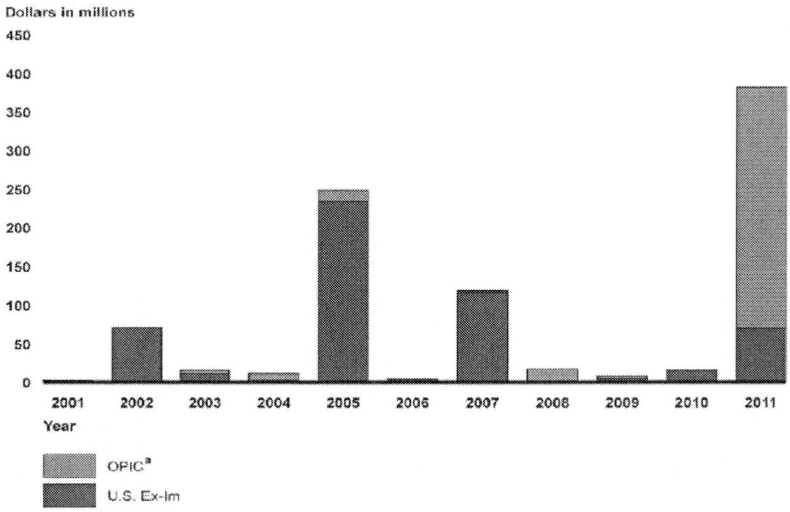

Source: GAO analysis of data from U.S. Ex-Im and OPIC.
Notes: Data are shown in nominal dollars by calendar year. In addition, these values are shown by calendar year, although U.S. Ex-Im and OPIC typically report data by fiscal year.
[a] OPIC may report data for some financing commitments, such as investment funds, only at the regional level. Data shown do not reflect OPIC investment funds for regional use in sub-Saharan Africa, possibly including Kenya. According to OPIC officials, because recipients of OPIC investment assistance may choose to invest in a set of countries, OPIC may initially lack information such as the countries where investments are made. In addition, according to OPIC officials, in countries with limited investment activity, business confidentiality agreements may prevent the disclosure of data that would reveal details of individual transactions.

Figure 30. U.S. Government Loans and Related Financing Committed for U.S.-made Products and U.S. Firms' Investments in Kenya, 2001-2011.

United States' and China's Grants and Loans to Kenya

U.S. Grants to Kenya Exceed China's in Recent Years

The U.S. government committed more grant assistance to Kenya than China did in 2009 and 2010. From 2001 to 2010, the United States committed almost $4 billion in aid to Kenya, including about $1.7 billion beginning in 2009, predominantly in the form of grants (see figure 29).[40]

The level of U.S. aid to Kenya generally increased from 2001 through 2010, largely because of an increase in funding in the health sector through initiatives such as the President's Emergency Plan for AIDS Relief and the President's Malaria Initiative as well as an increase in humanitarian assistance, primarily food aid. U.S. health programs in Kenya are among the largest U.S. government health portfolios globally, according to the Department of State. China does not publish data on its grants to countries, but Kenyan government documents indicate that China committed almost $39 million in grants from July 2009 through June 2012, (see table 5).[41]

Most of China's grants were for infrastructure such as roads, a hospital, and a sports center. China also committed assistance for emergency food aid in Kenya's fiscal year 2009/2010.

Table 6. China's Loans for Projects in Kenya, July 2009–June 2012

Types of projects	Year committed[a]	Loans committed
Nairobi eastern and northern bypass road project	2009/2010	$26,075,070
	2010/2011	54,567,474
	2011/2012	24,778,831
Subtotal		**$105,421,375**
Nairobi-Thika highway improvement project (one of three segments)	2010/2011	57,053,326
	2011/2012	45,052,420
Subtotal		**$102,105,746**
Drilling of Olkaria IV geothermal wells	2010/2011	52,797,063
	2011/2012	36,041,936
Subtotal		**$88,838,999**
Kenya power and distribution system modernization project	2009/2010	7,483,545
	2010/2011	18,189,158
	2011/2012	46,178,731
Subtotal		**$71,851,434**
Kenya e-government	2009/2010	16,900,197
	2010/2011	7,275,663
	2011/2012	1,312,152
Subtotal		**$25,488,012**
Enterprise messaging and collaboration system	2011/2012	43,700,848
Rehabilitation and upgrading of equipment in universities and technical training institutes	2011/2012	27,819,870
Procurement for equipment	2009/2010	17,767,813
Kenya rural telecommunication development program	2009/2010	54,992
Total		**$483,049,089**

Source: GAO analysis of Kenyan government data.

[a] Loan commitments are shown for each Kenyan fiscal year (July–June).

U.S. Government Committed Loans for U.S. Exports and Investments in Various Sectors, while China Committed Loans Mainly for Infrastructure Construction

The U.S. government committed about $896 million in loans and related financing, such as loan guarantees and insurance, between 2001 and 2011, primarily to support the export of U.S.-made aerospace products and parts and for U.S. investments in geothermal power and other sectors in Kenya (see figure 30).[42]

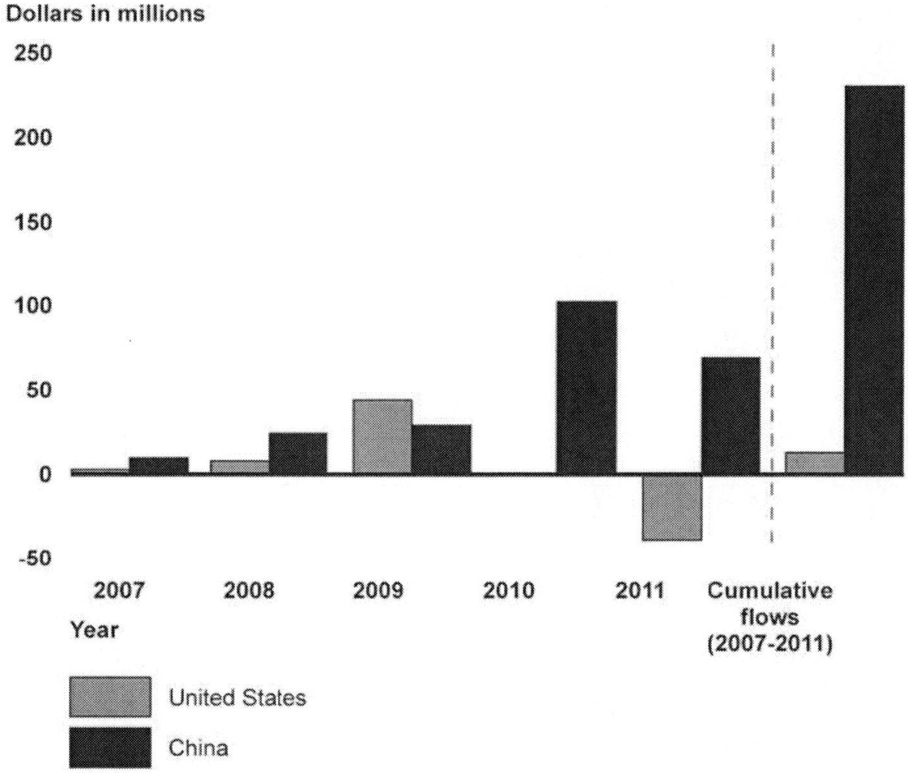

Source: GAO analysis of data from BEA, China's Ministry of Commerce, China's National Bureau of Statistics, and Haver Analytics.

Note: Data are shown in nominal values.

Figure 31. Reported Flows of Foreign Direct Investment from the United States and China to Kenya, 2007-2011.

China authorized about $480 million in loans from July 2009 to June 2012, primarily for infrastructure such as roads, geothermal wells, and power distribution (see table 6). China also committed funds for an e-government initiative, upgrading of equipment at universities and training institutes, rural telecommunication development, and purchase of other equipment. As a result of its recent funding, China has become one of the top donors to Kenya in the last 5 years, primarily providing highly concessional loans, according to a senior official at Kenya's Ministry of Finance.

U.S. and Chinese Investments in Kenya

From 2007 through 2011, cumulative U.S. foreign direct investment flows were $12 million, while China's reported foreign direct investment flows totaled about $230 million (see figure 31). According to experts, data on China's foreign direct investments are generally underreported,[43] and according to BEA, data on U.S. foreign direct investments may be underreported,[44] limiting precise comparisons of the United States' and China's investments.

From 2006 through 2011, according to BEA, the majority of U.S. foreign direct investment stock in Kenya was in finance and insurance and grew at an average annual rate of 20 percent. Growth in finance and insurance investments was primarily driven by investment in banks. Manufacturing, led by chemicals and transportation-equipment manufacturing, was the second largest sector but declined at an average annual rate of 3 percent during this period. Sectoral data for China's foreign direct investment stock in Kenya were not available.

End Notes

[1] This supplemental report was prepared in conjunction with GAO-13-199, in response to a request from Representative Jack Kingston and Senator James Inhofe—then Ranking Member, Senate Foreign Relations Subcommittee on East Asian and Pacific Affairs—to review U.S. and Chinese engagement in sub-Saharan Africa.

[2] We generally report data from 2001 through 2010 or 2011, but used data for shorter periods in some cases due to data availability. For comparability, and given challenges in determining appropriate deflators for some data, we used nominal rather than inflation-adjusted values for data on trade, grants and loans, and investments. All information sources reported nominal data in U.S. dollars. All of the data we report are for calendar years, except where noted otherwise. All percentages noted in this document are rounded to the nearest number.

[3] According to the U.S. Department of Energy, Angola has been a large oil producer for decades and is a member of the Organization of Petroleum Exporting Countries.

[4] In addition to importing crude oil, both countries have imported diamonds since 2003; in 2011, the United States imported $169 million in diamonds and China imported $99 million in diamonds. The United States also imported $510 million in noncrude oil (which includes refined oil) in 2011, whereas China imported none. As in 2011, crude and noncrude oil were the top imports for the United States and crude oil was the top import for China in 2001.

[5] To calculate estimates of total trade in services, including imports and exports of services, we used the higher value when ranges of estimates were provided for sectors of services such as business, professional, and technical services. Therefore, the averages we report represent the higher end of values in underlying tabulations from the Bureau of Economic Analysis (BEA) and other sources and our analysis of BEA's survey data.

[6] From 2006 through 2011, annual U.S. imports averaged $212 million for transportation services and $98 million for travel and passenger fares. From 2009 through 2011 annual U.S. exports averaged approximately $1 billion to $1.5 billion annually for business, professional, and technical services.

[7] Services provided by U.S. firms under World Bank–funded contracts represent a small fraction (less than 1 percent) of annual U.S. trade in service exports to Angola. However, World Bank contracts represent one of the few instances where data are available for examination of potential competition between U.S. and Chinese firms. According to the World Bank, the data include only contracts reviewed by World Bank staff prior to award, which constitute about 40 percent of total World Bank investment lending. The nationality of a firm reflects the country where it is registered, although the firm's parent may be headquartered in another country.

[8] According to USAID officials, the U.S. government committed almost all of its grants to organizations operating in Angola, not to the government of Angola.

[9] U.S. development assistance data for 2011 were not available at the time of this report's publication.

[10] A credit line represents funding available to a borrower, who incurs a loan by drawing funds from the credit line. Comprehensive information on disbursement of China's credit lines and loans to Angola is not available. However, data published by the Angolan Ministry of Finance indicate that as of June 2008, about 30 percent of China's credit lines of $2 billion in 2004 and $2.5 billion in 2007 had been disbursed. Additionally, according to a U.S. official, data from Angolan Ministry of Finance indicate that as of September 2010, Angola owed China about $3 billion.

[11] China's total lending and some additional information about the loans to Angola is corroborated by other sources.

[12] Brazilian and Portuguese firms are also constructing infrastructure in Angola, according to an official from an Angolan firm, an Angolan NGO, and a U.S. official.

[13] According to an Angolan NGO, Chinese-made materials must also constitute 70 percent of the materials used for these construction projects.

[14] Angola's Ministry of Finance published a list of projects that were being financed by the Export-Import Bank of China's credit lines as of the second quarter of 2008. This list includes information such as the number of Chinese and Angolan workers associated with projects but may not include all projects financed by the Export-Import Bank of China's credit lines and does not include information on the number of Chinese and Angolan workers for every project. However, in contrast to statements by an Angolan NGO and the former Chinese ambassador, the available information for the listed projects indicated that 36 percent of workers were Chinese and 64 percent were Angolans.

[15] According to a survey of Angolan workers employed at both Western (including Brazilian) and Chinese construction and oil firms, workers at Chinese firms tend to be younger, have less work experience, work longer hours per day, be less educated, and earn less compared with workers at Western firms. Worker turnover is also higher at Chinese firms.

[16] According to Angolan NGOs and an official from an Angolan firm, during the initial stages of Angola's reconstruction, Chinese contractors received little supervision. Inadequate supervision contributed to low quality of Chinese construction, according to Angolan NGOs and donor agency officials.

[17] According to the Organization for Economic Cooperation and Development (OECD), foreign direct investment is the ownership by a foreign person or business of 10 percent or more of the voting equity of a firm located in the host country. Foreign direct investment flows provide information for foreign direct investment activity within a given *period* of time, while foreign direct investment stock indicates the level of foreign direct investment at a given *point* in time. U.S. foreign direct investment flows during 2007 through 2011 were volatile, with a negative flow in 2007 and a spike in 2010.

[18] According to experts, Chinese firms set up subsidiaries, in places such as Hong Kong and the British Virgin Islands, that can be used to make investments in sub-Saharan Africa. Such investments are not captured by China's data on foreign direct investment and may be a significant source of underreporting. In addition, many small and medium-sized enterprises may not register their foreign direct investments, which therefore may not be reflected in China's data. According to an International Monetary Fund (IMF) working paper, China's foreign direct investment data also show inconsistencies between investment flows and changes in investment stock that are difficult to explain (see Montfort Mlachila and Misa Takebe, "FDI from BRICs to LICs: Emerging Growth Driver?" *IMF Working* Paper, WP/11/178 [2011], 11). Finally, China does not define foreign direct investment when reporting its data. However, the types of data that China reports for its foreign direct investments (e.g., equity investment data, reinvested earnings data) are similar to data reported for U.S. foreign direct investment. Moreover, China's reported foreign direct investment data represent official information published by the Chinese government and, despite their limitations, have been used in various reports, including those published by international organizations (e.g., the IMF), government agencies, academic experts, and other research institutions, to describe China's foreign direct investment activities in Africa.

[19] BEA noted that these data may not include investments in Sub-Saharan Africa by U.S. firms through subsidiaries in locations such as the Netherlands. According to BEA, U.S. foreign direct investment data are based on a 2009 benchmark survey that covers the value of all U.S. foreign direct investment, but these data may not reflect foreign direct investments by smaller firms.

[20] An oil block is a geographic area delineated by the licensing authorities for oil exploration and production. The licensing authority grants exploration and/or production rights to the oil company or joint venture within the boundaries of the block, usually on an exclusive basis.

[21] An operator is generally the oil company that engages in drilling, service, and other operations; an operator has primary responsibility for maintaining well operations and ensuring compliance with required rules and regulations. A nonoperator generally has an ownership stake, similar to a minority and noncontrolling interest.

[22] According to the U.S. Department of Energy, Chinese firms are gaining experience managing offshore oil operations in other sub-Saharan African countries and in Asia.

[23] From 2001 to 2011, tariffs on a combined total of nearly $906 million in U.S. imports (approximately 39 percent of total U.S. imports) from Ghana were eliminated under AGOA and GSP.

[24] From 2006 through 2011, annual U.S. imports averaged between $50 million to $200 million for business, professional, and technical services, $350 million for travel and passenger fares, $31 million for education services, and $3 million for transportation services. During the same period, annual U.S. exports averaged between $50 million and $200 million for business, professional, and technical services, $118 million for travel and passenger fares, $91 million for education services, and $22 million for transportation services. To calculate total trade, imports, and exports to Ghana, we used the higher value when ranges of estimates were provided for sectors of services such as business, professional, and technical services. The averages reported are the highest of possible values in underlying tabulations from BEA and other sources and our analysis of BEA's survey data.

[25] MCC does not favor companies by nationality in competing for contracts, and procurement guidelines specify open, fair, and competitive procedures consistent with delivering effective aid. In 2010, MCC revised its guidelines to exclude state-owned enterprises from competing for MCC-funded contracts to ensure level competition with firms that otherwise would not receive government support. At the time the regulation was put into effect, the success of Chinese state-owned enterprises in winning MCC contracts received particular attention. The regulation went into effect after a number of MCC contracts in Ghana were awarded, and MCC and Ghanaian government officials said it did not affect their work. Ghanaian firms won about $192 million in MCC contracts, 38 percent of the total amount of contracted work performed, more than half of which was for construction work. Portuguese firms won nearly $114 million in contracts, or approximately 22 percent of the total contracted work, all of which was for construction.

[26] Services provided by U.S. firms under World Bank–funded contracts represent a small fraction (less than 1 percent) of annual U.S. trade in service exports to Ghana. However, World Bank contracts represent one of the few instances where data are available for examination of potential competition between U.S. and Chinese firms. According to the World Bank, the data include only contracts reviewed by World Bank staff prior to award, which constitute about 40 percent of total World Bank investment lending. The nationality of a firm reflects the country where it is registered, although the firm's parent may be headquartered in another country.

[27] MCC compact funds are committed up front when compacts are signed with the partner country and obligated after a compact enters into force.

[28] According to information published by the government of Ghana, the terms of China's $3 billion loan to Ghana indicate that a Chinese state-owned oil company will purchase crude oil from Ghana's national petroleum company to support repayment of the loan. A Ghanaian ministry official said that oil also would be used as collateral on the loan. According to a World Bank report, cocoa exports make up part of the repayment of China's loan for the construction of the Bui Dam in Ghana.

[29] BEA has not released U.S. foreign direct investment flows to Ghana from 2007 to 2009 for reasons of confidentiality.

[30] According to experts, Chinese firms set up subsidiaries, in places such as Hong Kong and the British Virgin Islands, that can be used to make investments in sub-Saharan Africa. Such investments are not captured by China's data on foreign direct investment and may be a significant source of underreporting. In addition, many small and medium-sized enterprises may not register their foreign direct investments, which therefore may not be reflected in China's data. According to an International Monetary Fund (IMF) working paper, China's foreign direct investment data also show inconsistencies between investment flows and changes in investment stock that are difficult to explain (see Montfort Mlachila and Misa Takebe, "FDI from BRICs to LICs: Emerging Growth Driver?" *IMF Working* Paper, WP/11/178 [2011], 11). Finally, China does not define foreign direct investment when reporting its data. However, the types of data China reports for its foreign direct investments (e.g., equity investment data, reinvested earnings data) are similar to data reported for U.S. foreign direct investment. However, China's reported foreign direct investment data represent official information published by the Chinese government and, despite their limitations, have been used in various reports, including those published by international organizations (e.g., the IMF), government agencies, academic experts, and other research institutions, to describe China's foreign direct investment activities in Africa.

[31] BEA noted that these data may not include investments in Sub-Saharan Africa by U.S. firms through subsidiaries in locations such as the Netherlands. According to BEA, U.S. foreign direct investment data are based on a 2009 benchmark survey that covers the value of all U.S. foreign direct investment, but these data may not reflect foreign direct investments by smaller firms.

[32] In one oil block in Ghana, one U.S. firm was in an operator role and another U.S. firm was in a nonoperator role.

[33] U.S. exports of machinery and transport equipment declined from $469 million in 2001 to $110 million in 2011. This category includes exports of aircraft and related equipment, which dropped from $413 million in 2001 to $6 million in 2011.

[34] From 2001 to 2011, approximately $2.4 billion in U.S. imports from Kenya— approximately 75 percent of total U.S. imports from the country in that period— had tariffs eliminated under AGOA and GSP combined.

[35] Data on U.S imports of travel and passenger fares to Kenya are unavailable and are not included in the estimates for total U.S. trade in services and imports of services. However, given that Kenya received more U.S. travelers than Ghana in 2010, according to the Kenyan Ministry of Tourism and U.S. Department of Homeland Security, we estimate that U.S. imports from Kenya of travel and passenger fares in 2006 through 2010 likely equaled or exceeded this category of U.S. imports from Ghana, which averaged $350 million per year during that period. From 2006 to 2011, annual U.S. imports averaged approximately $50 million to $200 million per year from Kenya for business, professional, and technical services. During the same period, annual U.S. exports to Kenya averaged around $50 million to $200 million for business, professional, and technical services, $176 million for education services, and $109 million for travel and passenger fares. To calculate total trade, imports, and exports to Kenya, we used the higher value when ranges of estimates were provided for service sectors such as business, professional, and technical services. Our estimates are based on underlying tabulations from BEA and other sources and on our analysis of BEA's survey data.

[36]According to a March 2012 draft report by the Kenyan Association of Manufacturers, counterfeiting includes the violation of trademarks, industrial designs, geographical indications, copyright, and related rights. Kenyan Association of Manufacturers, *The Study to Determine Severity of the Counterfeit Problem In Kenya as It Affects Industries and Impact of Proliferation of Counterfeit Products from Other EAC Partner States And Far East* Countries *Into the Kenyan Market*, draft report (March 2012).

[37]The Kenyan Association of Manufacturers report also notes that manufacturers in Kenya lose more than $40 million annually because of counterfeit products. According to manufacturers interviewed for the report, about 30 percent of electrical components and electronics (such as motors and generators, switchgears, and batteries) sold in Kenya are counterfeits and are primarily from China.

[38]Although Kenya established an anticounterfeit agency in 2010, a representative for U.S. firms in Kenya and Kenyan officials noted that the agency has been underresourced and is unable to take necessary actions against counterfeits.

[39]Services provided by U.S. firms under World Bank–funded contracts represent a small fraction (less than 1 percent) of annual U.S. trade in service exports to Kenya. However, World Bank contracts represent one of the few instances where data are available for examination of potential competition between U.S. and Chinese firms. According to the World Bank, the data include only contracts reviewed by World Bank staff prior to award, which constitute about 40 percent of total World Bank investment lending. The nationality of a firm reflects the country where it is registered, although the firm's parent may be headquartered in another country.

[40]According to U.S. aid data reported to OECD, concessional loans comprised about 0.1 percent of U.S. aid to Kenya from 2001 through 2010. The United States has not committed any loans as aid to Kenya since 2008.

[41]The Kenyan government reported China's grant commitments for the Kenyan fiscal year (July-June).

[42] From 2001 to 2011, OPIC authorized about $363 million, more than half of which was authorized in 2011 for investment in a geothermal power plant. During this period, U.S. Ex-Im authorized about $533 million, with about 90 percent of those funds authorized for aerospace products and parts.

[43]According to experts, Chinese firms set up subsidiaries, in places such as Hong Kong and the British Virgin Islands, that can be used to make investments in sub-Saharan Africa. Such investments are not captured by China's data on foreign direct investment and may be a significant source of underreporting. In addition, many small and medium-sized enterprises may not register their foreign direct investments, which therefore may not be reflected in China's data. According to an International Monetary Fund (IMF) working paper, China's foreign direct investment data also show inconsistencies between investment flows and changes in investment stock that are difficult to explain (see Montfort Mlachila and Misa Takebe, "FDI from BRICs to LICs: Emerging Growth Driver?" *IMF Working* Paper, WP/11/178 [2011], 11). Finally, China does not define foreign direct investment when reporting its data. However, the types of data China reports for its foreign direct investments (e.g., equity investment data, reinvested earnings data) are similar to data reported for U.S. foreign direct investment. Moreover, China's reported foreign direct investment data represent official information published by the Chinese government and, despite their limitations, have been used in various reports, including those published by international organizations (e.g., the IMF), government agencies, academic experts, and other research institutions, to describe China's foreign direct investment activities in Africa.

[44] BEA noted that these data may not include investments in Sub-Saharan Africa by U.S. firms through subsidiaries in locations such as the Netherlands. According to BEA, U.S. foreign direct investment data are based on a 2009 benchmark survey that covers the value of all U.S. foreign direct investment, but these data may not reflect foreign direct investments by smaller firms.

In: Sub-Saharan Africa
Editor: Jacqueline S. Santiago
ISBN: 978-1-62618-433-6

Chapter 3

U.S. TRADE AND INVESTMENT RELATIONS WITH SUB-SAHARAN AFRICA AND THE AFRICAN GROWTH AND OPPORTUNITY ACT*

Vivian C. Jones and Brock R. Williams

SUMMARY

Following the end of the apartheid era in South Africa in the early 1990s, the United States sought to increase economic relations with sub-Saharan Africa (SSA). President Clinton instituted several measures that dealt with investment, debt relief, and trade. Congress passed legislation that required the President to develop a trade and development policy for Africa.

Between 1960 and 1973, Africa's economic growth was relatively strong, followed by a period of stagnation and decline for the subsequent two decades in many SSA countries. Current perspectives, however, indicate that many of the fastest-growing countries in the world are on the African continent, and the International Monetary Fund (IMF) projects that the SSA region will grow in terms of real GDP by 5.3% in 2012 and 2013.

In 2000, Congress approved new U.S. trade and investment legislation for SSA in the African Growth and Opportunity Act (AGOA; Title I, P.L. 106-200). According to U.S. trade statistics, U.S. trade with SSA has comprised 1% to 2% of U.S. total trade with the world. AGOA extends preferential treatment to U.S. imports from eligible countries that are pursuing market reform measures. Data show that U.S. imports under AGOA are mostly energy products, but imports of other products have grown significantly. AGOA mandated that U.S. officials meet regularly with their counterparts in SSA, and 11 of these meetings have been held to date. The 11th AGOA Forum was held from June 14 to June 15, 2012, in Washington, DC.

AGOA also directed the President to provide U.S. government technical assistance and trade capacity support to AGOA beneficiary countries. Government agencies that have roles

* This is an edited, reformatted and augmented version of the Congressional Research Service Publication, CRS Report for Congress RL31772, dated November 14, 2012.

in this effort include the U.S. Agency for International Development, the Assistant U.S. Trade Representative for Africa (established by statute under AGOA), the Overseas Private Investment Corporation, the Export-Import Bank, the U.S. and Foreign Commercial Service, and the Trade and Development Agency. In AGOA, Congress declared that free-trade agreements should be negotiated, where feasible, with interested SSA countries. Related to this provision, negotiations on a free-trade agreement with the Southern African Customs Union (SACU), which includes South Africa and four other countries, began in June 2003, but were suspended in April 2006.

The 112th Congress enacted legislation to extend through September 2015 an expiring provision in AGOA, which allows apparel made in lesser-developed countries to be made of yarns and fabrics from any country and still receive duty-free treatment, subject to a cap (P.L. 112-163). This amendment to AGOA also added South Sudan to the list of SSA countries eligible for AGOA benefits. Eligible countries may become AGOA beneficiaries subject to approval by the Administration.

Legislation is pending to further enhance U.S.-SSA trade relations. H.R. 4221 and S. 2215 seek to increase U.S. exports to Africa, in part, through strategies aimed at further developing relationships between the United States and African countries on a government-to-government level, fostering private sector U.S.-African ties, and targeting more U.S. export financing toward trade with Africa. An amended version of S. 2215 was ordered reported by the Senate Foreign Relations Committee in September 2012. H.R. 656, a separate initiative, would create at the State Department a Special Representative for United States-Africa Trade, Development, and Diaspora Affairs that would also promote U.S. trade and investment ties with SSA.

INTRODUCTION

A key element in U.S. policy toward Africa is the potential benefit from increased trade and commercial ties between the United States and Africa.[1] Interest in increasing bilateral commerce began after the end of the apartheid era in South Africa in the early 1990s. In 1993, Congress approved the end of anti-apartheid restrictions, and later that year then-Commerce Secretary Ron Brown led a business delegation to South Africa. In subsequent years, the Administration has also instituted several measures to help sub-Saharan African (SSA) countries and increase U.S. trade and investment in the region.

At the same time, Congress developed legislation that sought to improve U.S.-Africa trade relations. In the 1994 legislation to implement the Uruguay Round of multilateral trade agreements (P.L. 103-465), Congress directed the President to develop and implement a comprehensive trade and development policy for the countries of Africa, and subsequently introduced legislation to authorize a new trade and investment policy for sub-Saharan Africa. In 2000, Congress approved the African Growth and Opportunity Act (AGOA; Title I, P.L. 106-200). AGOA offers trade preferences and other economic benefits to SSA countries that meet certain criteria, including progress towards a market economy, respect for the rule of law, and human and worker rights. In AGOA, Congress also declared that free-trade agreements should also be negotiated, where feasible, with interested SSA countries.

AGOA has been amended several times since its initial enactment. In 2002, Congress amended AGOA to further increase market access for products from SSA.[2] In 2004, Congress passed legislation to extend AGOA benefits beyond the original deadline and to clarify certain provisions. This legislation also included directives to the President on investment initiatives and technical assistance. Congress passed legislation in 2006 to further amend AGOA and extend certain provisions concerning textile and apparel imports to 2012.[3] One of these provisions, the "third-country fabric provision," permits imports, subject to a cap, of apparel made in designated lesser-developed SSA countries of third-country yarns and fabrics (meaning that the yarns and fabrics may come from any country). This provision was recently extended through September 2015.[4]

This report examines African economic trends and U.S. trade and investment flows with SSA. It discusses the provisions of AGOA and the changes that have occurred since its enactment. It concludes with a brief discussion of issues for Congress.

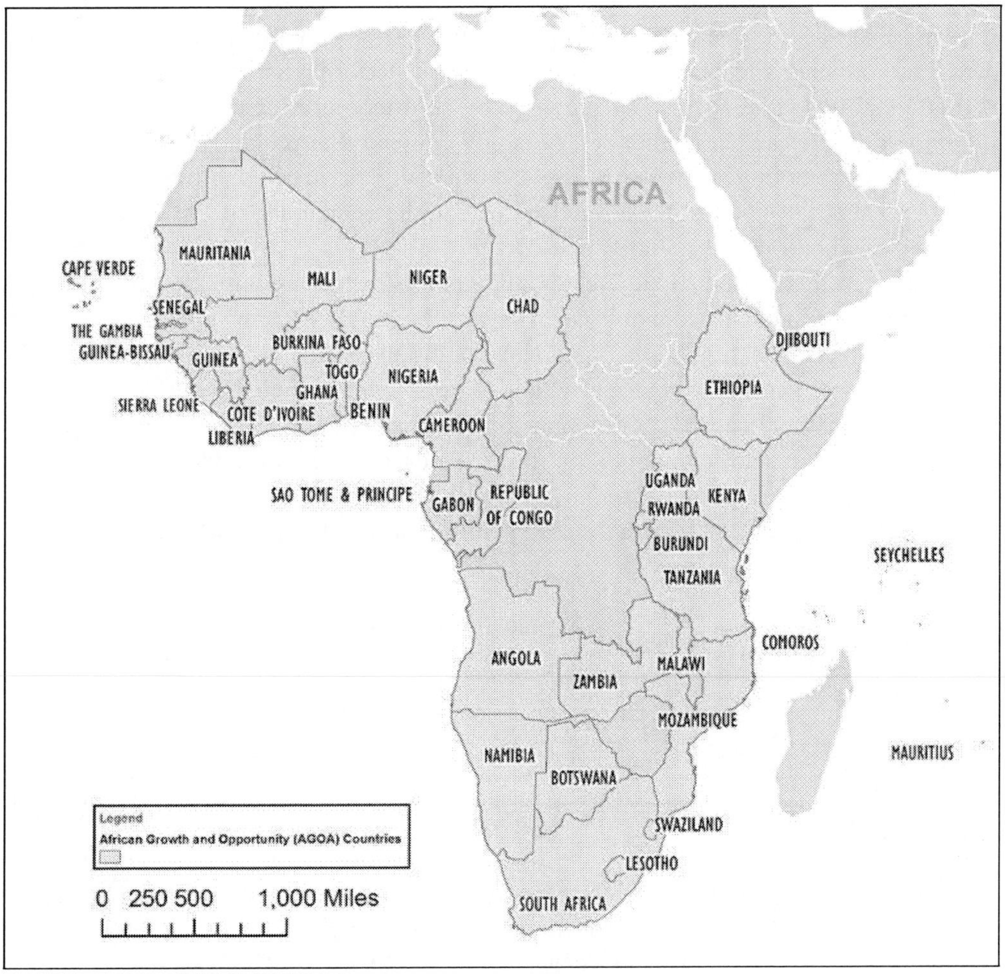

Source: Adapted by CRS (6/21/2012).

Figure 1. African Countries and AGOA Eligibility Status, 2012.

PERSPECTIVES ON THE SUB-SAHARAN AFRICAN ECONOMY

Historical Perspectives

The historical pattern of contemporary Africa's economic growth provides insights to help understand Africa's current economic situation and policy options. Between 1960 and 1973, which is the period immediately following independence in most African countries, economic growth was reasonably strong in many SSA countries. Most African countries experienced a sharp decline in their growth trends at some point between 1973 and 1980, followed by persistent stagnation until the early 1990s. Average SSA per-capita GDP (PPP data) reached its minimum point in the mid-1990s, and still had not recovered to 1970s levels in 2005.[5] Another factor that characterized growth in many African countries—and in many cases continues to affect economic development patterns—is high economic growth volatility, a common feature in SSA countries' historical trends. A 2007 World Bank study found that SSA has experienced more growth volatility than other regions, resulting in dampened investments and obscuring periods of good performance for some countries. The report found that this volatility has been caused by conflict, poor governance, and fluctuating world commodity prices. The authors of the study contend that reducing volatility is at least as important as promoting growth.[6] In the 1990s, many African countries made a modest recovery until about 1994, but the growth rates for the remainder of the period tended to remain far below the first post-colonial phase.[7]

The causes of this period of slow economic growth in the region have been a source of debate among development economists. Analysts have cited poor governance, political instability, geographic features, and historical conditions such as colonialism as different reasons for Africa's economic malaise. Other factors cited included slow accumulation of both human and physical capital, dependence on single commodity exports, low productivity growth and pressures from high population growth rates, and high dependence on foreign aid.

Table 1. Real GDP Growth in sub-Saharan Africa (percent change)

Country Group	2004-2008 (average)	2009	2010	2011	2012 (projected)	2013 (projected)
Oil Exporters	8.6	5.1	6.6	6.3	6.7	6.0
Middle Income	5.0	-0.6	3.8	4.5	3.4	3.8
Low Income	7.3	5.4	6.4	5.5	5.9	6.1
Fragile	2.5	3.1	4.2	2.3	6.6	6.5
Total SSA	6.5	2.8	5.3	5.2	5.3	5.3
World	4.6	-0.6	5.1	3.8	3.3	3.6

Source: International Monetary Fund, Regional Economic Outlook, sub-Saharan Africa, October 2012.

Notes: IMF Country Groupings: **Oil Exporting Countries:** Angola, Cameroon, Chad, Equatorial Guinea, Gabon, Nigeria, Republic of Congo. **Middle Income Countries:** Botswana, Cape Verde, Ghana, Lesotho, Mauritius, Namibia, Senegal, Seychelles, South Africa, Swaziland, Zambia. **Non-Fragile Low Income Countries:** Benin, Burkina Faso, Ethiopia, the Gambia, Kenya, Madagascar, Mali, Mozambique, Niger, Rwanda, Sierra Leone, Tanzania, Uganda. **Fragile Countries:** Burundi, Central African Republic, Comoros, Democratic Republic of the Congo, Cote d'Ivoire, Eritrea, Guinea, Guinea-Bissau, Liberia, Sao Tome and Principe, Togo, Zimbabwe.

Following this period of stagnation, the past decade has seen considerable improvements in governance and economic growth in many parts of Africa, although many countries continue to experience political instability, poor economic performance, and lack of progress in improving social welfare indicators. Poverty and inequitable income distribution also remain common in many countries. Despite these challenges, many countries are experiencing rapid economic growth.

Current Perspectives

The International Monetary Fund (IMF) projects that the SSA region will grow in terms of real GDP by 5.3% in 2012 and 2013 (see **Table 1**).[8] These projections, however, mask significant disparities among the 44 countries the IMF considers in its regional analysis. For example, in its *Regional Economic Outlook*, released in October 2012, the IMF projected that oil-exporting countries in SSA would experience average real GDP growth of 6.7% in 2012, and 6.0% in 2013. Relatively stable, low-income, non-energy-producing countries (such as Ethiopia, Burkina Faso, and Kenya) are expected to grow on average by 5.9% in 2012 and 6.1% in 2013, while middle income countries (such as South Africa) are projected to grow by 3.4% in 2012 and 3.8% in 2013. The IMF also projects that more than half of the 12 SSA countries identified as “fragile” countries, due to prolonged institutional weakness or conflict (such as the Democratic Republic of Congo, Guinea, and Liberia), are expected to see stronger or stable growth in 2012 (6.6%) and 2013 (5.8%).[9] This improved economic performance may reflect many factors, including better governance, increased trade flows, strong commodity prices, rising aid flows, and debt forgiveness.[10] Rising incomes and expanding urban middle classes in some countries, economic diversification, increased access to communications technologies, and multiple other factors could also contribute to such trends.

U.S. foreign direct investment (FDI) flows to the region in 2011 amounted to about $3.1 billion, with South Africa ($722 million), Angola ($707 million), Ghana ($250 million), and Liberia ($113 million) as the major destinations of those investment flows.[11] According to United Nations (UN) data, total world FDI to SSA amounted to about $35 billion in 2011.[12] Leading SSA country destinations for worldwide direct investment in 2011 included Nigeria ($8.9 billion), South Africa ($5.8 billion), and Ghana ($3.2 billion).

Investment and Growth Challenges

Despite improved economic performance in many African countries in recent years, the economic challenges facing Africa remain significant. African countries are vulnerable to volatile weather conditions, commodity price fluctuations, and poor road and other infrastructure conditions, as well as ongoing political instability in parts of the continent. Many countries have also faced difficulties in reducing high rates of poverty, improving social welfare indicators, combating corruption, and diversifying their economies. In addition, limited integration of regional trade regimes and transport systems often inhibits intra-regional trade, as well as foreign investment. Many countries’ domestic market demand is not large enough to draw the attention of large foreign and U.S. firms, which may prefer to deal with larger regional markets.[13]

Much of sub-Saharan Africa's trade with the world is largely still based on primary product exports, such as oil and other mineral fuels (about 54% of its exports to the world by value in 2010); precious stones and metals (10%); and ores, slag, and ash (5%).[14] As a result, many sub- Saharan African countries continue to be vulnerable—as do many developing countries and regions—to the rise and fall of international commodity prices.

HIV/AIDS and Other Health Challenges

The HIV/AIDS pandemic is also straining some African economies and threatens to curtail future economic growth. SSA is the region most affected by HIV/AIDS. As of 2010, an estimated 22.9 million people were living with HIV-AIDS in SSA, accounting for 68% of all people living with HIV worldwide. Nine countries with the world's highest HIV prevalence rates worldwide are located in Southern Africa, where an estimated 11.1 million people were living with HIV in 2010. Swaziland has the world's highest prevalence rate (25.9%), and South Africa has the world's largest HIV-positive population (5.6 million).[15] In 2010, about 1.9 million people in SSA contracted HIV and approximately 1.2 million people in the region died from AIDS.[16] The pandemic not only diverts resources from investments in productive resources to social services to care for the sick and dying, but it also erodes human capital by striking some of the most productive members of society: skilled workers, teachers, and professionals.[17]

Africa also suffers disproportionately high disease burdens attributable to such illnesses as malaria, tuberculosis and other respiratory diseases, and water-born diarrheal infections, and many countries face severe health care delivery system constraints.[18]

Table 2. SSA Countries with Highest Estimated Adult (15-49) HIV Prevalence Rate (Percentage), 2009

Country	Estimate (%)
Swaziland	25.9
Botswana	24.8
Lesotho	23.6
South Africa	17.8
Zimbabwe	14.3
Zambia	13.5
Namibia	13.1
Mozambique	11.5
Malawi	11.0
Kenya	6.3
SSA Average	5.9

Source: UNAIDS Report on the Global AIDS Epidemic, 2010.

Table 3. SSA Government Debt (as percent of GDP)

Country Grouping	2004 – 2008 (average)	2009	2010	2011
Oil Exporters	29.4	21.8	20.5	20.5
Middle Income	32.6	31.5	34.9	37.8
Low Income	50.6	34.8	37.2	37.3
Fragile	112.5	88.8	58.3	65.1
Total SSA	38.7	32.3	31.5	33.1

Source: International Monetary Fund, Regional Economic Outlook, sub-Saharan Africa, October 2012.

Notes: IMF Country Groupings: **Oil Exporting Countries:** Angola, Cameroon, Chad, Equatorial Guinea, Gabon, Nigeria, Republic of Congo. **Middle Income Countries:** Botswana, Cape Verde, Ghana, Lesotho, Mauritius, Namibia, Senegal, Seychelles, South Africa, Swaziland, Zambia. **Non-Fragile Low Income Countries:** Benin, Burkina Faso, Ethiopia, the Gambia, Kenya, Madagascar, Mali, Mozambique, Niger, Rwanda, Sierra Leone, Tanzania, Uganda. **Fragile Countries:** Burundi, Central African Republic, Comoros, Democratic Republic of the Congo, Cote d'Ivoire, Eritrea, Guinea, Guinea-Bissau, Liberia, Sao Tome and Principe, Togo, Zimbabwe.

Foreign Debt Burden

The debt burden carried by SSA countries has been identified as a drag on the economies of the region. In 2010, the states of SSA owed foreign creditors an estimated total of $143 billion.[19] SSA's total government debt as a percentage of GDP averaged 33.1% in 2011 (see **Table 3**).[20] Declines in some SSA countries' external debt are due to ongoing comprehensive debt relief initiatives begun in 1996, including the Heavily Indebted Poor Countries Initiative (HIPC), the Multilateral Debt Relief Initiative (MDRI), and the Paris Club agreement with Nigeria.[21]

U.S.-AFRICA TRADE AND INVESTMENT TRENDS

U.S. Trade with sub-Saharan Africa

U.S. imports from SSA countries fell in 2008 and 2009, possibly due to the spillover effects of the global financial crisis and falling demand.[22] According to the IMF, however, the SSA region is currently showing solid macroeconomic performance, and economic activity had expanded strongly in 2010 through 2012 to date.[23] This is illustrated, in part, by an expansion in total U.S. trade (imports plus exports) with SSA countries in 2010 and 2011, which grew by 29.5% and 17% respectively, after a decrease in total trade by 40% in the 2008-2009 time frame (see **Table 4**), as well as a continuing large increase in trade with China.

The United States conducts a small share of its total trade with SSA countries. In 2011, the United States imported $74 billion from SSA countries, or about 3.4% of total U.S. global imports of $2.2 trillion. The United States exported $20.3 billion to the region in 2011, or 1.5% of total U.S. exports of $1.3 trillion. Nevertheless, total trade (exports plus imports) between the United States and sub-Saharan Africa grew 51% between 2009 and 2011, up from $62.4 billion in 2009 to $94.3 billion in 2011 (see **Table 4**). Certain external factors, including increases in oil and other prices for natural resources, may also account, in part, for the dramatic growth (by value) in U.S.- SSA trade.

Comparing Chinese and U.S. Trade with Africa[24]

The value of total trade between China and Africa stood at $8.9 billion in the year 2000. In 2009, Chinese-African trade, totaling $70.4 billion, surpassed that of U.S.-Africa trade ($62 billion), and reached $127.3 billion in 2011, an increase of 1,423% over the 2000 level.[25] Africa's share of global Chinese trade also grew over the past decade, from 1.9% of Chinese global trade in 2000 to 3.5% of China's global trade in 2011. China is also Africa's largest single source of imports, while the United States is its largest export destination. In 2011, about 62% of African exports to China consisted of crude oil (over $24.77 billion of which came from Angola, the source of over 9% of China's oil imports in 2011). Another 34% was made up of raw materials, mostly metal commodities and wood. Oil also dominates Africa's exports to the United States; crude oil made up about 75% of U.S. imports from Africa in 2011. Both China and the United States export a highly diverse, variable array of products to Africa, notably equipment, machinery, vehicles, and other technology. U.S.-African trade has also grown over the past decade, but not as rapidly as Sino-African trade.[26]

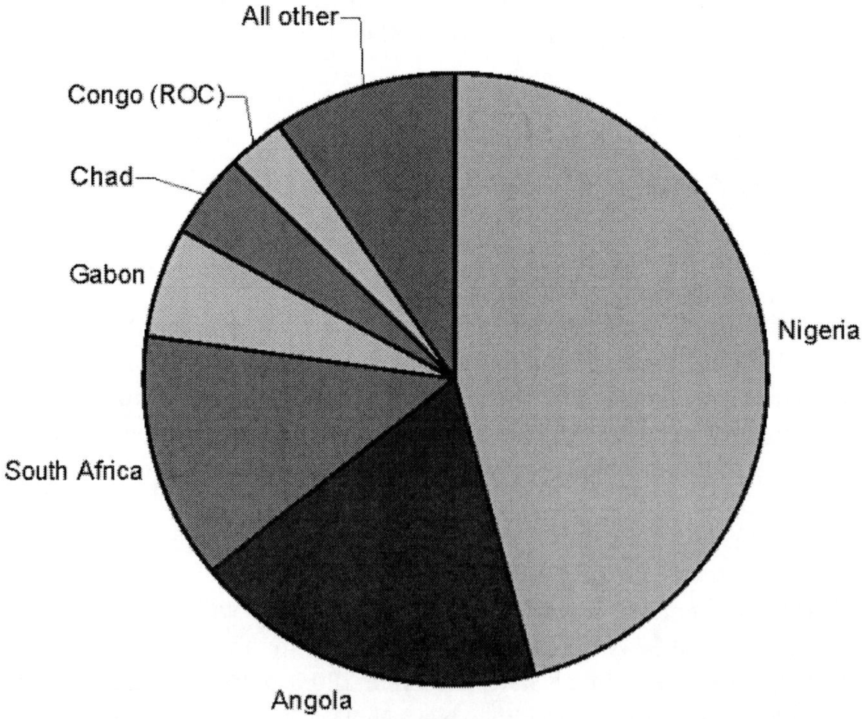

Source: U.S. International Trade Commission Trade Dataweb, http://www.usitc.gov.

Figure 2. U.S. Imports from sub-Saharan Africa by Country, 2011.

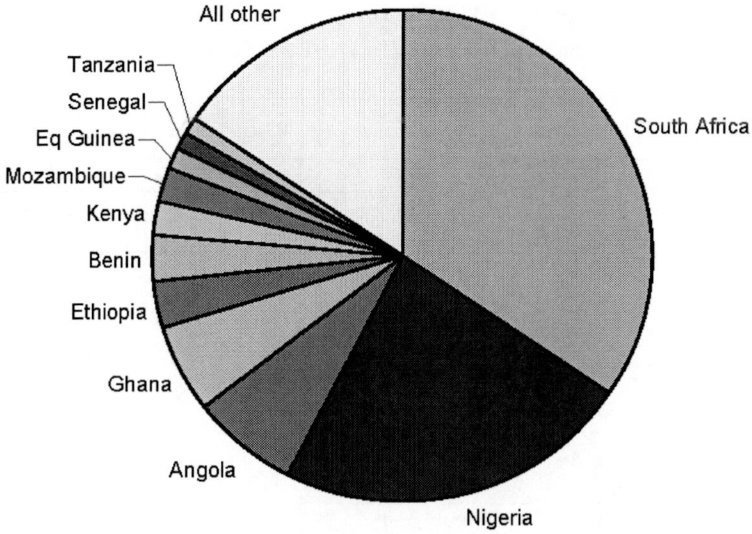

Source: U.S. International Trade Commission Trade Dataweb, http://dataweb.usitc.gov.

Figure 3. U.S. Exports to sub-Saharan Africa by Country, 2011.

A significant portion of U.S. trade with sub-Saharan Africa is with a small number of countries. About 79% of U.S. imports from the region were from three SSA countries in 2011: Nigeria (47%), Angola (19%), and South Africa (13%). Exports were similarly concentrated, with three countries receiving 68%: South Africa (34%), Nigeria (22%), and Angola (12%). All other countries accounted for less than 6% each of U.S. imports from the region (see **Figure 3**).

Natural resources continue to dominate U.S. imports from SSA. The leading U.S. imports from SSA in 2011 were mineral fuels and mineral oils ($58.97 billion, see **Table 5**). Nigeria was the greatest source of U.S. oil imports and was the fifth-largest global supplier (by value) of U.S. oil imports (of a total of $454 billion worldwide).[27] In 2011, Nigeria supplied 56% of U.S. petroleum imports from SSA, which accounted for about 7.4% of global U.S. oil imports. Angola supplied another 23% of U.S. petroleum from the region, Chad supplied 5%, and Congo (ROC) supplied 4%.[28]

Table 4. U.S. Goods Trade with SSA Countries (in $ billions)

Trade Flow	2008	2009	2010	2011	Percentage Change 2010 and 2011 (%)
Total U.S. Exports	18.0	14.6	16.4	20.3	24%
Total U.S. Imports	86.1	47.9	64.4	74.0	15%
Total Trade (Imports + Exports)	104.1	62.4	80.8	94.3	17%
Imports under AGOA (includes GSP)	*65.1*	*33.5*	*43.9*	*53.8*	*23%*

Source: U.S. International Trade Commission Trade Dataweb, http://dataweb.usitc.gov.

Notes: Domestic Exports, FAS value; Imports for Consumption, Customs Value. Total Imports under AGOA is a subset of total U.S. imports from SSA countries.

Table 5. Top Ten U.S. Imports from sub-Saharan Africa, 2010 and 2011 (in $ billions)

HTS Number	2010	2011	Percent Change 2010-2011
27-Mineral fuels and oil	51.38	58.97	14.80%
71-Pearls, Precious Stones, Precious Metals, etc., Coin	3.95	4.33	9.80%
87-Vehicles, Except Railway Or Tramway, And Parts	1.61	2.16	34.10%
18-Cocoa and cocoa preparations	1.04	1.27	22.60%
29-Organic chemicals	1.22	1.16	-4.70%
72-Iron and steel	0.76	0.89	16.70%
26-Ores, slag, and ash	0.67	0.79	17.70%
62-Articles of apparel and clothing accessories, not knitted or crocheted	0.40	0.46	14.70%
84-Nuclear Reactors, Boilers, Machinery and Parts	0.36	0.46	26.30%
61-Articles of apparel and clothing accessories, knitted or crocheted	0.39	0.44	14.30%
Subtotal	61.77	70.94	14.80%
All Other	2.58	3.08	19.40%
Total	64.35	74.02	15.00%

Source: U.S. International Trade Commission Trade Dataweb, http://www.usitc.gov.
Note: U.S. Imports for Consumption.

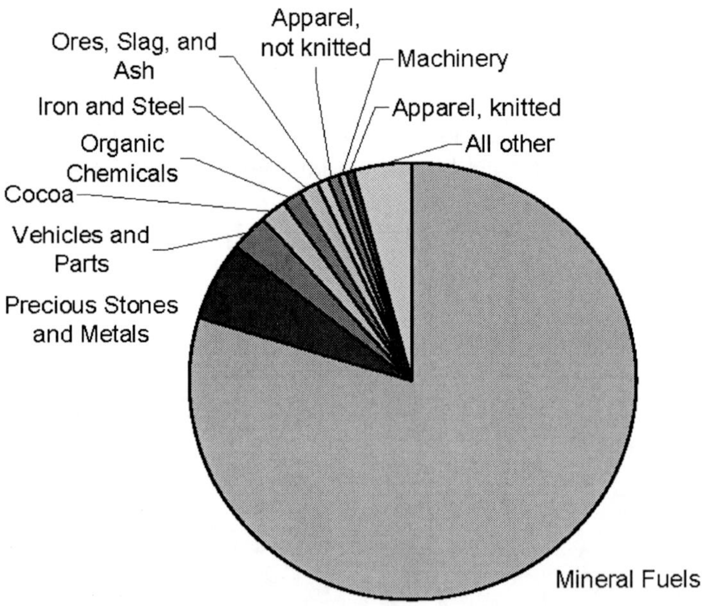

Source: U.S. International Trade Commission Trade Dataweb, http://www.usitc.gov.

Figure 4. U.S. Imports from sub-Saharan Africa by Product Category, 2011.

Precious stones and metals were another major U.S. import from SSA in 2011.[29] South Africa led this category (imports included platinum, diamonds, other semi-precious stones, and coins) with about $4.2 billion in U.S. imports; followed by Botswana, Angola, and Namibia—all diamond producers—at about $275 million, $169 million, and $100 million, respectively (see **Table 5** and **Figure 4**).[30]

Although natural resources are the major category of U.S. imports from SSA countries, there have also been marked increases in imports of other products, including textiles and apparel, vehicle parts and transportation equipment, and agricultural products. A 2009 report by the U.S. International Trade Commission (USITC) indicated that certain SSA countries have the potential to competitively produce certain textile and apparel inputs. Since cotton is the primary fiber currently used in the production of yarn and fabric in SSA countries, and is grown in large quantities in the region, the USITC found that cotton products seem to have the most competitive potential. The report also stated that certain niche apparel products manufactured in small quantities could also be successful in the U.S. market, including organic cotton products; yarn and knit fabric of modal and other specialty manmade fibers; hand-loomed fabric of cotton and silk for home furnishings and apparel; African print fabrics; and zippers and ornamental trim products.[31]

U.S. exports to sub-Saharan Africa were more diverse. Machinery and parts was the leading export sector in 2011 (22% of U.S. exports to the region), followed by transportation equipment (17%), cereals (8%), mineral fuels (8%), aircraft and parts (7%), and electrical machinery (6%) (see **Figure 5**).

U.S. Investment in sub-Saharan Africa

U.S. foreign direct investment (FDI) in Africa is characterized by the following:

Table 6. Top Ten U.S. Exports to sub-Saharan Africa (in $ billions)

HTS Number	2010	2011	Percent Change
84-Nuclear Reactors, Boilers, Machinery and Parts	3.43	3.93	14.30%
87-Vehicles, Except Railway Or Tramway, And Parts	2.40	3.45	43.60%
27-Mineral Fuels and Oil	1.41	1.84	30.30%
10-Cereals	1.36	1.79	31.60%
88-Aircraft, Spacecraft, and Parts	1.11	1.51	35.70%
85-Electric Machinery; Sound and TV Equipment and Parts	0.81	0.75	-7.70%
98-Special Classification Provisions	0.60	0.72	18.50%
71-Pearls, Precious Stones, Precious Metals, etc., Coin	0.42	0.62	44.90%
90-Optical, Photography, Medical or Surgical Instruments	0.60	0.58	-3.50%
39-Plastics and Articles Thereof	0.47	0.56	20.40%
Subtotal	12.63	15.73	24.60%
All Other	3.81	4.57	19.80%
Total	16.44	20.30	23.50%

Source: U.S. International Trade Commission Trade Dataweb, http://www.usitc.gov

- SSA countries are a relatively minor destination of U.S. FDI. Africa, as a whole, hosts about 1% of total U.S. FDI (see **Figure 6**).[32]
- U.S. FDI in Africa is largely concentrated in mining and extractive industries, which together comprise some $33 billion of the $57 billion total stock of U.S. FDI in Africa (see **Figure 7**).[33]
- U.S. FDI in African manufacturing industries has mostly been directed toward South Africa, which has received about 67% of total U.S. FDI in Africa's manufacturing sector.[34]

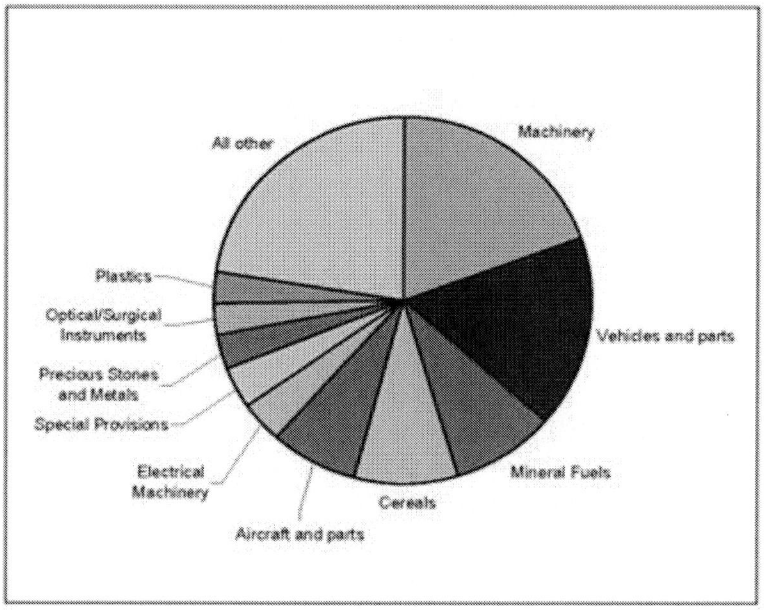

Source: U.S. International Trade Commission Trade Dataweb, http://www.usitc.gov.

Figure 5. U.S. Exports to sub-Saharan Africa by Product Category, 2011.

Table 7. Major Destinations of U.S. Foreign Direct Investment (FDI) in SSA, 2011 (in $ millions)

Leading Countries	Flow	Stock
Mauritius	45	7,330
South Africa	722	6,546
Angola	707	5,696
Nigeria	-35	4,994
Ghana	250	2,334
Equatorial Guinea	37	2,076
Liberia	113	964
Kenya	-40	292
Zambia	-1	138

Source: Analysis by CRS based on data from the Bureau of Economic Analysis (BEA).

In 2011, the latest year for which annual investment data are available, outflows of U.S. FDI abroad to SSA ($3.4 billion) were only about one-third greater than inflows of FDI into the United States from SSA ($2.1 billion). The three countries in SSA with the largest stock of U.S. FDI in 2011 were Mauritius, South Africa, and Angola (stock column, **Table 7**). This stock of FDI represents an accumulation over time. In terms of one-year flows for 2011, the top recipients were South Africa, Angola, and Ghana (see flow column).

(share of total, 2011)

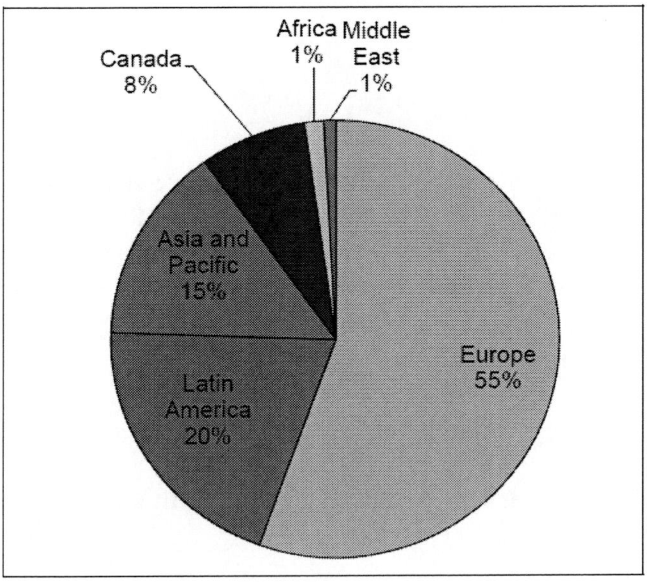

Source: Analysis by CRS based on data from the Bureau of Economic Analysis (BEA).

Figure 6. Stock of U.S. FDI Abroad, by Destination.

(in $ millions)

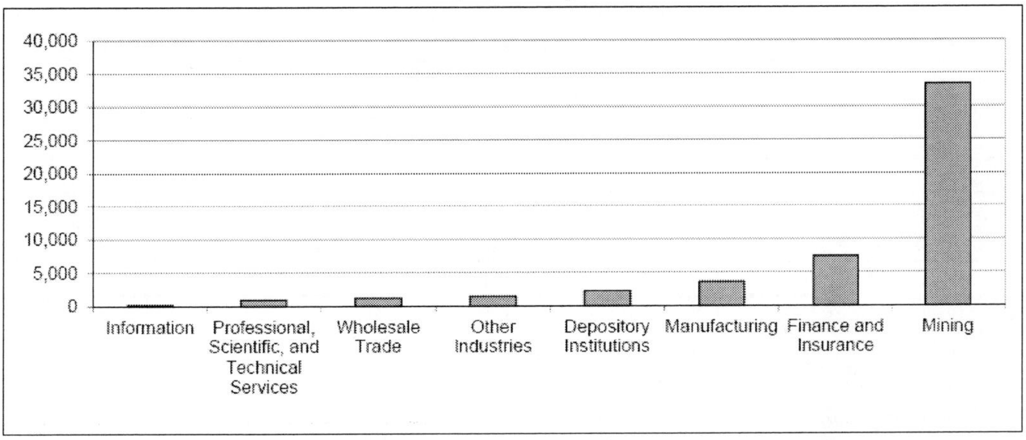

Source: Analysis by CRS based on data from the Bureau of Economic Analysis (BEA).
Note: Excludes U.S. stock of direct investment in holding companies.

Figure 7. Stock of U.S. FDI in Africa by Industry Sector, 2011.

AGOA Legislation and Key Provisions

The original AGOA legislation, the African Growth and Opportunity Act (AGOA; Title I, Trade and Development Act of 2000; P.L. 106-200), was approved by Congress in 2000, to assist the economies of sub-Saharan Africa and to improve economic relations between the United States and the region. The following section of this report examines the major provisions of AGOA, developments since enactment, and AGOA related legislation in the 112th Congress.

Beneficiary Countries

Subtitle A of AGOA authorized the President to designate sub-Saharan African countries as beneficiary countries eligible to receive duty-free treatment for certain articles that are the growth, product, or manufacture of that country. It directed that in designating a beneficiary country, the President must determine that the country (1) has established, or is making continual progress toward establishing a market-based economy and is taking other designated actions; (2) does not engage in activities that undermine U.S. national security and foreign policy interests; and (3) does not engage in gross violations of internationally recognized human rights or provide support for international terrorism.

Table 8. Beneficiary Countries under the African Growth and Opportunity Act (as of October 2012)

Republic of Angola	Republic of Ghana **	Democratic Republic of Sao Tome and Principe
Republic of Benin **	Republic of Guinea	Republic of Senegal **
Republic of Botswana **	Republic of Guinea-Bissau	Republic of Seychelles
Burkina Faso **	Republic of Kenya **	Republic of Sierra Leone **
Republic of Burundi	Kingdom of Lesotho **	Republic of South Africa
Republic of Cameroon **	Republic of Liberia **	Kingdom of Swaziland **
Republic of Cape Verde **	Republic of Malawi **	United Republic of Tanzania **
Republic of Chad **	Republic of Mali **	Republic of Togo
Union of the Comoros	Islamic Republic of Mauritania	Republic of Uganda **
Republic of Congo	Republic of Mauritius **	Republic of Zambia **
Republic of Cote d'Ivoire	Republic of Mozambique **	
Republic of Djibouti	Republic of Namibia**	
Ethiopia **	Republic of Niger **	
Gabonese Republic	Federal Republic of Nigeria **	
Republic of the Gambia **	Republic of Rwanda **	

Source: Harmonized Tariff Schedule of the United States, Supplement 1, Revision 1, October 31, 2012.

Notes: Eligible SSA countries, not currently AGOA-beneficiaries: Democratic Republic of Congo, Eritrea, Equatorial Guinea, Madagascar, Somalia, South Sudan, Sudan, and Zimbabwe.

** Beneficiary country is eligible for the lesser-developed country special rule for apparel (third-country fabric provision).

AGOA requires that the President monitor and report annually on the progress of each country in meeting the terms for AGOA eligibility. Under this requirement, Presidents have made, at the end of each year, annual designations of the countries eligible for AGOA benefits for the following year. The last presidential proclamation made with respect to AGOA was Proclamation 8741 of October 25, 2011.[35] This proclamation, among other things, reinstated the AGOA eligibility of Cote d'Ivoire, Guinea, and Niger, and also designated them each "lesser developed beneficiary sub-Saharan African countries." Thus, 40 SSA countries are now AGOA beneficiaries.

Benefits

Subtitle B of AGOA describes the trade-related benefits that are available to AGOA-eligible countries. Among these benefits is preferential duty-free treatment for certain articles under the U.S. Generalized System of Preferences (GSP). The GSP program is a unilateral trade preference regime that allows certain products from designated developing countries to enter the United States duty-free. In the AGOA Acceleration Act of 2004 (P.L. 108-274), GSP benefits were extended to AGOA countries until September 30, 2015.[36] Therefore, AGOA countries will continue to receive GSP benefits until that date, regardless of any expiration of the GSP program. AGOA beneficiaries are exempt from certain caps on allowable duty-free imports under the GSP program ("competitive need limitations").[37]

"Import-Sensitive" Articles Ineligible for GSP Preferences

1. Textile and apparel articles which were not eligible articles for purposes of this subchapter on January 1, 1994, as this subchapter was in effect on such date.
2. Watches, except those watches entered after June 30, 1989, that the President specifically determines, after public notice and comment, will not cause material injury to watch or watch band, strap, or bracelet manufacturing and assembly operations in the United States or the United States insular possessions.
3. Import-sensitive electronic articles.
4. Footwear, handbags, luggage, flat goods, work gloves, and leather wearing apparel which were not eligible articles for purposes of this subchapter on January 1, 1995, as this subchapter was in effect on such date.
5. Import-sensitive semi-manufactured and manufactured glass products.
6. Any other articles which the President determines to be import-sensitive in the context of the Generalized System of Preferences.

Source: 19 U.S.C. 2463(b).

AGOA-eligible countries may also receive duty-free treatment for certain "import sensitive" categories of products (see box above) that are identified as ineligible for duty-free treatment under GSP, provided that the President determines, after consultation with the International Trade Commission, that the product is not import-sensitive in the context of imports from AGOA beneficiaries.[38] However, the President may not grant duty-free treatment for textile or apparel products; rather, the AGOA statute provides specific benefits for certain limited categories of textiles and apparel.

Textile and Apparel Provisions

AGOA, as amended, allows duty-free and quota-free treatment for eligible textile and apparel articles in qualifying SSA countries through 2015. Qualifying articles include

- Apparel assembled in one or more AGOA beneficiary countries from U.S. yarn and fabric;
- Apparel made of SSA (regional) yarns and fabrics, subject to a cap until 2015;
- Apparel made in a designated lesser-developed country (LDC) of third-country yarns and fabrics, subject to a cap until 2015 ("Third-Country Fabric Provision Extended");
- Apparel made of yarns and fabrics not produced in commercial quantities in the United States (determination must be made that the yarn or fabric cannot be supplied by the U.S. industry in a timely manner, and to extend preferential treatment to the eligible fabric);
- Certain cashmere and merino wool sweaters;
- Eligible handloomed, handmade, or folklore articles and ethnic printed fabrics (certain countries only);
- Textiles and textile articles produced entirely in an LDC SSA beneficiary country; and
- Certain handloomed, handmade, ethnic printed fabrics, or folklore articles (certain countries only).[39]

To receive the duty-free and quota-free treatment for textile and apparel products as described above, beneficiary countries must first adopt an efficient visa ("tracking") system to prevent unlawful transshipment. They also must work with the U.S. Customs Service to report exports and prevent illegal trade. AGOA also provides that the Secretary of Commerce must monitor U.S. imports under AGOA for surges in textile and apparel imports, with the possible withdrawal of duty-free treatment if imports surge beyond a certain level.[40]

AGOA Non-Textile Rules of Origin

Non-textile products from AGOA countries must also meet certain rules of origin (ROO) requirements in order to qualify for duty-free treatment. First, duty-free entry is only allowed if the article is imported directly from the beneficiary country into the United States.

Second, at least 35% of the appraised value of the product must be the "growth, product or manufacture" of a beneficiary developing country, as defined by the sum of (1) the cost or value of materials produced in the beneficiary developing country (or any two or more beneficiary countries that are members of the same association or countries and are treated as one country for purposes of the U.S. law) plus (2) the direct costs of processing in the country.[41] Up to 15% of the required 35% of the appraised value may be of U.S. origin, and any amount of production in other beneficiary SSA countries may also contribute to the value-added requirement.[42]

Amendments to AGOA

Congress has passed legislation to amend AGOA five times since its initial passage. This legislation includes the Trade Act of 2002, the AGOA Acceleration Act of 2004, the Miscellaneous Trade and Technical Corrections Act of 2004, the Africa Investment Incentive Act of 2006, and most recently in August 2012, the amendment to AGOA that extended the third- country fabric provision ("AGOA Legislation in the 112th Congress").

Trade Act of 2002

In 2002, Congress amended AGOA for the first time through the Trade Act of 2002 (P.L. 107-210), which included adjustments to the textile and apparel provisions. An important change pertained to the cap that AGOA had set on imports of apparel assembled in an AGOA country from fabric made in an AGOA country (see the third bullet under "Textile and Apparel Provisions" above). The Trade Act of 2002 doubled this cap, increasing it to 7% in FY2008. The act, however, left the cap unchanged at 3.5% under the special rule for lesser-developed countries. The act also allowed Namibia and Botswana to qualify for the special rule for lesser-developed countries, even if their per capita incomes exceeded the limit set under AGOA. In addition, it specifically extended AGOA benefits to knit-to-shape articles and to garments cut in both the United States and an AGOA beneficiary country ("hybrid cutting") and made a correction to extend AGOA benefits to merino wool sweaters knit in AGOA beneficiary countries.

The Trade Act of 2002 also included other AGOA-related provisions. It stated that U.S. workers could be found eligible for trade adjustment assistance if U.S. production shifted to an AGOA beneficiary country and other conditions were met.[43] It authorized $9.5 million to the then-U.S. Customs Service for textile transshipment enforcement, and further specified that two permanent positions be assigned to South Africa for AGOA enforcement and that additional travel funds be allocated for verification in sub-Saharan Africa. The act also required that $1.317 million of the Customs Service budget be spent on programs to help sub-Saharan African countries develop visa and anti-transshipment systems.

AGOA Acceleration Act of 2004

In 2004, Congress further amended AGOA through the AGOA Acceleration Act of 2004 (P.L. 108-274). This legislation extended the deadline for AGOA benefits to 2015, and it also extended the special rule for LDCs from September 2004 to September 2007. It further stipulated that the cap on the volume of allowable U.S. apparel imports under this rule would be decreased starting in the year beginning September 2004, with a major reduction in the year beginning October 2006 (from 2.9% to 1.6%). The rationale behind this change was to encourage fabric production and vertical integration of the apparel industry in Africa. For apparel imports meeting the yarn forward rules of origin, the cap was set to remain at 7% until the expiration of the benefits in 2015.

The AGOA Acceleration Act also clarified certain apparel rules of origin to reflect the intent of Congress. Apparel articles containing fabric from both the United States and AGOA beneficiary countries were specifically allowed, as were otherwise eligible apparel articles containing cuffs, collars, and other similar components that did not meet the strict rules of origin. There was also clarification that ethnic printed fabric would qualify for duty-free treatment, as long as the fabric met certain standards regarding its size, form, and design characteristics. In addition, apparel articles containing fabrics and yarns recognized in the North American Free Trade Agreement (NAFTA) as being in short supply in the United States were declared as eligible for duty-free treatment, regardless of the source of such fabric and yarns. The legislation also increased the maximum allowable content of non-regional or non-U.S. fibers or yarns in AGOA eligible apparel imports, otherwise known as the *de minimis* rule, from 7% to 10%.

The AGOA Acceleration Act of 2004 also included a number of directives for the President related to trade capacity building. One such directive was to provide agricultural technical assistance by assigning U.S. personnel to at least 10 AGOA beneficiary countries, to help exporters meet U.S. technical standards for agricultural imports. Another directed the President to develop policies to encourage investment in agriculture and agricultural processing, as well as investment in infrastructure projects aimed at improving transportation and communication links both within Africa and between Africa and the United States. There was also a directive to foster improved relationships between African and U.S. customs and transportation authorities. An additional directive was to encourage technical assistance and infrastructure projects to assist in the development of the ecotourism industry in sub-Saharan Africa. Finally, another directed the President to conduct a study on each beneficiary country, identifying potential sectors for growth, barriers to such growth, and how U.S. technical assistance can assist each country in overcoming these barriers.

Miscellaneous Trade and Technical Corrections Act of 2004

In December 2004, the Miscellaneous Trade and Technical Corrections Act of 2004 (P.L. 108-429) was passed, which included a technical correction to the AGOA Acceleration Act. The legislation also allowed Mauritius to qualify for the special rule for LDCs for the one year beginning October 1, 2004, with a cap of 5% of total eligible imports under this rule.

Table 9. U.S. imports from Lesser Developed AGOA Countries under the Third-Country Fabric Provision (in millions of square meter equivalents (M2))

	2010	2011	YTD September 2011	YTD September 2012
Total Quota Allowance	814.400	866.700	866.700	938.700
Total Imports	191.648	199.857	153.464	143.131
Kenya	68.097	74.476	58.321	53.513
Lesotho	71.702	64.630	48.635	50.838
Swaziland	26.800	19.991	16.957	10.948
Mauritius	11.731	17.930	13.447	12.858
Tanzania	3.332	6.942	5.216	7.02
Ethiopia	2.949	6.128	4.292	3.313
Malawi	4.066	4.689	3.097	1.445
Botswana	2.431	3.292	2.433	2.771
Ghana	0.188	1.610	1.61	0.913
Uganda	0.087	0.138	0.138	0.000
Cameroon	0.001	0.016	0.001	0.000
Mozambique	0.000	0.014	0.014	0.000
Liberia	0.000	0.000	0.000	0.000

Source: Office of Textiles and Apparel, Department of Commerce.

Africa Investment Incentive Act of 2006

Congress passed the Africa Investment Incentive Act of 2006 in December 2006 (Title VI of P.L. 109-432), which extended the textile and apparel benefits of AGOA until 2015. This act also extended until 2012 the special rule for LDCs, which allows textiles and apparel quota- and duty-free access to the U.S. market regardless of the source of materials used, as long as assembly takes place within an AGOA-eligible LDC. The act also increases the cap on square meter equivalents under this rule back to the initial level of 3.5%. It also contains an "abundant supply" provision stipulating that if a certain fabric is determined by the U.S. International Trade Commission to be available in commercial quantities in AGOA beneficiary countries, then the special rule will no longer apply to apparel and textiles containing that particular fabric.

AGOA Legislation in the 112th Congress

Third-Country Fabric Provision Extended

A provision in AGOA that allows duty-free treatment of apparel assembled in one or more lesser- developed SSA countries regardless of the country of origin of the fabric ("third-country fabric provision"), subject to a cap, was recently extended by Congress through September 2015 (P.L. 112-163). This amendment also added South Sudan to the list of SSA countries eligible for AGOA benefits, though full beneficiary status also requires approval by the Administration.

Lesser-developed countries are defined in AGOA as those with a per capita gross national product of less than $1,500 per year as measured by the World Bank.[44] In subsequent amendments to AGOA, Botswana, Namibia, and Mauritius were added to the list of lesser-developed countries (§112 of P.L. 106-200, as amended). At present, 27 AGOA-eligible countries qualify for the third- country fabric provision (see **Table 8**).

Table 10. Top Ten Apparel Exporters under AGOA (actual $ U.S.)

Country	2011 (Value)
Lesotho	314,311,152
Kenya	258,886,230
Mauritius	153,428,075
Swaziland	76,579,510
Botswana	15,475,230
Malawi	13,483,949
Ethiopia	9,966,621
South Africa	5,277,269
Tanzania	5,118,819
Ghana	1,267,006
Total Above	853,793,861
All Other	1,021,392
Total	854,815,253

Source: U.S. International Trade Commission Trade Dataweb, http://www.usitc.gov.
Note: Imports for Consumption.

The quantitative limitation on third-country fabric, set each fiscal year, is announced annually by the Committee for the Implementation of Textile Agreements (CITA).[45] The AGOA Acceleration Act of 2004 raised the quantitative limit to a maximum of 3.5% (by quantity) of all U.S. apparel imports. In October 2012, CITA announced that the amount imported under this provision, for the 12-month period beginning October 1, 2012, must be no more than 867,929,963 square meters equivalent (SMEs), half of all apparel imports allowed under AGOA provisions.[46] Any imports from qualifying SSA countries in excess of these quantities are subject to otherwise applicable tariffs.[47] As **Table 9** indicates, imports under the provision from eligible countries are far below the quota allowance.[48]

The fact that only 23% of the allowable third-country fabric provision quota is currently being used could mask the fact that several SSA countries, including Lesotho, Kenya, Mauritius, Swaziland, and Botswana, have exported a significant amount (both by quantity and value) of apparel under the provision (see **Table 10**). For the countries above—all of whom, with the exception of Botswana, are major beneficiaries of AGOA by percentage of utilization (see **Table 11**)—U.S. apparel imports represent the major portion of their benefits under the AGOA preference.

Pending Legislation

H.R. 656 (introduced February 11, 2011), in part, directs the President to establish a Special Representative for United States-Africa Trade, Development, and Diaspora Affairs within the U.S. Department of State. The role of the representative would be to promote U.S.-African trade and investment relations; facilitate international learning exchanges; establish a database for information sharing; and consult with African governments, the private sector, and United Nations agencies regarding economic development in Africa. This bill is currently in committee.

Table 11. Total U.S. Imports, Imports under AGOA (including GSP), and Utilization Rate of Preference, 2011 (actual $ U.S.)

AGOA Beneficiary (in 2011)	Total U.S. Imports	Imports Under AGOA (including GSP)	Utilization Rate of Preference (%)
Chad	3,188,885,282	2,991,225,667	93.80%
Swaziland	83,289,612	77,192,451	92.68%
Nigeria	33,834,587,752	31,008,519,187	91.65%
Angola	13,756,357,845	11,534,181,604	83.85%
Malawi	72,353,659	60,141,734	83.12%
Lesotho	384,351,085	314,335,330	81.78%
Congo (ROC)	2,376,790,086	1,935,228,815	81.42%
Kenya	380,463,239	292,594,742	76.90%
Mauritius	250,482,636	169,190,565	67.55%
Ghana	778,992,716	454,534,351	58.35%
Cameroon	322,218,673	173,784,645	53.93%
South Africa	9,473,431,885	3,797,405,595	40.08%

AGOA Beneficiary (in 2011)	Total U.S. Imports	Imports Under AGOA (including GSP)	Utilization Rate of Preference (%)
Namibia	436,337,789	134,316,828	30.78%
Cape Verde	1,467,584	165,226	11.26%
Gabon	4,432,128,840	477,555,593	10.77%
Tanzania	58,244,222	5,751,382	9.87%
Ethiopia	144,404,059	13,874,923	9.61%
Senegal	6,766,267	490,660	7.25%
Gambia	82,442	5,352	6.49%
Botswana	293,285,806	17,063,293	5.82%
Uganda	45,881,727	2,540,952	5.54%
Mali	4,078,609	132,542	3.25%
Sao Tome & Principe	981,624	24,482	2.49%
Mozambique	34,966,794	692,543	1.98%
Rwanda	30,857,888	597,270	1.94%
Djibouti	4,053,092	58,050	1.43%
Sierra Leone	26,480,435	193,761	0.73%
Benin	1,970,887	14,019	0.71%
Zambia	47,321,448	220,669	0.47%
Burkina Faso	3,603,288	6,623	0.18%
Togo	31,744,687	57,584	0.18%
Liberia	158,178,415	0	0.00%
Burundi	9,558,071	0	0.00%
Seychelles	6,265,409	0	0.00%
Comoros	1,778,891	0	0.00%
Mauritania	965,142	0	0.00%
Guinea-Bissau	261,369	0	0.00%

Source: U.S. International Trade Commission Trade Dataweb (http://dataweb.usitc.gov).

Note: "Utilization Rate of Preference" is the value of U.S. imports under AGOA divided by the total amount of U.S. imports from AGOA countries expressed as a percentage. U.S. Imports for Consumption

H.R. 4221 (introduced March 20, 2012) and its companion bill in the Senate, S. 2215 (introduced March 21, 2012), seek to increase U.S. exports to Africa, in part, through strategies aimed at further developing relationships between the United States and African countries on a government-to-government level, as well as fostering private sector U.S.-African ties and targeting more U.S. export financing toward U.S.-SSA trade. Hearings were held on this legislation in the House Committee on Foreign Affairs Subcommittee on Africa, Global Health, and Human Rights on April 17, 2012, and in the Senate Committee on Foreign Relations Subcommittee on African Affairs on July 25, 2012. The Senate Committee on Foreign Relations voted to report out an amended version of S. 2215 on September 19, 2012. The House version of the bill is still in committee.

AGOA Trade Trends

According to the United States Trade Representative (USTR), over 93% of U.S. imports from SSA from AGOA-eligible countries in 2010 entered the United States duty-free, either under AGOA or GSP, or under zero-duty most-favored-nation (MFN) tariff rates.49 In 2011, U.S. imports under AGOA and GSP amounted to $53.8 billion (see **Table 11**).

In 2011, oil and mineral fuels (mostly crude oil) accounted for about 93% of all U.S. imports (by value) under the African Growth and Opportunity Act (AGOA), and about 81% of all U.S. imports from all SSA countries.50 Vehicles and parts were the next-largest category of AGOA imports at 4%. Apparel products (HTS chapters 61 and 62 combined) amounted to about 2%.[51]

As shown in **Figure 8**, the largest portion, by far, of U.S. exports to SSA are to AGOA-eligible countries. Except for decreases in 2002 and 2009-2010, arguably due to periods of worldwide recession, these exports have increased markedly over time. As **Table 13** indicates, the top destinations for U.S. products are South Africa, Nigeria, Angola, and Ghana.

Table 12. Top Ten U.S. Imports under AGOA (Excluding GSP) (actual $ U.S.)

HTS Number	2010	2011	Percent Change
27-Mineral fuels and oil	35,833,825,932	48,497,450,862	35.30%
87- Vehicles, Except Railway Or Tramway, And Parts	1,538,204,237	2,038,110,536	32.50%
62-Articles of apparel and clothing accessories, not knitted or crocheted	368,059,665	445,373,100	21.00%
61-Articles of apparel and clothing accessories, knitted or crocheted	358,416,707	409,442,153	14.20%
72-Iron and steel	141,893,313	204,501,643	44.10%
08-Edible fruit and nuts; peel of citrus fruit or melons	104,371,648	100,871,339	-3.40%
38-Miscellaneous chemical products	41,692,091	47,955,570	15.00%
22-Beverages, spirits, and vinegar	52,759,899	47,657,887	-9.70%
24-Tobacco and manufactured tobacco substitutes	33,362,905	39,949,659	19.70%
20-Preparations of vegetables, fruit, nuts, or other parts of plants	18,275,960	17,720,158	-3.00%
Subtotal	38,490,862,357	51,849,032,907	34.70%
All Other	26,903,235	34,021,330	26.50%
Total	**38,517,765,592**	**51,883,054,237**	**34.70%**

Source: U.S. International Trade Commission Trade Dataweb, http://www.usitc.gov.

Notes: Imports under AGOA are a subset of imports from SSA.

AGOA TECHNICAL ASSISTANCE AND CAPACITY BUILDING

Section 122 of AGOA directed the President to target U.S. government technical assistance and trade capacity building in AGOA beneficiary countries. This mandate includes assistance to both government and non-governmental actors. The act directs the President to target technical assistance to governments to (1) liberalize trade and exports; (2) harmonize laws and regulations with WTO membership; (3) engage in financial and fiscal restructuring; and (4) promote greater agribusiness linkages. The act also includes assistance for developing private sector business associations and networks among U.S. and sub-Saharan African enterprises. Technical assistance is also to be targeted to increasing the number of reverse trade missions, increasing trade in services, addressing critical agricultural policy issues, and building capabilities of African states to participate in the World Trade Organization, generally, and particularly in services. In FY2010 (latest available data), the United States reported obligating approximately $588 million in trade capacity building (TCB) assistance to AGOA countries.[52] Of this amount, about $341 million was obligated for physical infrastructure development and $200 million on trade-related agriculture projects.[53]

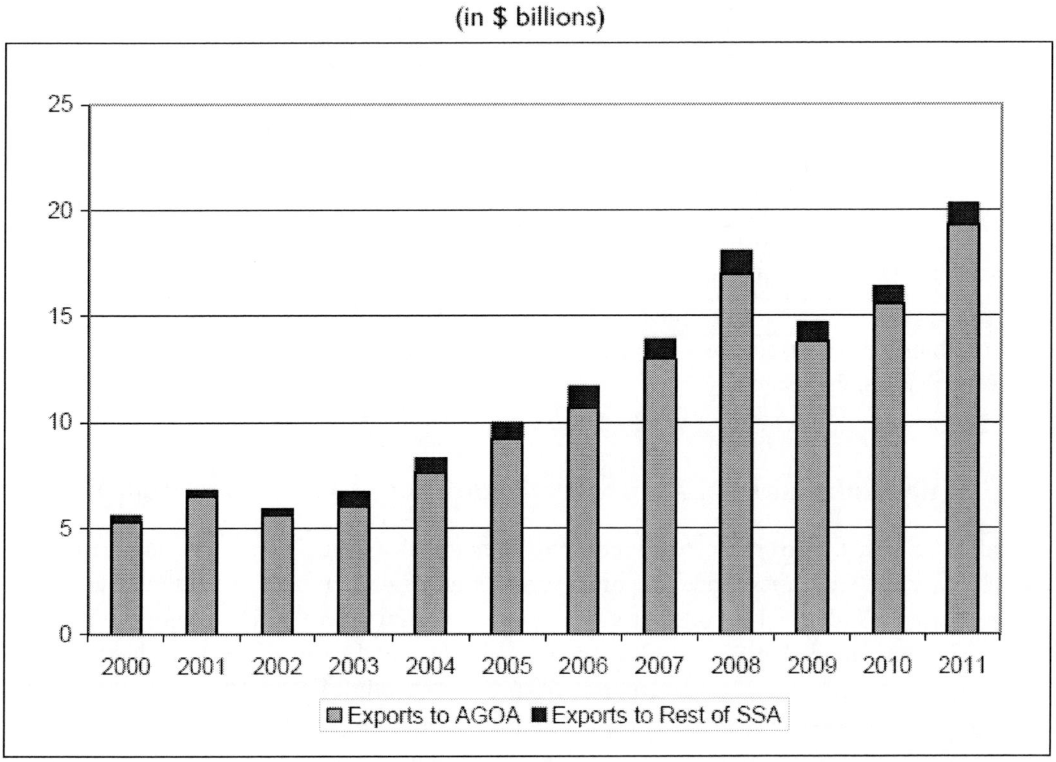

Source: U.S. International Trade Commission Trade Dataweb, http://dataweb.usitc.gov.
Note: U.S. Domestic Exports, FAS Value.

Figure 8. U.S. Exports to AGOA-Eligible Countries as a Portion of Total U.S. Exports to sub-Saharan Africa.

Table 13. U.S. Exports to AGOA Countries, 2011 (actual $ U.S.)

Country	2011
South Africa	6,848,590,454
Nigeria	4,706,183,368
Angola	1,458,062,000
Ghana	1,155,466,454
Ethiopia	684,957,626
Benin	610,363,392
Kenya	447,392,579
Mozambique	445,907,638
Senegal	258,781,861
Tanzania	250,729,324
Mauritania	241,472,844
Congo (ROC)	222,429,871
Cameroon	216,235,118
Togo	212,522,913
Gabon	197,360,657
Liberia	184,975,506
Djibouti	130,577,790
Zambia	123,078,281
Namibia	121,006,058
Rwanda	118,576,796
Subtotal Above Countries	18,634,670,530
All Other	590,328,884
Total Exports	19,224,999,414

Source: U.S. International Trade Commission Trade Dataweb (http://dataweb. usitc.gov).
Notes: Total Exports, FAS value

United States–sub-Saharan Africa Trade and Economic Cooperation Forum

Under AGOA, the President was required to establish within a year of enactment, after consultation with Congress and the other governments concerned, a United States-sub-Saharan Africa Trade and Economic Cooperation Forum (hereinafter referred to as the Forum). The act stated that the President was to direct certain top officials to host the first Forum meeting with their counterparts from AGOA-eligible countries and countries attempting to meet AGOA eligibility requirements.[54] The purpose of the Forum is to "discuss expanding trade and investment relations between the United States and sub-Saharan Africa and the implementation of [AGOA] including encouraging joint ventures between small and large businesses."

AGOA also required the President to encourage non-governmental organizations and the private sector to hold similar annual meetings, and it required the President to instruct U.S. delegates to the Forum to promote a review of HIV/AIDS in each sub-Saharan African country and the effect on economic development. It required the President to meet, to the extent practicable, with heads of governments of sub-Saharan African countries at least every two years to discuss expanding trade and investment relations, and the first such meeting should be within one year of enactment.

AGOA was enacted May 18, 2000, and on May 16, 2001, President Bush established the Forum and announced plans for its first meeting in Washington in October 2001. The first Forum was held October 29-30, 2001, in Washington, DC. President Bush addressed the Forum and announced several initiatives: (1) a $200 million Overseas Private Investment Corporation (OPIC) support facility to give U.S. firms access to loans, guarantees, and political risk insurance for investment projects; (2) a regional office of the Trade and Development Agency (TDA) in Johannesburg to help attract new investment; and (3) the Trade for African Development and Enterprise Program, initially funded at $15 million, to establish regional hubs to help African businesses in the global market. (These initiatives were implemented; see discussion below.)

AGOA forums have been held annually since 2001, alternately in the United States or in an SSA partner country. The 10th AGOA forum was held in Zambia on June 9-10, 2011. The theme of the Forum was "Enhanced Trade Through Increased Competitiveness, Value Addition, and Deeper Regional Integration."

The 11th AGOA Forum was held in Washington, DC, June 14-15, 2012. The theme for this year's event was "Enhancing Africa's Infrastructure for Trade," and it focused on various aspects designed to promote trade, including improvements in both physical infrastructure, such as roads and ports, and institutional infrastructure, such as the business climate. The Forum also focused on advancing African initiatives in regional economic integration and increasing awareness among U.S. businesses of opportunities in Africa. In a speech at the Forum, Secretary of State Hillary Rodham Clinton called for "urgent" efforts to renew the AGOA third country fabric provision. Continuing with the Forum's focus on improved infrastructure, she also highlighted the need for more "human infrastructure," or investments in human capital, especially among young people, throughout the region.

The Forum was followed by a one-time event, the *U.S.-Africa Business Conference 2012*, held in Cincinnati, OH, June 21-22. Hosted by the State Department and several other U.S. government agencies and private business promotion groups,[55] the conference sought

> to expand on the AGOA Forum by providing an opportunity to both showcase U.S. business expertise to potential African clients, and to highlight trade and investment opportunities in Africa to U.S. exporters and investors ... [focused] broadly on infrastructure development, including energy, transportation, and water and sanitation.[56]

U.S. Agency for International Development (USAID)

AGOA's mandate to encourage trade-related technical assistance is primarily implemented by USAID through the African Global Competitiveness Initiative (AGCI), a Presidential Initiative which supplanted the Trade for African Development and Enterprise (TRADE) initiative in 2006. The TRADE initiative succeeded the Africa Trade and Investment Policy Program (ATRIP), which operated from 1998 to 2003. These initiatives are generally used to focus activities around a common goal, but there are AGOA-related activities funded by other initiatives within USAID.

USAID funds various technical assistance programs throughout Africa aimed at improving trade within the region and between the region and the United States. USAID supports regional efforts through its regional missions and the four Regional Hubs for Global Competitiveness (Trade Hubs), located in Ghana, Senegal, Kenya, and Botswana. USAID bilateral missions support projects in individual African countries. The missions and hubs work on improving trade policy both regionally and within country governments. They also have programs to improve trade infrastructure, such as in transportation and energy, and they have enterprise development programs which often target specific industries, such as handicrafts and shea butter.

As mentioned above, AGOA encourages the establishment of private sector linkages between U.S. and SSA businesses. To this end, USAID funds an international business linkage program, South African International Business Linkages (SAIBL), which is implemented by the Corporate Council on Africa. SAIBL assists black-owned South African companies to prepare business plans, achieve International Standards Organization (ISO) certification, participate in U.S.-led trade delegations, attend trade shows in the United States, and identify public and private sector export financing. It also assists U.S. firms by identifying trade and investment opportunities in South Africa, by steering U.S. firms to appropriate government and private sector contacts, and by identifying sources of financing. USAID formerly funded a similar linkage program for West Africa, the West African International Business Linkages (WAIBL), but it no longer funds this program. The regional trade hubs implement many of the same types of activities as SAIBL, except that they focus more on promoting trade in general and not just exports to the United States.

Assistant U.S. Trade Representative for Africa (AUSTRA)

Section 117 of AGOA supported the creation of this position to serve as the "primary point of contact in the executive branch for those persons engaged in trade between the United States and sub-Saharan Africa," and the chief adviser to the U.S. Trade Representative (USTR) on trade and investment issues pertaining to Africa. This position previously had been established by President Clinton in 1998. One primary function of AUSTRA is to make the yearly determinations as to which countries are eligible for AGOA benefits generally, and also its special textile and apparel benefits. The AUSTRA also sponsors projects for WTO training for SSA trade negotiators and provides support for the Trade Advisory Committee on Africa.

Overseas Private Investment Corporation (OPIC)

Section 123 of AGOA expressed the sense of Congress that OPIC should exercise its authority to support projects in SSA and directed OPIC to increase funds directed to SSA countries. OPIC, a U.S. development finance agency, seeks to promote economic growth in developing and emerging economies and expand U.S. exports by providing political risk insurance, project financing, investment funds support, and other services for U.S. businesses in those countries, in support of U.S. foreign policy goals. OPIC's programs are intended to promote U.S. private investment by mitigating risks, such as political risks (including currency inconvertibility, expropriation, political violence, and terrorism), for U.S. firms making qualified investment overseas. Since 1974, OPIC has supported investments of nearly $6.3 billion in projects in Africa (of about $200 billion worldwide).[57]

Export-Import Bank (Ex-Im Bank)

Ex-Im Bank is the official export credit agency of the U.S. government. It maintains finance and insurance programs to facilitate U.S. exports to developing countries, especially in circumstances in which alternative commercial financing is not available, in order to contribute to U.S. employment. Some Ex-Im Bank programs are used to counter officially backed subsidized export financing offered by other countries. Its main program instruments are direct loans, loan guarantees, working capital guarantees, and export credit insurance, all backed by the full faith and credit of the U.S. government.[58]

Section 124 of AGOA expressed the sense of Congress that the Ex-Im Bank should continue to expand its financial commitments to its loan guarantee and insurance programs to African countries. The legislation also commended the Bank's sub-Saharan Africa Advisory Committee for its work in fostering economic cooperation between the United States and SSA. This committee's work was extended to September 30, 2014, in recent legislation reauthorizing the Ex-Im Bank (§23 of P.L. 112-122).[59]

In FY2011, the Ex-Im Bank authorized nearly $1.4 billion to support U.S. exports to SSA countries ($804 million in direct loans, $466 million in loan guarantees, $68 million in export credit insurance, and $40 million working capital guarantees), which supported approximately 8% of U.S. exports to SSA.[60] Ex-Im Bank-supported exports to SSA have tripled since 2007 from $434 million to about $1.4 billion in FY2011. About 80% of the number of those transactions directly supported small businesses.[61]

U.S. and Foreign Commercial Service (CS)

The U.S. and Foreign Commercial Service is the main export promotion arm of the U.S. Department of Commerce's International Trade Administration. CS services are primarily targeted at small and medium-sized U.S. businesses, providing export promotion services such as trade counseling, market intelligence, business matchmaking, and commercial diplomacy tools to assist them in exporting abroad. In 2011, CS employed about 500 staff working in the United States, operating 108 "U.S. Export Assistance Centers." CS also staffs 115 offices in more than 70 countries (down from 125 offices in 75 countries in 2010), which employ about 900 overseas staff, including Foreign Service officers and locally employed staff.[62] In 45 other countries where the CS does not have a presence, it has an agreement with the State Department to fulfill these functions through its Foreign Service officers and locally employed staff.[63]

In Section 125 of AGOA, Congress found that the CS presence in SSA had been reduced since the 1980s and that the level of staffing in 1997 (seven officers in four countries) did not "adequately service the needs of U.S. businesses attempting to do business in sub-Saharan Africa."[64] Accordingly, the legislation required the posting of at least 20 CS officers in not less than 10 countries in SSA by December 31, 2001, "subject to the availability of appropriations."[65] According to the U.S. Commercial Service Annual Report for 2011, there are currently eight CS staff in Africa. CS staff are located in Accra, Ghana; Nairobi, Kenya; and Cape Town and Johannesburg, South Africa.[66]

Section 125(c) of P.L. 106-200 (AGOA) also directed the International Trade Administration (ITA) to develop an initiative to (1) identify the best U.S. export prospects in the region; (2) identify tariff and non-tariff barriers that impede U.S. exports to Africa; and (3) undertake discussions with African states to increase market access for these goods and services. These activities are being carried out, in part, by the ITA's Market Access and Compliance Unit (MAC). The ITA also maintains the AGOA website at http://www.agoa.gov.

U.S. Trade and Development Agency (TDA)

Though its role is not specifically mentioned in AGOA legislation, the TDA is an independent agency that operates under a dual mission of promoting economic development and U.S. commercial interests in developing and middle-income countries. The agency links U.S. businesses to export opportunities by funding project planning activities, feasibility studies, and pilot projects overseas; and by sponsoring reverse trade missions, while creating sustainable infrastructure and economic growth in partner countries. TDA supports projects in economic sectors such as transportation, energy, and telecommunications. It provides grants to overseas project sponsors (both public and private sector grantees) who select U.S. companies to conduct TDA-funded activities. These programs are designed to assist project sponsors to make informed investment decisions, while opening markets for increased exports of U.S.-manufactured goods and services. Since 1981, TDA has provided over $90 million for projects in SSA, which the agency states have resulted in over $1 billion in U.S. exports related to partnerships between African project sponsors and U.S. firms. In FY2010, TDA obligated funds for 39 projects in SSA totaling $9.3 million, or approximately 19% of its total program expenditures ($49.7 million).[67]

Multilateral Initiatives

In addition to domestic agency programs, the United States participates in several multilateral institutions that provide trade capacity building in Africa and other developing-country regions and indirectly support the aims of AGOA. The World Bank and regional development banks all provide trade capacity building assistance, mainly in the form of loans.

The Enhanced Integrated Framework (EIF) is the main multilateral initiative in trade capacity building. It is a process that assists least developed countries (LDCs) to integrate trade issues into their national development strategies. The EIF process begins with a diagnostic study of trade challenges and opportunities in the LDC, and is meant to result in better targeted and coordinated assistance by all donors. Six international institutions collaborate on the EIF, including the International Monetary Fund (IMF), the International Trade Center (ITC), the United Nations Conference on Trade and Development (UNCTAD), the United Nations Development Program (UNDP), the World Bank, and the WTO. The EIF is funded by an Multi-Donor Trust Fund, composed of voluntary contributions from multilateral and bilateral donors. Total contribution receipts to this trust fund equaled $165.1 million as of April 2012, of which the United States contributed $600,000.[68]

The United States has also provided SSA countries with technical assistance and TCB support on a wide range of WTO-related issues such as trade facilitation, services, and sanitary and phytosanitary measures, in coordination with the other multilateral institutions mentioned above.[69] The United States has also provided technical support for the efforts of some SSA countries, such as Ethiopia (still in negotiations) and Togo (WTO accession July 2007), to accede to the WTO.[70]

Regional Cooperation and Free Trade Agreements

P.L. 105-200, the original AGOA legislation, contained a section encouraging exploration of new agreements to encourage trade and investment. AGOA, however, directed the President specifically toward FTA negotiations, and required more concrete steps regarding potential actions to be taken to establish such an agreement.

Discussion of potential partners for free trade agreements has revolved around South Africa and the South African Customs Union (SACU), but several other regional groupings are potential partners for future trade agreements with the United States. The Southern African Development Community (SADC), the Common Market for Eastern and Southern Africa (COMESA), the East African Community (EAC), and the West African Economic and Monetary Union (WAEMU) have all taken steps to begin the process of economic integration, either through trade liberalization or through steps to promote monetary union. While these groups are being encouraged in their attempts at regional integration, they are not immediate prospects for FTAs with the United States. Background on these groups appears in **Appendix A**.

FTA Negotiations with SACU

On November 4, 2002, then-USTR Robert B. Zoellick notified Congress that negotiations would be initiated with the SACU member countries.[71] These negotiations began in June 2003, but were postponed indefinitely in April 2006. Observers cited several possible reasons for the unsuccessful FTA negotiations, including the capacity of SACU nations to negotiate a U.S.-style (comprehensive and high-standard) FTA, and disagreements between the parties on the scope and level of ambition of the negotiations.

The United States and SACU signed a Trade, Investment, and Development Cooperation Agreement (TIDCA) on July 16, 2008, designed to build on and potentially capture some of the progress made in previous FTA negotiations.[72] The TIDCA establishes a forum for consultative discussions and cooperative work, and creates a framework for discussions on customs and trade facilitation, technical barriers to trade, sanitary and phytosanitary measures, and trade and investment relations.[73]

The U.S. decision to negotiate an FTA with SACU, rather than just with South Africa, may have reflected the large degree of economic integration that exists among the SACU states. The original SACU agreement dates from the colonial government in 1910 and was renegotiated with the apartheid government in 1969. A new agreement to more fully integrate the smaller states into decision-making for the area, which was previously dominated by South Africa, was signed on October 21, 2002. The agreement is characterized by free movement of goods within SACU, a common external tariff, and the common revenue pool which is apportioned among the member states. However, South Africa remains the dominant economy of the region, accounting for 87% of the population and 91% of the gross domestic product of the customs area (2010 figures).[74]

U.S. merchandise exports to SACU totaled $7.0 billion in 2011, led by machinery, motor vehicles and parts, precious metals and stones, mineral fuels and oils, precision equipment (e.g., photographic and optical devices), electrical machinery and parts, and aircraft. U.S. merchandise imports from SACU in 2011 totaled $10.7 billion, and included precious metals and stones, motor vehicles and parts, iron and steel, and machinery.[75]

U.S. Trade and Investment Framework Agreements (TIFAs)

Although TIFAs were not specifically addressed in AGOA legislation, the USTR regards TIFAs as important tools for strengthening trade and economic relations with key SSA countries and regional organizations.[76] As of this writing, the United States has negotiated TIFAs with Angola, Ghana, Liberia, Mauritius, Mozambique, Nigeria, Rwanda, and South Africa, and with the COMESA,[77] East African Community, and the WAEMU[78] regional arrangements. Generally, TIFAs commit the signatories to expand trade of goods and services, to encourage private sector investment, and to resolve problems and disputes through consultation and dialogue. To facilitate these objectives, the signatories of each agreement have established a Council on Trade and Investment to provide a venue for consultation on trade issues of interest or concern to the parties, and to work toward the removal of impediments to trade and investment flows. TIFAs are often considered to be first steps to the negotiation of free trade agreements.

U.S. Bilateral Investment Treaties (BIT)

BITs were not specifically addressed in AGOA, but are regarded as important tools for advancing bilateral trade. BITs help protect U.S. foreign direct investment and promote economic growth by advancing important reforms and encouraging the adoption of policies that facilitate and support foreign investment.[79] As of this writing, the United States has signed BITs with Cameroon, Republic of the Congo (Brazzaville), Democratic Republic of the Congo (Kinshasa), Mozambique, Rwanda, and Senegal, and is currently pursuing a BIT with the East African Community (EAC). The goals of the BIT are to protect U.S. investments abroad, and to encourage market-oriented domestic policy in host countries. Generally, BITs ensure national treatment for U.S. investments, limit expropriations, enable free repatriation of funds, place limitations on the imposition of trade-distorting or inefficient practices on U.S. investments—including requirements in hiring—and provide the right of submission of investment disputes to international arbitration. These treaties are promoted by the U.S. government as a method of encouraging the development of international law and trade standards within the partner country.[80]

AGOA IN COMPARATIVE PERSPECTIVE: EUROPEAN UNION TRADE FRAMEWORKS WITH AFRICA

Like the United States, the European Union (EU) has also been active in promoting trade between itself and SSA countries. The EU-South Africa Agreement on Trade, Development, and Cooperation entered into force on January 1, 2000. This agreement creates a free-trade area between the participants during a 12-year asymmetric transition period. The EU pledged to remove tariffs on 95% of imports from South Africa during a 10-year period with most products granted duty-free status in 2002. South Africa will remove duties on 86% of its tariff lines during a 12-year period with most eliminations occurring between 2006 and 2012. Notably, the agreement does not provide tariff relief to several important South African agricultural exports, nor to aluminum.

The Cotonou Agreement, signed in Cotonou, Benin, between the European Union and 71 African, Caribbean, and Pacific nations (ACP) in February 2000, extended non-reciprocal, duty-free access for industrial and processed agricultural goods to the EU market granted by the 4th Lomé Convention to the end of 2007. The extent of the duty-free access conferred by Cotonou was subsequently enhanced in March 2001 by the "Everything but Arms" initiative, which granted LDCs tariff-free access to all goods, except for sugar, rice, and bananas, for which products a tariff-rate quota system was maintained during a phase-out period ending in 2009. Provisions of the Cotonou Agreement call for the negotiation of trade liberalization agreements with regional economic partnerships that could include the regional African groupings discussed in **Appendix A**.

Preliminary negotiations on the Regional Economic Partnership Agreements (EPAs) began on September 27, 2002, and were supposed to conclude before the expiration of the Cotonou Agreement on December 31, 2007. Many African countries opposed signing EPAs because that would mean opening up their markets to EU imports. In the end, a temporary compromise was reached: most African countries signed "interim EPAs" to keep their EU trade preferences as they were under the Cotonou Agreement.

On May 14, 2012, the first EPA between the EU and Mauritius, Madagascar, Seychelles, and Zimbabwe went into effect. These countries will have duty-free/quota-free access to the EU market for exports. In exchange, these countries agreed to open their markets to EU exports in a 15-year time frame, but may exclude products they consider import sensitive.[81]

AGOA: CURRENT AND FUTURE CHALLENGES

Several issues may be important to Congress in the oversight of AGOA and in consideration of a potential renewal of the preference program. These issues concern the diversification of beneficiary country and industry participants, the continued eligibility of certain countries for AGOA benefits, the HIV/AIDS epidemic, and the participation of U.S. small business in AGOA.

- **Diversification of AGOA Exports.** While textile and manufacturing industries make up a growing part of U.S. imports under AGOA, these imports are dwarfed by AGOA imports from the petroleum and mining sectors. These industries are highly capitalized and do not provide extensive employment opportunities for African workers. AGOA benefits are also concentrated in few countries. Moreover, several AGOA-eligible countries export very little under the program. Increasing African economic diversification and export levels, key goals of AGOA, could arguably be enhanced by continuing and potentially expanding targeted trade capacity building and technical assistance to countries in the sub- region, particularly in the sectors where economic activity and production is concentrated. Agriculture, for instance, is a crucial component of many African economies and an important source of income for African workers. Increasing agricultural exports under AGOA, notably of processed goods, could help raise incomes and spur economic growth. Similarly, targeted technical assistance aimed at improving productive capacity, infrastructure, and investment policies, could also spur growth in light manufactured product exports.
- **Eligibility Standards.** A country's eligibility for AGOA benefits may become a subject of controversy. Some observers feel that the President must strictly enforce eligibility requirements to ensure continued adherence to reforms. However, others have cited the unpredictability of a country's AGOA benefits from year-to-year as a source of investment risk, and have suggested minimum eligibility terms of greater than the current one-year period. Another suggestion includes allowing Congress to override the President's decision to terminate AGOA benefits through legislation. Several countries have been considered candidates for losing AGOA eligibility.[82]
- **HIV/AIDS.** The HIV/AIDS pandemic continues to destabilize the economies of Africa and threatens any progress achieved by AGOA as additional income is spent, not to raising living standards, but to treat a population afflicted with the disease. Due to the disease, life expectancy is falling in several AGOA-eligible countries and in the region as a whole. Even with the advantages that AGOA preferences confer, investors may be deterred from the region by high medical costs, by constant replacement of workers stricken with the disease and the attendant training costs, and by the destabilizing risks associated with a society containing a large, dying population.
- **Lack of Uniform Trade Effects Reporting.** The initial AGOA legislation required an annual comprehensive report on U.S.-Africa trade and investment policy and on implementation of AGOA. The resulting annual report was a unique and invaluable oversight and trade trend tracking tool for policy-makers, but the reporting requirement sunsetted in 2008. Congress may wish to consider reinstating the annual AGOA reporting requirement.
- **Small Business Participation.** Small business accounts for about 55% of the U.S. GDP, and employs a large portion of American workers. U.S. small businesses, however, only participate in limited trade with Africa, and reportedly very few in the small business community know about AGOA. Some observers have noted that U.S. small businesses may benefit from AGOA, and in the process help provide avenues for diversifying African exports. Small business is also important in Africa, and increased partnership may result in better participation on both continents. There are

multiple ways that U.S. agencies could become more involved in increasing awareness of AGOA among the small business community, and providing opportunities for partnership. Examples include increased investment in and emphasis on the use of USAID's trade hubs as a mechanism for U.S. small business entrance into Africa, or an increased small business emphasis within the mandate of the U.S. Foreign Commercial Service. The provision of appropriations adequate to enable greater CS compliance with the original AGOA goal of deploying at least 20 CS officers in not less than 10 African countries could also further attainment of the goals laid out under AGOA.

APPENDIX A. REGIONAL ECONOMIC INTEGRATION AMONG SUB-SAHARAN AFRICA NATIONS

Southern African Development Community (SADC)

This group is composed of the nations of Angola, Botswana, Democratic Republic of the Congo, Lesotho, Madagascar, Malawi, Mauritius, Mozambique, Namibia, South Africa, Swaziland, Tanzania, Zambia, and Zimbabwe. Originally formed by front-line states to lessen economic dependence on the apartheid regime in South Africa, the group expanded to include South Africa in 1994. The 1996 Protocol on Trade committed each signatory to remove duties and non-tariff barriers to SADC members within 12 years, to provide national treatment for each other's goods, and to bind existing tariffs at current levels.

Common Market for Eastern and Southern Africa (COMESA)

Founded in 1982 as the Preferential Trade Area of Eastern and Southern Africa, current member states of the COMESA include Burundi, Comoros, Democratic Republic of the Congo, Eritrea, Ethiopia, Kenya, Madagascar, Malawi, Mauritius, Rwanda, Seychelles, Sudan, Swaziland, Uganda, Zambia, and Zimbabwe. The goal of COMESA is to attain a "fully integrated, competitive, regional economic community with high standards of living for all its people ready to merge into an African Economic Community."[83] The goal of monetary union by 2025 is expected to be advanced by the introduction of limited currency convertibility and improved coordination of fiscal and monetary policy during this time period.

East African Community (EAC)

Comprised of Burundi, Kenya, Rwanda, Tanzania, and Uganda, this organization sought to revive historic regional integration arrangements that had existed since 1917. This cooperation broke down in the 1970s due to widespread transshipments and the varied economic paths of its participants. The community was established once again by the three original members (Kenya, Tanzania, and Uganda) in 1999.[84] On July 1, 2010, the community established an EAC Common Market providing for free movement of goods, labor, services and capital within the region.[85] In the agreement, the partner states agreed to eliminate tariff, non-tariff, and technical barriers to trade; harmonize and mutually recognize standards; implement a common trade policy; and ease cross-border movement of persons through an integrated border management system.[86]

West African Economic and Monetary Union (WAEMU)

WAEMU[87] is made up of Benin, Burkina Faso, Côte d'Ivoire, Mali, Niger, Senegal, Togo, and Guinea-Bissau, the sole non-francophone member. This grouping was originally created to promote economic integration among countries that share the CFA franc (*Communauté financière africaine*), a currency formerly tied to the French franc prior to its disappearance in 2000 (but still backed by the French treasury). The member states have espoused the long-term goal of a full economic union with a common market, macroeconomic convergence, regulatory harmonization, and a common investment policy. A preferential tariff arrangement was concluded for member states in 1995, and a customs union with a common external tariff of 22% became operational in 2000. WAEMU countries have established a common accounting system, periodic reviews of member countries' macroeconomic policies, a regional stock exchange, and the legal and regulatory framework for a regional banking system.[88]

Appendix B. U.S.–SSA Trade Relationship

Table B-1. SSA Countries Trade Relationship with United States and Preference Program Status

Countries	GSP	GSP-Least Developed	AGOA	AGOA- Lesser Developed	BIT	TIFA
Angola	√	√	√			2009
Benin	√	√	√	√		2002[b]
Botswana	√		√	√		2008[c]
Burkina Faso	√	√	√	√		2002[b]
Burundi	√	√	√			2001[a], 2008[d]
Cameroon	√		√	√	1989	
Cape Verde	√		√	√		
Central African						
Republic	√	√				
Chad	√	√	√	√		
Comoros	√	√	√			2001[a]
Democratic Republic of Congo (Kinshasa)	√	√			1989	2001[a]

Countries	GSP	GSP-Least Developed	AGOA	AGOA- Lesser Developed	BIT	TIFA
Republic of Congo (Brazzaville)	√		√		1994	
Cote d'Ivoire	√		√			2002[b]
Djibouti	√	√	√			2001[a]
Equatorial Guinea						
Eritrea	√					2001[a]
Ethiopia	√	√	√	√		2001[a]
Gabon	√		√			
Gambia	√	√	√	√		
Ghana	√		√	√		1999
Guinea	√	√	√	√		
Guinea-Bissau	√	√	√			2002[b]
Kenya	√		√	√		2001[a], 2008[d]
Lesotho	√	√	√	√		2008c
Liberia	√	√	√	√		2007
Madagascar	√	√				2001[a]
Malawi	√	√	√	√		2001[a]
Mali	√	√	√	√		2002[b]
Mauritania	√	√	√			
Mauritius	√		√	√		2001[a], 2006
Mozambique	√	√	√	√	2005	2005
Namibia	√		√	√		2008[c]
Niger	√	√	√	√		2002b
Nigeria	√		√	√		2000
Rwanda	√	√	√	√	2012	2001[a], 2006, 2008[d]
Sao Tomei and						
Principe	√	√	√			
Senegal	√		√	√	1990	2002[b]
Seychelles	√		√			2001[a]
Sierra Leone	√	√	√	√		
Somalia	√	√				
South Africa	√		√			1999, 2008[c],2012
South Sudan	√	√				
Sudan						2001[a]
Swaziland	√		√	√		2001[a], 2008[c]
Tanzania	√	√	√	√		2008B
Togo	√	√	√			2002[b]
Uganda	√	√	√	√		2001[a], 2008[d]
Zambia	√	√	√	√		2001[a]
Zimbabwe	√					2001[a]

Source: Analysis by CRS. Data from USTR and USITC.

a. As part of the U.S. TIFA with the Common Market for Eastern and Southern Africa (COMESA).

b. As part of the U.S. TIFA with the West African Economic and Monetary Union (WAEMU).

c. As part of the U.S. Trade, Investment, and Development Cooperation Agreement with the Southern African Customs Union SACU, which is actually a TIDCA

d. As part of the U.S. TIFA with the East African Community (EAC).

End Notes

[1] The White House, *U.S. Strategy Toward Sub-Saharan Africa*, June 2012, p. 4, http://www. whitehouse.gov/sites/ default/files/docs/africa_strategy_2.pdf.

[2] Section 3108 of the Trade Act of 2002, P.L. 107-210.

[3] Section 6002 of the Tax Relief and Health Care Act of 2006, P.L. 109-432.

[4] P.L. 112-163

[5] Jorge Saba Arbache and John Page, "Patterns of Long Term Growth in Sub-Saharan Africa," World Bank, November 2007. Purchasing Power Parity (PPP) estimates attempt to determine comparative prices across countries for similar baskets of goods, taking into account exchange rates and various cost of living measures. This generates an artificial, but uniform, global exchange rate, which can be used to measure the local purchasing value of national currencies.

[6] Jorge Saba Arbache and John Page, "More Growth or Fewer Collapses? A New Look at Long Run Growth in SSA," World Bank, October 2007.

[7] *The Economist*, May 13-19, 2000.

[8] International Monetary Fund *Regional Economic Outlook: Sub-Saharan Africa*, October 2012, http://www.imf.org.

[9] Ibid, p. 95

[10] The World Bank, *Global Development Finance*, 2006 and 2007.

[11] Bureau of Economic Analysis (BEA), Foreign Direct Investment database.

[12] United Nations Conference on Trade and Development, *World Investment Report 2012: Towards a New Generation of Investment Policies*, p. 169.

[13] Based on remarks of representatives from the Chamber of Commerce and GE Africa speaking on U.S. economic engagement in Africa, June 19, 2012.

[14] CRS analysis using the Global Trade Atlas Navigator database.

[15] UNAIDS, *Report on the Global AIDS Epidemic, 2010*, CRS Report R41645, *U.S. Response to the Global Threat of HIV/AIDS: Basic Facts*.

[16] Ibid.

[17] CRS Report RL33584, *AIDS in Africa*, by Nicolas Cook.

[18] See CRS Report R41644, *U.S. Response to the Global Threat of Malaria: Basic Facts*; CRS Report R41802, *The Global Challenge of HIV/AIDS, Tuberculosis, and Malaria*; and CRS Report R41851, *U.S. Global Health Assistance: Background and Issues for the 112th Congress*, by Tiaji Salaam-Blyther.

[19] World Bank Global Development Finance data, http://data.worldbank.org. Foreign debt is defined as total external debt stock, comprising public and publicly guaranteed long-term debt.

[20] International Monetary Fund, *Regional Economic Outlook: Sub-Saharan Africa*, October 2012, http://www.imf.org

[21] United States Trade Representative, 2008 *Comprehensive Report on U.S. Trade and Investment Policy Toward Sub- Saharan Africa and Implementation of the African Growth and Opportunity Act*, May 2008. See also CRS Report RS22534, *The Multilateral Debt Relief Initiative*, by Martin A. Weiss.

[22] CRS Report R40778, *The Global Economic Crisis: Impact on Sub-Saharan Africa and Global Policy Responses*, by Alexis Arieff, Martin A. Weiss, and Vivian C. Jones.

[23] International Monetary Fund, *Regional Economic Outlook*, October 2012, http://www.imf.org.

[24] Contribution from Nicolas Cook, CRS African Affairs Specialist.

[25] Sino-African trade in 2011 also eclipsed the record $104.7 billion in U.S.-African trade attained in 2008.

[26] U.S.-African trade also stood at $29.4 billion in the year 2000 and $94.3 billion in 2011, having increased 221%. In the year 2000, trade with Africa made up 1.5% of total U.S global trade, and Africa's share had grown to 2.6% by 2011. U.S.-Africa trade peaked in 2008 at $104.7 billion.

[27] Harmonized Tariff Schedule Chapter 27, Mineral Fuels, Mineral Oils and Products of their Distillation; Bituminous Substances; Mineral Waxes. The top five oil suppliers to the United States in 2011 were Canada ($101.9 billion), Saudi Arabia ($46.2 billion), Mexico ($44 billion), Venezuela ($42 billion), and Nigeria ($34 billion) according to U.S. trade statistics (U.S. imports for consumption using the Global Trade Atlas).

[28] CRS calculations based on trade statistics (U.S. imports for consumption) from the U.S. International Trade Commission Trade Dataweb (http://dataweb.usitc.gov) and the Global Trade Atlas trade database.

[29] Harmonized Tariff Schedule Chapter 71, Natural or Cultured Pearls, Precious or Semi-Precious Stones, Precious Metals; Precious Metal Clad Metals, Articles Thereof; Imitation Jewelry; Coin.

[30] CRS calculations based on trade statistics from the U.S. International Trade Commission Trade Dataweb (http://dataweb.usitc.gov).

[31] U.S. International Trade Commission, *Sub-Saharan African Textile and Apparel Inputs: Potential for Competitive Production,* Investigation No. 332-502, May 2009.

[32] Data from the Bureau of Economic Analysis (BEA). Analysis by CRS. BEA industry-specific data were not provided in sufficient detail to break out SSA countries from Africa as a whole.

[33] Ibid.
[34] Ibid.
[35] 76 *Federal Register* 67035.
[36] P.L. 106-200, as amended by §7 of P.L. 108-274.
[37] See CRS Report RL33663, *Generalized System of Preferences: Background and Renewal Debate*, by Vivian C. Jones.
[38] P.L. 93-618, §506A, as added by §111(a) of P.L. 106-200, and as amended by §7 of P.L. 108-274. The USITC conducts a study to determine the import activity and sensitivity of the targeted product(s) from AGOA countries, and reports its determinations to the President. The President may also grant this status, with respect to certain import sensitive articles, to all GSP-qualifying countries.
[39] Department of Commerce, Office of Textiles and Apparel (OTEXA) Summary of AGOA textile and apparel provisions at OTEXA website, http://otexa.ita.doc.gov.
[40] Ibid.
[41] §506A of P.L. 93-618, as added by §111 of P.L. 106-200, and amended by §7 of P.L. 108-274.
[42] Ibid.
[43] For more information, see CRS Report R41922, *Trade Adjustment Assistance (TAA) and Its Role in U.S. Trade Policy*, by J. F. Hornbeck and Laine Elise Rover.
[44] 19 U.S.C. § 3721(c)(3). The statute refers to the International Bank for Reconstruction and Development, one of the five institutions that make up the World Bank Group.
[45] CITA is an interagency group chaired by the Department of Commerce that is responsible for matters affecting textile trade policy and supervising the implementation of all textile trade agreements. CITA was established by Executive Order 11651 on March 3, 1972 (44 *Federal Register* 4699).
[46] The cap for AGOA apparel imports under the special rule for lesser-developed countries is 3.5% of all U.S. apparel articles imported in the previous 12-month period. The cap for all AGOA apparel imports, including those under the special rule, is 7% of all U.S. apparel articles imported in the previous 12-month period.
[47] 77 *Federal Register* 59914, October 1, 2012.
[48] Data from the Office for Textiles and Apparel, Department of Commerce website, http://otexa.ita.doc.gov.
[49] United States Trade Representative website , http://www.ustr.gov/tradeprograms/african-growth-and-opportunity-act-agoa.
[50] CRS calculations based on data from the U.S. International Trade Commission Trade Dataweb, http://dataweb.usitc.gov.
[51] U.S. Census data from the Global Trade Atlas.
[52] U.S. Agency for International Development, Trade Capacity Building Database, http:// tcb.eads.usaidallnet.gov/.
[53] Ibid.
[54] Representatives from appropriate Sub-Saharan African regional organizations and government officials from other appropriate countries in Sub-Saharan Africa also could be invited.
[55] Sponsors included the Departments of State, Transportation, and Energy, USDA, USAID, Millennium Challenge Corporation, Export-Import Bank, U.S. Trade and Development Agency, Executive Office of the President, Greater Cincinnati World Affairs Council, Department of Commerce, The Corporate Council on Africa, U.S. Small Business Administration, and U.S. Environmental Protection Agency.
[56] It also provided "structured networking opportunities for African government officials and business leaders with U.S. state and local government officials and business leaders; informational sessions on U.S. government opportunities and services from various federal agencies; and site visits to companies and organizations." State Department, *U.S.-Africa Business Conference 2012*.
[57] CRS Report 98-567, *The Overseas Private Investment Corporation: Background and Legislative Issues*, by Shayerah Ilias.
[58] CRS Report R42472, *Export-Import Bank: Background and Legislative Issues*, by Shayerah Ilias.
[59] Export-Import Bank Reauthorization Act, 12 U.S.C. 635(b)(9)(B)(iii).
[60] Export-Import Bank of the United States, *2011 Annual Report*, http://www.exim.gov/about/reports/ar/2011/exim_2011annualreport.pdf.
[61] Ibid.
[62] *Powering Export Growth*, U.S. Commercial Service Annual Report, 2011.
[63] The Commerce and State departments agreed to expand this program additional 11 countries in September 2011.
[64] AGOA, §125(a)(4).
[65] AGOA, §125(b).
[66] U.S. Commercial Service, *Powering Export Growth*, U.S. Commercial Service Annual Report, 2011.CS staff are also located in Cairo, Egypt; Tripoli, Libya; and Casablanca, Morocco.
[67] U.S. Trade and Development Agency, *2010 Annual Report*. Examples of specific USTDA projects in SSA are available on the USTDA website at http://www.ustda.gov/program/ regions/subsaharanafrica/.
[68] Enhanced Integrated Framework website, http://www.enhancedif.org/documents/ EIF% 20toolbox/ EIF%20Trust%20Fund%20Current%20Status.pdf.
[69] 2008 USTR Report, p. 40.

[70] Ibid.
[71] SACU countries are Botswana, Lesotho, Namibia, South Africa, and Swaziland.
[72] U.S. International Trade Representative website, http://www.ustr.gov.
[73] Ibid.
[74] International Monetary Fund, *International Financial Statistics*, retrieved from Economist Intelligence Unit *All Country Data database*.
[75] U.S. International Trade Commission data website, at http://dataweb.usitc.gov.
[76] 2008 USTR SSA Report, p. 42.
[77] COMESA is made up of Burundi, Comoros, Democratic Republic of Congo, Djibouti, Egypt, Eritrea, Ethiopia, Kenya, Libya, Madagascar, Malawi, Mauritius, Rwanda, Seychelles, South Sudan, Sudan, Swaziland, Uganda, Zambia, and Zimbabwe.
[78] WAEMU/UEMOA members are Benin, Burkina Faso, Cape Verde, Cote d'Ivoire, Gambia, Ghana, Guinea-Bissau, Liberia, Mali, Niger, Nigeria, Senegal, Sierra Leone, and Togo.
[79] Ibid.
[80] U.S. Trade Representative website, http://www.ustr.gov/trade
[81] European Union, *EU's First Economic Partnership with an African Region Goes Live*, Press Release, May 14, 2012, http://europa.eu/newsroom/press-releases/index_en.htm.
[82] In 2003, the President declared Eritrea and the Central African Republic to be ineligible for AGOA. In 2004, Cote d'Ivoire was declared ineligible as well, but was reinstated in 2011. In 2009, benefits for Guinea, Madagascar, and Niger were terminated because the President determined that they were not making continual progress in meeting AGOA requirements (Guinea and Niger were reinstated in 2011). Also in 2009, Mauritania was removed from AGOA eligibility, but was reinstated later that year. Lesotho, which is considered an AGOA success story, has been the subject of persistent complaints from indigenous labor groups regarding working conditions in newly developed textile plants. In some years, Swaziland has received warnings from the State Department that its human rights record does not meet AGOA eligibility requirements. Several countries have questionable commitment to privatization and tariff reform.
[83] Common Market for Eastern and Southern Africa (COMESA) website.
[84] East African Community (EAC) website, http://www.eac.int.
[85] Ibid.
[86] Ibid.
[87] WAEMU is also known as UEMOA from its French name, *Union Economique et Monetaire Oest-Africaine*.
[88] 2008 USTR SSA Report, p. 39.

In: Sub-Saharan Africa
Editor: Jacqueline S. Santiago
ISBN: 978-1-62618-433-6

Chapter 4

U.S. STRATEGY TOWARD SUB-SAHARAN AFRICA*

The White House

Nearly 3 years ago, I remarked in front of the Ghanaian Parliament that Africa is a fundamental part of our interconnected world. Since that time, we have partnered with leaders, youth, and civil society in Africa to deepen the principles of democracy and human rights, to expand economic opportunity, and to support those who seek peace where war and deprivation have plagued communities. Africa and its people are partners with America in creating the future we want for all of our children—a future that is grounded in growth, mutual responsibility, and mutual respect.

As we look toward the future, it is clear that Africa is more important than ever to the security and prosperity of the international community, and to the United States in particular. Africa's economies are among the fastest growing in the world, with technological change sweeping across the continent and offering tremendous opportunities in banking, medicine, politics, and business. At the same time, the burgeoning youth population in Africa is changing economies and political systems in profound ways.

Addressing the opportunities and challenges in Africa requires a comprehensive U.S. policy that is proactive, forward-looking, and that balances our long-term interests with near-term imperatives. This *U.S. Strategy Toward Sub-Saharan Africa* solidifies and advances many of the initiatives that we have launched since I took office in order to help achieve that balance, and elevates two efforts that will be critical to the future of Africa: strengthening democratic institutions and boosting broad-based economic growth, including through trade and investment. Strong, accountable, and democratic institutions, sustained by a deep commitment to the rule of law, generate greater prosperity and stability, and meet with greater success in mitigating conflict and ensuring security. Sustainable, inclusive economic growth is a key ingredient to security, political stability, and development, and it underpins efforts to alleviate poverty, creating the resources that will bolster opportunity and allow individuals to reach their full potential.

While many countries on the continent have made tremendous strides to broaden political participation and reduce corruption, there is more work to be done to ensure fair electoral processes, transparent institutions that protect universal rights, and the provision and

* This is an edited, reformatted and augmented version of The White House publication, dated June 2 012.

protection of security and public goods. Our message to those who would derail the democratic process is clear and unequivocal: the United States will not stand idly by when actors threaten legitimately elected governments or manipulate the fairness and integrity of democratic processes, and we will stand in steady partnership with those who are committed to the principles of equality, justice, and the rule of law.

America believes in Africa as a region of growing opportunity and promise, for Africa, for America, and for our people and our economies. We believe that Africa can be the world's next major economic success story. We will work with our African partners to build strong institutions, to remove constraints to trade and investment, and to expand opportunities for African countries to effectively access each other's markets and global markets, to embrace sound economic governance, and diversify their economies beyond a narrow reliance on natural resources, and—most importantly—create opportunities for Africa's people to prosper.

As we support these efforts, we will encourage American companies to seize trade and investment opportunities in Africa, so that their skills, capital, and technology will further support the region's economic expansion, while helping to create jobs here in America.

Across all of these efforts, the United States will prioritize efforts to empower the next generation of African leadership.

These young men and women have shown time and again the willingness and ability to change their communities and their countries for the better, and the United States will continue to be their steadfast ally and partner. America's partnership with this new generation of Africans will extend beyond our Government to the broad and deepening relationships between our peoples, businesses, and institutions. These roots will drive our path to a future of democracy, peace, and prosperity for generations to come.

INTRODUCTION

Upon taking office, President Obama committed to supporting strong, open, and accountable governments and sustainable development in Africa. In his speech before the Ghanaian Parliament in July 2009, the President asserted that Africa is a fundamental part of our interconnected world, and called for a partnership with Africa that is "grounded in mutual responsibility and mutual respect."

The National Security Strategy, released in May 2010, reinforces this vision, and calls for partnership with African nations as they grow their economies and strengthen their democratic institutions and governance. In June 2012, the President approved a Presidential Policy Directive that outlines his vision with respect to U.S. policy toward sub-Saharan Africa. This document is drawn from and reflects that Directive.

Over the last three and a half years, we have worked to translate the President's words to the Ghanaian Parliament into action.

We have supported democratic development by strengthening institutions and challenging leaders whose actions threaten peaceful political transitions, including in Cote d'Ivoire. We have advanced peace and security by playing an integral role in the birth of South Sudan, supporting the African Union Mission in Somalia, and working with regional partners to counter the predatory Lord's Resistance Army. We have engaged young African leaders who will shape the continent's future. We have invested in development partnerships to foster sustained economic growth, promote food security, increase resilience to climate change, and improve the capacity of countries and communities to address HIV/AIDS, malaria, and other health threats.

We have been the world's leader in responding to humanitarian crises, including in the Horn of Africa, while at the same time working with our African partners to promote resilience and prevent future crises.

The economies of sub-Saharan Africa are among the world's most rapidly growing. An increasing number of African governments and regional organizations are taking a lead role in addressing the security and political challenges within their borders and beyond and are increasingly influential players in international fora. The African Union serves as an important leader on political, diplomatic, and peacekeeping issues across the continent. At the same time, urbanization and a burgeoning youth population are changing the region's demographics in profound ways, and young people are increasingly making their voices heard.

While the continent has made important gains on democracy and institution building, those gains are fragile.

There are still too many countries where the transition to democracy is uneven and slow, and leaders who resist relinquishing power. In many countries, corruption is endemic, and state institutions remain weak. In addition to eroding the legitimacy of governments, these factors impede local business activity and foreign investment. Despite having much of the world's arable land and many of its richest fisheries, the agricultural sectors of many sub-Saharan African states are underperforming, and poverty still cripples the lives of too many. Transnational security challenges pose threats to regional stability, economic growth, and U.S. interests.

As the United States addresses these opportunities and challenges, we will be guided by our core interests in sub-Saharan Africa: ensuring the security of the United States, our citizens, and our allies and partners; promoting democratic states that are economically vibrant and strong partners of the United States on the world stage; expanding opportunities for U.S. trade and investment; preventing conflict and mass atrocities; and fostering broad-based, sustainable economic growth and poverty alleviation.

Given the growing strategic importance of sub-Saharan Africa to the United States, over the next 5 years we will elevate our focus on and dedicate greater effort to strengthening democratic institutions and spurring economic growth, trade, and investment, while continuing to pursue other objectives on the continent.

Stronger democratic institutions lead countries to achieve greater prosperity and stability; are more successful in mitigating conflict and countering transnational threats; and serve as stronger partners of the United States.

Additionally, promoting sustainable, inclusive economic growth is a key ingredient of security, political stability, and development, and it underpins efforts to alleviate poverty, creating the resources to support health care, education, and other public goods.

The Four Pillars of the U.S. Strategy Toward Sub-Saharan Africa

The United States will partner with sub-Saharan African countries to pursue the following interdependent and mutually reinforcing objectives: (1) strengthen democratic institutions; (2) spur economic growth, trade, and investment; (3) advance peace and security; and (4) promote opportunity and development. Across all objectives, we will: deepen our engagement with Africa's young leaders; seek to empower marginalized populations and women; address the unique needs of fragile and post-conflict states; and work closely with the U.N. and other multilateral actors to achieve our objectives on the continent.

I. Strengthen Democratic Institutions

As the President said in Ghana, "Africa doesn't need strong men, it needs strong institutions." We will work to advance democracy by strengthening institutions at every level, supporting and building upon the aspirations of Africans for more open and accountable governance, promoting human rights and the rule of law, and challenging leaders whose actions threaten the credibility of democratic processes. As the National Security Strategy states, our support for democracy is critical to U.S. interests and is a fundamental component of American leadership abroad. We will pursue the following actions:

- *Promote Accountable, Transparent, and Responsive Governance.* The United States will expand efforts to support and empower key reformers and institutions of government at all levels to promote the rule of law, strengthen checks on executive power, and incorporate responsive governance practices. We will also seek to expand African membership in the Open Government Partnership and the Extractive Industries Transparency Initiative, which promote sound governance, transparency, and accountability.
- *Bolster Positive Models.* The United States recognizes that Africans must forge lasting solutions, and build their own democracies. To this end, we will support those leaders and actors who are creating vibrant democratic models, including elected leaders as well as young Africans who are leaders in civil society and entrepreneurship. We will use the facilitating power of the United States Government to help young African leaders network with one another, share innovative solutions, and demonstrate America's support for their efforts.
- *Promote and Protect Human Rights, Civil Society, and Independent Media.* The United States will amplify and support voices calling for respect for human rights, rule of law, accountability and transitional justice mechanisms, and independent media. Further, we will continue to focus on empowering women and marginalized populations, and opposing discrimination based on disability, gender, or sexual orientation.
- *Ensure a Sustained Focus on the Credibility of Democratic Processes*. The United States will take a strong and consistent stand against actions that undermine democratic institutions or the legitimacy of democratic processes. We will evaluate

elections against the highest possible standards of fairness and impartiality. The United States will seek to expand adherence to the principle of civilian control of the military, and will support strong measures against individuals or groups that threaten legitimately elected governments.

- *Promote Strong Democratic Norms.* The United States will support efforts by regional and international bodies to enforce the consistent application of democratic practices, particularly the African Union's African Charter on Democracy, Elections, and Governance and other multilateral standards. We will support basic and civic education to ensure future generations are active, informed, and committed to the rights and responsibilities of democratic citizenship.

II. Spur Economic Growth, Trade, and Investment

It is in the interest of the United States to improve the region's trade competitiveness, encourage the diversification of exports beyond natural resources, and ensure that the benefits from growth are broad-based. We will pursue the following actions as we seek to accelerate inclusive economic growth, including through trade and investment:

- *Promote an Enabling Environment for Trade and Investment.* Building on U.S. programs such as the Partnership for Growth and New Alliance for Food Security and Nutrition, as well as international programs such as the Open Government Partnership and the Extractive Industries Transparency Initiative, we will encourage legal, regulatory, and institutional reforms that contribute to an environment that enables greater trade and investment in sub-Saharan Africa. We will also encourage sub-Saharan Africa's private sector to engage governments to undertake these necessary reforms.
- *Improve Economic Governance.* We will help to build the public sector's capacity to provide services and improve protections against illicit financial activity. Greater economic governance facilitates effective management of public finances, more efficient and transparent use of (and less reliance on) donor aid, and increased transparency and accountability. In turn, strong public financial management helps increase transparency and effectiveness in government operations and broaden the revenue base.
- *Promote Regional Integration.* Increased African regional integration would create larger markets, improve economies of scale, and reduce transaction costs for local, regional, and global trade. We will work with regional economic communities, including through the U.S.- East African Community Trade and Investment Initiative, and national governments to reduce the barriers to trade and investment flows across the continent. In particular, we will promote trade facilitation, customs modernization, and standards harmonization; support regulatory coherence and transparency; improve infrastructure that strengthens regional trade and access to global markets; and explore ways to remove impediments to efficient operation of supply chains in the region.

- *Expanding African Capacity to Effectively Access and Benefit from Global Markets.* Notwithstanding the tariff advantages afforded by the United States to sub-Saharan Africa, non-oil exports from Africa to the United States continue to grow slowly and have not reached their full potential. To increase Africa's capacity to produce goods for export that are diverse, competitive, and meet global standards, we will (1) work with the Congress to extend the unilateral preferences under the African Growth and Opportunity Act beyond 2015 and extend the Generalized System of Preferences beyond 2013, while also exploring ways to update these programs and enhance African capacity to fully utilize and benefit from these programs, including through the African Competitiveness and Trade Expansion Initiative; (2) increase cooperation and technical assistance on a range of issues, including building Africa's capacity to meet product standards, food safety and sanitary and phytosanitary requirements, product testing, and certification requirements; and (3) take steps to increase productive capacity and improve the competitiveness of African exports, including by helping to address a range of supply-side constraints that raise costs and reduce the efficiency of exports.
- *Encourage U.S. Companies to Trade with and Invest in Africa.* Many U.S. businesses – particularly small- and medium-sized enterprises – are unaware of opportunities for trade with and investment in Africa, or face challenges establishing business relationships in sub-Saharan African countries. In harmony with the National Export Initiative, we will develop a "Doing Business in Africa Campaign" to harness the resources of the United States Government to assist U.S. businesses in identifying and seizing opportunities in sub-Saharan Africa. We will also engage with members of the sub-Saharan African Diaspora in the United States, who are showing an increasing level of interest in investing in their countries of origin.

III. Advance Peace and Security

African states are showing increasing capacity to take the lead on security issues on the continent. Nonetheless, international and domestic conflict and the inability of some governments to meet the basic security needs of their people continue to be key obstacles to effective democratic governance, economic growth, trade and investment, and human development. Only Africa's governments and people can sustainably resolve the security challenges and internal divisions that have plagued the continent, but the United States can make a positive difference. Recognizing this fact, we will pursue the following actions:

- Counter al-Qa'ida and Other Terrorist Groups. In our approach to counterterrorism, we will continue to be guided by the President's affirmation in the National Security Strategy that he bears no greater responsibility than ensuring the safety and security of the American people. Consistent with the National Strategy for Counterterrorism, we will concentrate our efforts on disrupting, dismantling, and eventually defeating al-Qa'ida and its affiliates and adherents in Africa to ensure the security of our citizens and our partners. In doing so, we will seek to strengthen the capacity of civilian bodies to provide security for their citizens and counter violent extremism through more effective governance, development, and law enforcement efforts.

- Advance Regional Security Cooperation and Security Sector Reform. We will deepen our security partnerships with African countries and regional organizations and their stand-by forces by expanding efforts to build African military capabilities through low-cost, small-footprint operations, consistent with the vision set forth in "Sustaining U.S. Global Leadership: Priorities for 21st Century Defense." We will also seek to strengthen the capacity of civilian bodies and institutions to improve the continent's ability to provide security and respond to emerging conflicts. Moreover, U.S. military and civilian agencies will help establish effective partner nation security forces, intelligence organizations, and law enforcement and border control agencies that are subordinate to and operating jointly with their constitutional civil authorities.
- Prevent Transnational Criminal Threats. We will build comprehensive partnerships that leverage our land border, maritime, aviation, cybersecurity, and financial sector expertise to counter illicit movement of people, arms, drugs, and money, as well as guard against the criminal facilitation of weapons of mass destruction material and technology. We will work to curb armed robbery at sea and protect fisheries, and continue to implement our Counter-Piracy Action Plan off the coast of Somalia. Consistent with the Strategy to Combat Transnational Organized Crime, we will support efforts and build partner capacity to combat corruption and instability as well as to combat trafficking in persons.
- Prevent Conflict and, Where Necessary, Mitigate Mass Atrocities and Hold Perpetrators Accountable. Consistent with the objectives of Presidential Study Directive-10, we will address atrocity risks at the earliest stage possible to help prevent violence before it emerges, and bolster domestic and international efforts to bring perpetrators to justice. We will also cultivate deeper and broader support among governments and multilateral organizations to work toward the same objectives.
- Support Initiatives to Promote Peace and Security. We will support U.N. peacebuilding and peacekeeping missions in sub-Saharan Africa, including by working to ensure that peacekeeping missions are well-led, well-supported, and appropriately resourced in order to maximize their effectiveness. Within African countries, we will support those who work to overcome communal divisions in pursuit of sustainable and peaceful political processes.

IV. Promote Opportunity and Development

This Administration, including through the Presidential Policy Directive on Global Development, has charted a new approach that focuses on sustainable development outcomes and a new operational model for U.S. development assistance and builds on our work to date. Africa is the focus of three key Presidential development initiatives: the Global Health Initiative, Feed the Future, and the Global Climate Change Initiative. Additionally, two of the four Partnership for Growth countries (Ghana and Tanzania) are in Africa. In each of these efforts, we have highlighted the importance of reform and transparency to development and prioritized good economic and project management to promote sustainability. We are investing in a growing number of good-performing countries and seeing the evidence in clear outcomes and the increased capacity and commitment of our partners. We will pursue the following actions as we strive to further accelerate development progress:

- *Address Constraints to Growth and Promote Poverty Reduction*. We will leverage our engagement via multilateral financial institutions to advocate for increased financing for poorer countries, and will focus on addressing constraints to growth. We will encourage governments to use revenues, particularly from energy sources, to more broadly benefit their populations, and we will continue to support the expansion and improvement of sub-Saharan Africa's education services.
- *Promote Food Security*. Food security will remain a priority, consistent with the commitments made by the United States at the L'Aquila Summit, through the Feed the Future Initiative, and the New Alliance for Food Security and Nutrition launched at the 2012 G-8 Summit. We will build on the progress achieved thus far, while also intensifying our efforts to promote policy reforms, drive increased private capital to African agriculture, scale innovation, and reduce risk.
- *Transform Africa's Public Health*. We will work through the Global Health Initiative and our disease-specific programs, including the President's Emergency Plan for AIDS Relief and the President's Malaria Initiative, to tackle other diseases and malnutrition while strengthening health systems for sustainable impact. We will continue to leverage the leadership being demonstrated by a growing number of African countries on global health in order to bolster our efforts to promote good governance, development, and economic growth, including as we pursue the expanded AIDS prevention targets announced on World AIDS Day in 2011 and through the June 2012 Child Survival Call to Action.
- *Increase Opportunities for Women and Youth*. We will continue to use our diplomacy and assistance programs to empower women, including through the African Women Entrepreneurship Program, implementing the U.S. National Action Plan on Women, Peace, and Security, and focusing on maternal and child health as a centerpiece of the Global Health Initiative. This includes enhancing efforts to protect women in the context of conflict and humanitarian emergencies. We will also continue engaging with Africa's next generation of leaders by advancing the President's Young African Leaders Initiative to provide tools to support leadership development, promote entrepreneurship, and connect young leaders with one another and the United States.
- *Respond to Humanitarian Crises While Promoting Resilience*. While continuing to lead the world in response to humanitarian crises in Africa, we will promote and bring to scale resilience policies and programs. In that context, we will work to prevent the weakening or collapse of local economies, protect livestock, promote sustainable access to clean water, and invest in programs that reduce community-level vulnerability to man-made and natural disasters.
- *Promote Low-emissions Growth and Sustainable Development, and Build Resilience to Climate Change*. We will continue promoting resilience and adaptation to impacts

of climate change on food, water, and health in vulnerable African countries, supporting the adoption of low-emissions development strategies, and mobilizing financing to support the development and deployment of clean energy. We will also work to protect and encourage sustainable use of Africa's natural resources.

INDEX

A

access, 8, 11, 51, 55, 127, 133, 142, 145, 148
accountability, 36, 144, 145
accounting, 108, 132, 136
adaptation, 148
ADC, 131, 135
adjustment, 50, 119
advocacy, 35, 46, 66, 80, 95
aerospace, 34, 67, 78, 94, 98, 102
African Growth and Opportunity Act, v, viii, 2, 9, 10, 42, 59, 63, 103, 104, 116, 124, 138, 146
agencies, vii, viii, 1, 4, 7, 10, 30, 31, 34, 44, 45, 46, 51, 53, 54, 57, 60, 92, 100, 101, 102, 103, 122, 127, 135, 139, 147
AGOA Forum, viii, 103, 127
agricultural exports, 133, 134
agricultural sector, 6, 143
agriculture, 5, 13, 44, 46, 55, 56, 77, 81, 120, 125, 148
AIDS, 20, 97, 108, 134, 138, 148
airports, 68
annual rate, 99
apparel industry, 119
apparel products, 113, 118
appraised value, 118
appropriations, 130, 135
arbitration, 132
Argentina, 51
Asia, 100
Asian countries, 37, 89
assessment, 4, 42, 60
assets, 54
atrocities, 143
audit, 4, 46, 60
audits, 9
authorities, 51, 54, 100, 120, 147
authority, 54, 100, 128
awareness, 127, 135

B

banking, 136, 141
banks, 20, 99
barriers, 51, 120, 130, 131, 135, 136, 145
base, 145
batteries, 36, 56, 92, 102
BEA, 2, 24, 25, 27, 28, 42, 45, 50, 53, 54, 56, 59, 70, 84, 85, 98, 99, 100, 101, 102, 114, 115, 138
Beijing, 12
benchmarks, 44
beneficiaries, viii, 104, 116, 117, 118, 122
benefits, viii, 10, 51, 104, 105, 117, 118, 119, 121, 122, 128, 133, 134, 140, 145
Bilateral, 132
bilateral ties, 11
bonuses, 54
border control, 147
borrowers, 31, 44
Botswana, 106, 108, 109, 113, 116, 119, 120, 121, 122, 123, 128, 135, 136, 140
Brazil, 27, 28, 51, 71
bribes, 7, 51
Bulgaria, 51
Burkina Faso, 106, 107, 109, 116, 123, 136, 140
Burundi, 106, 109, 116, 123, 135, 136, 140
business environment, 6, 11, 36, 41
business partners, 39
businesses, 4, 10, 36, 46, 60, 126, 127, 128, 129, 130, 134, 142, 146
buyer, 20, 53
buyers, 20

C

Cairo, 139
Cameroon, 52, 106, 109, 116, 120, 122, 126, 132, 136
candidates, 134
capacity building, 11, 120, 125, 130, 134
carbon, 92
Caribbean, 133
case studies, 4, 42, 60
case study, 22, 26
cashmere, 118
Census, 42, 139
Central African Republic, 106, 109, 140
certification, 128, 146
Chad, 17, 50, 106, 109, 111, 116, 122, 136
challenges, 4, 6, 36, 38, 40, 42, 50, 99, 107, 130, 141, 143, 146
Chamber of Commerce, 41, 138
chemical, 124
chemicals, 72, 99, 112
child labor, 51
child mortality, 4
children, 141
Chinese firms, 2, 11, 12, 13, 19, 25, 26, 27, 29, 30, 31, 32, 33, 34, 36, 38, 39, 40, 42, 43, 45, 51, 52, 53, 55, 56, 63, 66, 69, 70, 71, 77, 78, 80, 84, 85, 91, 92, 93, 94, 99, 100, 101, 102
Chinese government, 2, 3, 7, 8, 9, 11, 12, 13, 14, 20, 22, 26, 29, 30, 31, 32, 36, 39, 40, 41, 44, 45, 46, 47, 48, 49, 50, 51, 53, 54, 55, 56, 57, 60, 67, 69, 92, 94, 100, 101, 102
citizens, 146
citizenship, 145
civil society, 11, 141, 144
civil war, 5, 30, 39, 69
classification, 55
clean energy, 149
clients, 127
climate, 6, 11, 39, 51, 127, 143, 149
climate change, 6, 51, 143, 149
climate change issues, 6
clothing, 89, 112, 124
cocoa, 72, 84, 101, 112
coherence, 145
collaboration, 7, 97
collateral, 101
color, 36, 92
commerce, 9, 104
commercial, 7, 8, 10, 36, 40, 51, 53, 54, 85, 104, 118, 121, 129, 130
commercial ties, 104
commodity, 106, 107, 108
common external tariff, 132, 136
Common Market, 52, 131, 135, 136, 137, 140
communication, 55, 83, 91, 92, 120
communities, 11, 39, 141, 142, 143, 145
community, 3, 39, 134, 135, 141, 148
competition, 2, 26, 33, 34, 43, 51, 53, 55, 56, 92, 99, 101, 102
competitive need limitations, 117
competitiveness, 7, 145, 146
competitors, 34, 94
complexity, 76
compliance, 8, 27, 28, 100, 135
composition, 43, 63, 66, 81, 89
conference, 127
confidentiality, 23, 25, 28, 45, 68, 82, 96, 101
conflict, 10, 106, 107, 141, 143, 144, 148
Congo, 17, 52, 106, 109, 111, 116, 122, 126, 132, 137
Congress, vii, viii, 9, 52, 103, 104, 105, 116, 119, 121, 126, 128, 129, 131, 133, 134, 138, 146
consensus, 51
construction, 5, 9, 12, 19, 20, 25, 26, 29, 30, 32, 33, 34, 38, 39, 44, 46, 53, 55, 56, 57, 63, 67, 69, 77, 78, 81, 84, 93, 100, 101
consulting, 19, 34, 53, 63, 77, 78, 93
consumption, 138
convention, 51
convergence, 136
cooperation, 6, 11, 12, 20, 82, 83, 135, 146
coordination, 52, 131, 135
copper, 52
copyright, 56, 102
corruption, 5, 6, 36, 51, 92, 107, 141, 143, 147
cost, 5, 26, 29, 31, 32, 33, 36, 41, 49, 55, 118, 138, 147
cost of living, 5, 138
Côte d'Ivoire, 17, 136
Cotonou Agreement, 133
cotton, 17, 113
counseling, 129
counterfeiting, 56, 102
counterterrorism, 146
country of origin, 121
covering, 25
creditors, 109
crises, 143

critical state, 13
crude oil, 5, 13, 16, 26, 54, 60, 63, 72, 75, 99, 101, 110, 124
currency, 129, 135, 136
Customs Service, 118, 119
Customs Union, viii, 52, 104, 131, 137
cybersecurity, 147

D

data availability, 99
database, 42, 50, 53, 122, 138, 140
deaths, 5
decision-making process, 71
deepwater drilling, 54
delegates, 126
democracy, 9, 141, 142, 143, 144
Democratic Republic of Congo, 107, 116, 136, 140
Denmark, 27, 28, 71
Department of Commerce, 2, 8, 16, 35, 38, 42, 59, 62, 66, 75, 80, 91, 120, 139
Department of Energy, 42, 54, 71, 86, 99, 100
Department of Homeland Security, 56, 101
Department of the Treasury, 2, 8
deprivation, 141
depth, 4, 42
developed countries, viii, 11, 17, 52, 53, 56, 63, 75, 104, 119, 121, 130, 139
developing countries, 12, 53, 108, 117, 129
development assistance, 1, 6, 8, 9, 10, 11, 12, 20, 37, 40, 43, 53, 56, 57, 99, 147
development banks, 8, 130
development policy, vii, 103, 104
diamonds, 52, 99, 112
diplomacy, 7, 8, 129, 148
diplomatic engagement, 41
direct cost, 118
direct costs, 118
direct investment, 22, 23, 24, 25, 27, 28, 45, 52, 54, 70, 84, 99, 100, 101, 102, 107, 115
directives, 105, 120
disability, 144
disbursement, 44, 47, 48, 49, 50, 55, 57, 99
disclosure, 23, 68, 82, 96
discrimination, 144
diseases, 108, 148
distribution, 97, 98
diversification, 107, 133, 134, 145
diversity, 4, 42, 60
division of labor, 51
domestic conflict, 146
domestic policy, 132
domestic resources, 12
donors, 4, 29, 32, 37, 46, 52, 57, 60, 93, 98, 130
draft, 41, 56, 102
drawing, 99
drought, 6
drugs, 147
duty free, 17, 52
duty-free access, 121, 133
duty-free treatment, viii, 11, 13, 52, 54, 104, 116, 117, 118, 120, 121

E

earnings, 25, 45, 100, 101, 102
earnings data, 25, 45, 100, 101, 102
East Asia, 50, 99
economic activity, 109, 134
Economic and Monetary Union, 52, 131, 136, 137
economic assistance, vii, 1, 3
economic cooperation, 7, 9, 129
economic crisis, 13
economic development, 5, 10, 11, 53, 106, 122, 126, 130
economic growth, vii, 6, 10, 11, 41, 50, 103, 106, 107, 108, 128, 130, 132, 134, 141, 143, 144, 145, 146, 148
economic integration, 7, 10, 127, 131, 136
economic performance, 107
economic policy, 8
economic power, 40
economic relations, vii, 103, 116, 132
economic union, 136
economies of scale, 145
education, 1, 4, 5, 6, 10, 36, 42, 91, 92, 100, 101, 143, 145, 148
educational opportunities, 51
Egypt, 139, 140
elected leaders, 144
eligibility criteria, 52
eligible countries, viii, 9, 11, 52, 103, 117, 121, 122, 124, 126, 134
embassy, 36, 92
emergency, 12, 20, 97
employees, 36, 38, 56, 92
employment, 37, 38, 39, 89, 129, 134
employment opportunities, 134

energy, viii, 6, 30, 34, 36, 46, 66, 84, 92, 94, 103, 107, 127, 128, 130, 148
enforcement, 119
engineering, 17, 20, 63, 78
enrollment, 6
enrollment rates, 6
entrepreneurs, 8
entrepreneurship, 144, 148
environment, 51, 145
Environmental Protection Agency, 139
EPA, 133
epidemic, 133
equality, 11, 12, 142
Equatorial Guinea, 17, 50, 54, 106, 109, 114, 116, 137
equipment, 17, 20, 21, 30, 33, 34, 35, 52, 63, 65, 72, 78, 79, 84, 89, 92, 93, 97, 98, 99, 101, 110, 113, 132
equity, 8, 25, 45, 52, 54, 57, 100, 101, 102
Eritrea, 106, 109, 116, 135, 137, 140
EU, 133, 140
European Union, 133, 140
evidence, 4, 32, 34, 46, 66, 78, 94, 148
exchange rate, 138
executive branch, 128
Executive Order, 139
executive power, 144
exercise, 39, 128
expenditures, 12, 43, 130
expertise, 29, 127, 147
export promotion, 129
exporter, 6, 7, 55
exporters, 37, 89, 120, 127
exposure, 49, 57
extraction, 13, 20, 24, 70, 72

F

fairness, 142, 145
faith, 129
FAS, 111, 125, 126
FDI, 54, 57, 100, 101, 102, 107, 113, 114, 115
Federal Register, 139
fiber, 113
fibers, 113, 120
financial, 6, 19, 24, 46, 53, 71, 109, 125, 129, 145, 147, 148
financial sector, 147
fiscal year 2009, 97
fisheries, 83, 143, 147
fishing, 56
flat goods, 117
flexibility, 26, 31, 32
flour, 94
fluctuations, 107
folklore, 118
folklore articles, 118
food, 5, 6, 11, 51, 63, 94, 97, 143, 146, 149
food safety, 146
food security, 11, 51, 143
footwear, 17, 37, 52, 72, 75, 89
force, 101, 133
foreign affairs, 46
foreign aid, 8, 9, 11, 12, 20, 42, 51, 53, 106
foreign assistance, vii, 1, 2, 3, 11, 40
foreign companies, 54
foreign direct investment, 13, 22, 23, 24, 25, 27, 28, 45, 52, 54, 57, 70, 84, 85, 99, 100, 101, 102, 107, 113, 132
foreign firms, 7, 38, 39
foreign investment, 6, 25, 27, 51, 107, 132, 143
foreign person, 52, 54, 57, 100
foreign policy, 10, 116, 128
France, 27, 28, 35, 66, 71, 80, 95
free trade, 131, 132
funding, 4, 9, 29, 30, 37, 39, 41, 56, 81, 97, 98, 99, 130
funds, 8, 23, 29, 31, 39, 49, 50, 54, 68, 82, 96, 98, 99, 101, 102, 119, 128, 130, 132

G

Gabon, 17, 54, 106, 109, 123, 126, 137
GDP, viii, 2, 5, 6, 50, 51, 103, 106, 107, 109, 134
Generalized System of Preferences, 2, 51, 59, 63, 117, 139, 146
Germany, 35, 50, 80, 95
global economy, 7, 55
global markets, 142, 145
global trade, 1, 10, 110, 138, 145
goods and services, 10, 12, 32, 34, 44, 50, 63, 66, 78, 84, 93, 130, 132
governance, viii, 4, 8, 11, 106, 107, 142, 144, 145, 146, 147, 148
government budget, 30, 41
governments, viii, 4, 26, 28, 29, 30, 32, 33, 38, 39, 40, 42, 44, 47, 48, 52, 55, 56, 69, 92, 122, 125, 126, 127, 128, 142, 143, 145, 146, 147, 148
grant assistance, 2, 30, 97

grants, vii, 1, 2, 3, 8, 11, 12, 13, 20, 26, 29, 30, 37, 40, 41, 42, 50, 53, 54, 55, 56, 60, 66, 81, 97, 99, 100, 130
gross domestic product, 2, 6, 50, 132
gross national product, 121
grouping, 136
growth, 2, 3, 5, 7, 13, 20, 36, 50, 51, 52, 55, 72, 84, 106, 107, 110, 116, 118, 120, 134, 139, 141, 145, 148
growth rate, 5, 84, 106
guidance, 51
guidelines, 101
Guinea, 106, 107, 109, 116, 117, 123, 136, 137, 140

H

handbags, 117
harbors, 84
harmonization, 136, 145
harmony, 146
health, 1, 2, 5, 10, 11, 20, 26, 37, 51, 66, 81, 97, 108, 143, 148, 149
health care, 51, 108, 143
HIPC, 109
hiring, 2, 26, 38, 39, 69, 78, 93, 132
historical data, 44
HIV, 11, 53, 108, 126, 133, 134, 138, 143
HIV/AIDS, 11, 53, 108, 126, 133, 134, 138, 143
holding company, 54
Hong Kong, 25, 100, 101, 102
host, vii, 1, 2, 4, 22, 26, 30, 32, 33, 34, 36, 37, 41, 42, 43, 44, 46, 47, 48, 52, 54, 55, 57, 60, 63, 66, 78, 91, 94, 100, 126, 132
House, 3, 59, 123
House of Representatives, 3, 59
housing, 30, 67, 68, 93
hub, 6
human, 1, 5, 10, 51, 104, 106, 108, 116, 127, 140, 141, 144, 146
human capital, 108, 127
human development, 5, 146
Human Development Index, 5
human right, 1, 10, 51, 116, 140, 141, 144
human rights, 1, 10, 51, 116, 140, 141, 144
humanitarian aid, 20
humanitarian crises, 143, 148
hybrid, 119

I

image, 93
IMF, viii, 2, 4, 15, 16, 25, 42, 45, 46, 54, 57, 59, 87, 100, 101, 102, 103, 106, 107, 109, 130
import sensitive, 117, 133, 139
imports, viii, 2, 3, 5, 6, 7, 11, 13, 15, 16, 17, 19, 26, 27, 37, 42, 43, 52, 53, 54, 60, 61, 62, 63, 72, 75, 87, 89, 91, 99, 100, 101, 103, 105, 109, 110, 111, 112, 113, 117, 118, 119, 120, 122, 123, 124, 132, 133, 134, 138, 139
improvements, 4, 8, 55, 107, 127
income, 4, 5, 6, 50, 107, 130, 134
income distribution, 107
increased access, 107
independence, 6, 11, 50, 106
India, 54, 56
individuals, 141, 145
industrialized countries, 51, 54
industries, 6, 39, 56, 114, 128, 134
industry, 54, 118, 120, 133, 138
inflation, 5, 6, 42, 50, 99
information sharing, 122
information technology, 21, 34, 35, 65, 78, 79, 94
infrastructure, 2, 5, 8, 9, 11, 12, 20, 22, 26, 29, 30, 31, 33, 34, 37, 39, 40, 44, 50, 55, 56, 67, 77, 83, 84, 93, 97, 98, 100, 107, 120, 125, 127, 128, 130, 134, 145
injury, 117
institution building, 143
institutional infrastructure, 127
institutional reforms, 145
institutions, viii, 1, 9, 10, 41, 46, 52, 53, 57, 130, 131, 139, 141, 142, 143, 144, 147
integration, 7, 41, 107
integrity, 142
intellectual property, 36, 51, 56
intellectual property rights, 56
intelligence, 129, 147
interest rates, 49, 57
internal consistency, 43
International Bank for Reconstruction and Development, 54, 55, 139
international economic assistance, vii, 1
international law, 132
International Monetary Fund, viii, 2, 4, 42, 59, 100, 101, 102, 103, 106, 107, 109, 130, 138, 140
international standards, 6
international terrorism, 116

intra-regional trade, 107
investments, vii, 1, 3, 9, 10, 11, 13, 20, 22, 23, 25, 26, 27, 30, 36, 39, 41, 42, 45, 50, 52, 53, 67, 68, 70, 71, 82, 84, 96, 98, 99, 100, 101, 102, 106, 108, 127, 129, 132
investors, 8, 38, 56, 127, 134
iron, 52, 63, 89, 132
irrigation, 77
Israel, 80
issues, 4, 6, 8, 9, 10, 11, 13, 39, 56, 105, 128, 130, 131, 132, 133, 143, 146
Italy, 27, 28, 66, 86

J

joint ventures, 54, 126

K

kerosene, 74

L

law enforcement, 147
laws, 7, 42, 125
laws and regulations, 125
LDCs, 119, 120, 121, 130, 133
lead, 143, 146, 148
leadership, 142, 144, 148
leadership development, 148
learning, 11, 122
leather wearing apparel, 117
legislation, vii, viii, 41, 103, 104, 105, 116, 119, 120, 123, 129, 130, 131, 132, 134
lending, 21, 32, 35, 53, 55, 56, 57, 65, 79, 93, 99, 101, 102
lesser developed beneficiary countries, 52
Liberia, 18, 52, 106, 107, 109, 114, 116, 120, 123, 126, 132, 137, 140
life expectancy, 134
light, 134
livestock, 148
loan guarantees, 8, 20, 31, 53, 54, 67, 98, 129
loans, vii, 1, 2, 3, 8, 9, 11, 12, 13, 20, 22, 26, 29, 30, 31, 32, 37, 40, 41, 42, 44, 46, 47, 48, 49, 50, 53, 54, 55, 56, 57, 60, 67, 84, 98, 99, 102, 127, 129, 130
local government, 139
long-term debt, 138
lower-middle-income status, 6
luggage, 117

M

machinery, 17, 30, 63, 72, 84, 89, 101, 110, 113, 132
macroeconomic policies, 136
magnitude, 44, 46, 53, 54, 55, 57, 75
majority, 2, 17, 39, 54, 77, 78, 84, 85, 99
malaise, 106
malaria, 11, 108, 143
malnutrition, 148
man, 148
management, 6, 29, 54, 63, 71, 78, 93, 136, 145, 148
manufactured goods, 17, 63, 72, 89, 130
manufacturing, 6, 7, 25, 37, 54, 67, 70, 89, 99, 114, 117, 134
market access, 105, 130
market economy, 104
market share, 92
market-based economies, 51
market-based economy, 6, 116
mass, 143
materials, 12, 22, 32, 33, 38, 55, 78, 84, 93, 100, 118, 121
Mauritania, 17, 116, 123, 126, 137, 140
Mauritius, 52, 106, 109, 114, 115, 116, 120, 121, 122, 132, 133, 135, 137, 140
media, 22, 144
medical, 20, 21, 30, 35, 84, 93, 134
medicine, 141
membership, 52, 125, 144
merchandise, 132
metals, 16, 52, 108, 112, 132
meter, 120, 121
methodology, 4, 43, 45, 46, 60
Mexico, 138
middle class, 107
military, 145, 147
Millennium Challenge Corporation (MCC), 4, 8, 11, 41, 77
mission, 130
missions, 8, 125, 128, 130, 147
models, 144
modernization, 97, 145
monetary policy, 135
monetary union, 131, 135
Morocco, 139

Mozambique, 52, 106, 108, 109, 116, 120, 123, 126, 132, 135, 137
Multilateral, 109, 130, 138
multinational corporations, 34, 92
mutual respect, viii, 141, 142
mutual responsibility, viii, 141, 142

N

NAFTA, 120
Namibia, 106, 108, 109, 113, 116, 119, 121, 123, 126, 135, 137, 140
national income, 5, 50
national security, 83, 116
National Strategy, 146
nationality, 21, 35, 43, 53, 55, 56, 65, 76, 79, 93, 99, 101, 102
natural disaster, 148
natural disasters, 148
natural resources, vii, 1, 2, 3, 6, 7, 13, 84, 110, 113, 142, 145, 149
negotiation, 132, 133
Netherlands, 45, 95, 100, 101, 102
networking, 139
next generation, 142, 148
NGOs, 93, 100
Nigeria, 17, 18, 20, 21, 24, 28, 52, 53, 54, 55, 86, 106, 107, 109, 111, 114, 116, 122, 124, 126, 132, 137, 138, 140
nominal data, 42, 50, 99
nongovernmental organization, 2, 4, 41, 46, 59, 60, 69
non-OECD, 32
North America, 120
North American Free Trade Agreement, 120
Norway, 27

O

obstacles, 146
OECD, 2, 6, 7, 12, 25, 32, 44, 45, 47, 48, 49, 51, 52, 53, 54, 55, 56, 57, 59, 100, 102
Office of the United States Trade Representative, 51
officials, vii, viii, 1, 3, 7, 10, 12, 17, 19, 22, 23, 26, 29, 30, 31, 32, 33, 34, 36, 37, 39, 41, 42, 43, 44, 46, 47, 48, 49, 51, 52, 55, 56, 57, 60, 63, 67, 68, 69, 77, 78, 82, 89, 92, 93, 96, 99, 100, 101, 102, 103, 126, 139
OH, 127
oil, 5, 6, 15, 17, 20, 24, 26, 27, 28, 29, 34, 36, 38, 39, 40, 42, 44, 45, 46, 52, 54, 55, 56, 60, 61, 62, 63, 66, 67, 70, 71, 72, 74, 75, 84, 85, 86, 94, 99, 100, 101, 107, 108, 110, 111, 112, 124, 138, 146
oil production, 6
oilseed, 67
operations, 27, 28, 29, 30, 33, 34, 36, 71, 85, 92, 100, 117, 145, 147
opportunities, 3, 8, 11, 12, 39, 51, 52, 55, 127, 128, 130, 135, 139, 141, 142, 143, 146
ores, 16, 52, 72, 108
Organization for Economic Cooperation and Development, 2, 6, 44, 59, 100
overlap, 52, 78
overseas investment, 7
Overseas Private Investment Corporation, viii, 2, 4, 8, 41, 50, 59, 104, 127, 128, 139
oversight, 78, 133, 134
ownership, 11, 27, 28, 29, 52, 54, 57, 71, 85, 100

P

Pacific, 50, 99, 133
Pakistan, 55, 56
Paris Club, 109
Parliament, viii, 141, 142
participants, 54, 56, 133, 135
peace, 10, 141, 142, 143, 144, 147
peacekeeping, 143, 147
per capita income, 6, 119
perpetrators, 147
Persian Gulf, 53
petroleum, 13, 16, 38, 40, 52, 54, 56, 71, 75, 84, 85, 101, 111, 134
Petroleum, 2, 17, 52, 54, 56, 99
plants, 124, 140
platform, 12
platinum, 52, 112
playing, 143
policy, 2, 8, 9, 11, 12, 20, 26, 29, 42, 52, 78, 79, 104, 106, 125, 134, 136, 148
policy issues, 125
policy options, 106
policy reform, 148
political instability, 106, 107
political participation, 141
political pluralism, 51
political system, 141
politics, 141

population, 5, 106, 108, 132, 134, 141, 143
population growth, 106
poultry, 63
poverty, 4, 6, 37, 51, 69, 77, 107, 141, 143
poverty alleviation, 143
poverty reduction, 37
power generation, 20
preferential treatment, viii, 103, 118
present value, 31, 44, 46, 47, 48, 49, 50, 57
president, 13, 22
President, vii, viii, 10, 20, 51, 97, 103, 104, 105, 116, 117, 120, 122, 125, 126, 127, 128, 131, 134, 139, 140, 142, 144, 146, 148
President Clinton, vii, 103, 128
President Obama, viii, 10, 142
prevalence rate, 108
prevention, 53, 148
primary function, 128
principles, 10, 11, 12, 52, 141, 142
private enterprises, 7, 51
private investment, 128
private sector, viii, 7, 8, 11, 52, 92, 104, 122, 123, 125, 126, 128, 130, 132, 145
private sector investment, 132
privatization, 140
procurement, 76, 77, 101
producers, 113
productive capacity, 134, 146
productivity growth, 106
professionals, 108
profitability, 29
project, 8, 20, 29, 31, 33, 50, 53, 55, 83, 93, 94, 97, 100, 128, 130, 148
project sponsors, 130
prosperity, 141, 142, 143
protection, 51, 55, 142
public finance, 145
public goods, 142, 143
public officials, 7, 51
public sector, 5, 6, 145
public support, 51
publishing, 40
purchasing power, 5, 51
purchasing power parity, 5, 51

Q

quality standards, 78

R

raw materials, 110
recession, 124
recognition, 12
reconstruction, 69, 94, 100
recovery, 6, 94, 106
reform, viii, 12, 103, 140, 148
Reform, 147
reformers, 144
reforms, 132, 134, 145
regional integration, 131, 135, 145
regulations, 2, 7, 11, 26, 27, 28, 71, 85, 100
regulatory framework, 8, 136
reliability, 25, 43, 44
relief, vii, 12, 103, 109, 133
Republic of the Congo, 17, 52, 106, 109, 132, 135
reputation, 26, 34, 36, 91, 92
requirements, 2, 26, 38, 39, 69, 78, 118, 126, 132, 134, 140, 146
research institutions, 45, 54, 100, 101, 102
reserves, 5
resilience, 143, 148
resources, 6, 12, 16, 108, 111, 141, 143, 146
response, 40, 50, 99, 148
restrictions, 104
restructuring, 125
retail, 39
revenue, 56, 132, 145
rights, 54, 56, 100, 102, 141, 145
risk, 8, 34, 36, 41, 49, 55, 127, 128, 134, 148
risks, 36, 71, 128, 134, 147
roots, 142
rowing, 89
royalty, 54
rule of law, 51, 104, 141, 142, 144
rules, 27, 28, 32, 39, 49, 51, 55, 71, 85, 93, 100, 118, 119
rules of origin, 118, 119
Russia, 51
Rwanda, 52, 106, 109, 116, 123, 126, 132, 135, 137, 140

S

safety, 146
Saudi Arabia, 138
school, 20, 30, 39, 67, 68
scope, vii, 1, 4, 55, 56, 60, 131
Secretary of Commerce, 118

securities, 7
Securities Exchange Act, 7
security, vii, 1, 4, 9, 10, 52, 56, 141, 142, 143, 144, 146, 147, 148
security forces, 147
Senate, viii, 3, 50, 59, 99, 104, 123
Senate Foreign Relations Committee, viii, 104
sensitivity, 39, 139
services, 6, 7, 8, 12, 19, 20, 32, 34, 42, 43, 44, 46, 53, 54, 55, 63, 75, 76, 77, 78, 79, 81, 91, 93, 99, 100, 101, 125, 128, 129, 130, 131, 136, 139, 145, 148
sexual orientation, 144
Seychelles, 106, 109, 116, 123, 133, 135, 137, 140
shape, 119, 143
shareholders, 29, 36
short supply, 120
showing, 27, 43, 109, 146
Sierra Leone, 50, 106, 109, 116, 123, 137, 140
silk, 113
skilled workers, 108
slag, 108, 112
small businesses, 129, 134
social benefits, 20
social development, 11
social responsibility, 38, 39
social services, 39, 108
social welfare, 20, 107
society, 7, 108, 134
Somalia, 116, 137, 143, 147
South Africa, vii, viii, 13, 17, 18, 20, 24, 47, 48, 51, 52, 53, 54, 57, 95, 103, 104, 106, 107, 108, 109, 111, 112, 114, 115, 116, 119, 121, 122, 124, 126, 128, 130, 131, 132, 133, 135, 137, 140
South Korea, 12
Southern African Customs Union (SACU), viii, 104
Southern African Development Community, 131, 135
SP, 51, 63, 117
speech, viii, 13, 127, 142
spillover effects, 109
SSA, vii, viii, 103, 104, 105, 106, 107, 108, 109, 111, 112, 113, 114, 115, 116, 117, 118, 121, 122, 123, 124, 127, 128, 129, 130, 131, 132, 133, 136, 138, 139, 140
stability, 6, 36, 141, 143
staffing, 129
stakeholders, vii, 1
state, 7, 9, 29, 30, 45, 51, 52, 55, 83, 94, 101, 139, 143
state-owned enterprises, 7, 30, 51, 55, 101
states, 10, 11, 12, 20, 50, 55, 109, 125, 130, 131, 135, 136, 143, 144, 146
statistics, viii, 103, 138
steel, 63, 112, 124, 132
stock, 24, 25, 45, 52, 54, 70, 84, 99, 100, 101, 102, 114, 115, 136
stock exchange, 136
style, 131
substitutes, 124
Sudan, viii, 5, 17, 18, 50, 53, 104, 116, 121, 135, 137, 140, 143
supervision, 93, 100
supplier, 111
suppliers, 138
supply chain, 145
surplus, 19
sustainability, 148
sustainable development, viii, 6, 142, 147
Sustainable Development, 148
sustainable economic growth, 10, 143

T

Taiwan, 11, 56
tanks, 41, 46
Tanzania, 18, 21, 52, 106, 109, 116, 120, 121, 123, 126, 135, 137, 147
target, 125, 128
tariff, 51, 63, 124, 130, 133, 135, 136, 140, 146
tariff rates, 124
teachers, 108
technical assistance, viii, 8, 36, 92, 103, 105, 120, 125, 127, 128, 131, 134, 146
technical comments, 41
technical support, 131
technological change, 141
technology, 2, 13, 29, 33, 34, 40, 71, 84, 91, 92, 110, 142, 147
technology transfer, 13
telecommunications, 17, 34, 46, 53, 56, 67, 68, 78, 92, 130
terrorism, 129
testing, 146
textiles, 17, 37, 52, 75, 89, 113, 118, 121
theft, 36
third country fabric, 127

third-country fabric, 10, 37, 52, 89, 105, 116, 121, 122
threats, 143
time frame, 109, 133
time periods, 49, 55
Title I, viii, 103, 104, 116
Title V, 51, 121
tobacco, 124
Togo, 18, 106, 109, 116, 123, 126, 131, 136, 137, 140
tourism, 53
trade agreement, viii, 8, 104, 131, 139
Trade and Development Act of 2000, 116
trade benefits, 52
trade liberalization, 131, 133
trade policy, 10, 128, 136, 139
trade preference, 8, 9, 12, 52, 75, 89, 104, 117, 133
trademarks, 56, 102
trafficking, 147
trafficking in persons, 147
training, 34, 92, 97, 98, 128, 134
transaction costs, 145
transactions, 15, 16, 23, 30, 51, 55, 68, 82, 87, 96, 129
transformation, 7
transition period, 133
transmission, 89
transparency, 4, 6, 8, 31, 32, 40, 54, 144, 145, 148
transport, 17, 63, 72, 89, 101, 107
transportation, 17, 21, 34, 35, 42, 46, 55, 63, 65, 66, 77, 78, 79, 81, 84, 93, 99, 100, 113, 120, 127, 128, 130
transportation infrastructure, 84
transshipment, 119
Treasury, 2, 8, 41
treaties, 8, 11, 52, 132
treatment, 53, 54, 117, 118, 120, 132, 135
trust fund, 131
Trust Fund, 130
tuberculosis, 108
turnover, 100

U

U.S. assistance, 56
U.S. Department of Commerce, 4, 50, 52, 129
U.S. economy, 7
U.S. Export-Import Bank, 54
U.S. policy, viii, 40, 104, 141, 142
U.S. Treasury, 49
U.S. yarn, 118
UN, 2, 3, 5, 15, 16, 18, 19, 27, 42, 50, 51, 52, 53, 59, 61, 64, 72, 73, 87, 88, 90, 107
uniform, 138
unions, 39
United Kingdom, 27, 28, 35, 66, 71, 79, 86, 93, 95
United Nations, 2, 5, 7, 11, 42, 50, 59, 107, 122, 130, 138
universities, 97, 98
unlawful transshipment, 118
urban, 6, 7, 46, 107
urbanization, 143
Uruguay, 104
Uruguay Round, 104
USDA, 139

V

valuation, 25
value-added requirement, 118
variations, 25, 45
vegetables, 124
vehicles, 17, 72, 84, 110, 132
Venezuela, 138
venue, 132
vertical integration, 119
violence, 6, 129, 147
vision, viii, 142, 147
volatility, 106
voting, 52, 54, 57, 100
vulnerability, 148

W

war, 5, 69, 141
Washington, viii, 4, 11, 41, 46, 50, 51, 54, 55, 56, 60, 103, 127
watches, 117
water, 20, 30, 67, 93, 108, 127, 148, 149
weakness, 5, 107
weapons, 147
weapons of mass destruction, 147
welfare, 6, 53
wells, 54, 97, 98
West Africa, 52, 128, 131, 136, 137
White House, v, 51, 138, 141
White Paper, 51, 52, 53
withdrawal, 118
wood, 110

wool, 118, 119
work gloves, 117
worker rights, 51, 104
workers, 33, 38, 39, 43, 53, 69, 78, 93, 100, 119, 134
workforce, 6, 38
working conditions, 140
World Bank, 4, 5, 6, 7, 8, 9, 19, 21, 22, 32, 34, 35, 41, 42, 43, 44, 46, 47, 48, 49, 50, 51, 52, 53, 54, 55, 56, 57, 63, 65, 77, 79, 93, 99, 101, 102, 106, 121, 130, 138, 139
World Trade Organization, 7, 17, 42, 51, 52, 63, 125
worldwide, 4, 10, 12, 20, 107, 108, 111, 124, 129
WTO, 125, 128, 130, 131

Y

yarn, 113, 118, 119
young people, 127, 143

Z

Zimbabwe, 106, 108, 109, 116, 133, 135, 137, 140
zinc, 92
zippers, 113